WHAT YOUR COLLEAGUE

Young Scientists in Action is a timely and necessary book that challenges science educators to reimagine science teaching through the lens of social justice. It offers practical strategies to empower students to recognize, critique, and act on societal inequities by using science as a powerful tool for change. I highly recommend this book to every science educator and every leader committed to transforming science education into a force for equity, justice, and community empowerment

Kristopher J. Childs
CEO, The Mathematics Group
Winter Garden, FL

Young Scientists in Action is a practical guide for elementary educators striving to make science meaningful, equitable, and action-oriented. Moldavan and Nafziger offer a powerful framework and ready-to-use lessons that center student voice, critical thinking, and real-world relevance. This book supports teachers in creating classrooms where all students see themselves as scientists and change agents, capable of understanding and improving the world around them.

Stephanie Westhafer
Elementary Representative, Georgia Science Teachers Association
Braselton, GA

This book provides a resource I wish I had as a practicing teacher. Children are naturally curious about science, fairness, and their world, so connecting science and justice-centered teaching is a great fit. The authors provide key information about facilitating these connections and positioning learners to use their science knowledge to take action in their world.

Jennifer Ward
Associate Professor of Early Childhood and Elementary Mathematics
Kennesaw State University
Canton, GA

I had the opportunity to try a lesson in this book. It was engaging for all my students. I was able to scaffold and extend it to meet the needs of all learners. I appreciated the interdisciplinary elements woven into the lesson and that my students could easily connect the learning to their daily lives.

Karli Gilbertson
Fourth-Grade Teacher, ISD 622
St. Paul, MN

This book is very important for elementary science teachers. *Young Scientists in Action* shows how easily science as a tool for advocacy and for social justice can be brought into the classroom with young learners. I can't wait to bring the Elicit-Investigate-Interrogate-Act Framework for Social Justice Lessons format into my elementary science methods classroom.

Katie Brkich
Professor, Georgia Southern University
Statesboro, GA

In this relevant and timely book, the content and resources inspire teachers and administrators in engaging young students to tackle culturally relevant issues at early ages, which is critical in developing scientific literacy. Highly recommended!

Edralin Pagarigan
Resource Teacher, Adjunct Faculty,
Baltimore County Public Schools,
University of Maryland Baltimore County
Rosedale, MD

This book powerfully emphasizes the dual importance of fostering critical thinking and scientific knowledge. The "mirrors, windows, and sliding glass doors" metaphor brilliantly connects social justice to education, highlighting equity in science classrooms. It's an essential read for educators committed to inclusive, reflective, and transformative teaching practices.

Kimberly Morton
Content Specialist, Science & Social Studies K–12
Gilbert, AZ

Young Scientists in Action: Building Critical Thinkers for a Better World just makes sense from a mathematics and STEM education perspective, while leveraging creativity for active and engaged learning. The authors have built a strong framework for supporting the fundamental development of critical thinkers through an approachable and logical organization of complex ideas.

Robert Capraro
Professor Emeritus & Director Emeritus Aggie
STEM Center & Texas A&M University
College Station, TX

As a mathematics educator and STEM educator who has worked extensively with teachers and students, the development of critical thinking is a cornerstone for success in each STEM discipline. This book takes a fresh look at critical thinking, which situates learning from the perspective of investigation and scientific inquiry, as an important motivational factor in becoming an engaged and thoughtful thinker that transcends disciplines.

Mary Margaret Capraro
Professor Emerita & Director Emerita Aggie,
STEM Center & Texas A&M University
College Station, TX

Young Scientists in Action

Dedication

To Myla and Abby, our young scientists, whose curiosity, questions, and wonder remind us why this work matters. May you always explore boldly, think critically, and use your voices to build a better world.

Young Scientists in Action

Building Critical Thinkers for a Better World

Alesia Mickle Moldavan

Bailey Nafziger

CORWIN

FOR INFORMATION:

Corwin

A Sage Company

2455 Teller Road

Thousand Oaks, California 91320

(800) 233-9936

www.corwin.com

Sage Publications Ltd.

1 Oliver's Yard

55 City Road

London EC1Y 1SP

United Kingdom

Sage Publications India Pvt. Ltd.

10th Floor, Emaar Capital Tower 2

MG Road, Sikanderpur

Sector 26, Gurugram

Haryana - 122002

India

Sage Publications Asia-Pacific Pte. Ltd.

18 Cross Street #10-10/11/12

China Square Central

Singapore 048423

Vice President and
    Editorial Director: Monica Eckman

Senior Acquisitions Editor: Debbie Hardin

Senior Editorial Assistant: Nyle DeLeon

Production Editor: Aparajita Srivastava

Typesetter: C&M Digitals (P) Ltd.

Proofreader: Lawrence W. Baker

Indexer: Integra

Cover Designer: Candice Harman

Copyright © 2026 by Corwin Press, Inc.

All rights reserved. Except as permitted by U.S. copyright law, no part of this work may be reproduced or distributed in any form or by any means, or stored in a database or retrieval system, without permission in writing from the publisher.

When forms and sample documents appearing in this work are intended for reproduction, they will be marked as such. Reproduction of their use is authorized for educational use by educators, local school sites, and/or noncommercial or nonprofit entities that have purchased the book.

All third-party trademarks referenced or depicted herein are included solely for the purpose of illustration and are the property of their respective owners. Reference to these trademarks in no way indicates any relationship with, or endorsement by, the trademark owner.

No AI training. Without in any way limiting the author's and publisher's exclusive rights under copyright, any use of this publication to "train" generative artificial intelligence (AI) or for other AI uses is expressly prohibited. The publisher reserves all rights to license uses of this publication for generative AI training or other AI uses.

Printed in the United States of America

Library of Congress Control Number:

Paperback ISBN: 9781071976449

LCCN: 2025032361

Notice icon by Istock.com/Jobalou

Wonder icon by Istock.com/Dimitris66

This book is printed on acid-free paper.

26 27 28 29 30 10 9 8 7 6 5 4 3 2 1

DISCLAIMER: This book may direct you to access third-party content via web links, QR codes, or other scannable technologies, which are provided for your reference by the author(s). Corwin makes no guarantee that such third-party content will be available for your use and encourages you to review the terms and conditions of such third-party content. Corwin takes no responsibility and assumes no liability for your use of any third-party content, nor does Corwin approve, sponsor, endorse, verify, or certify such third-party content.

Table of Contents

Foreword *by Edna Tan and Angela Calabrese Barton* — xi

Preface — xv

Acknowledgments — xvii

About the Authors — xix

Introduction — 1
- Why This Book? — 2
- Our Lenses and Beliefs Framing This Book — 5
  - My Adaptation and *Why* Motivator: Alesia Mickle Moldavan's Lens — 6
  - Looking Back to Move Forward With My *Why*: Bailey Nafziger's Lens — 7
- A Collective Partnership — 8
- The Book's Audience — 9
- The Book's Organization — 10
- Your Teaching Manifesto — 12

PART I: USING SCIENCE TO SOLVE PROBLEMS: WHERE DO WE BEGIN? — 15

1. Connecting Minds and Hearts Through Critical Thinking and Engagement in Science — 17
   - Building Critical Thinkers — 18
   - Empathy in Science — 21
   - Science as a Human and Social Endeavor — 22
     - Tracing Pedagogical Approaches Illuminating Students' Assets and Communities — 25
     - Using Science to Explore Fairness — 26
     - Understanding Our World and Each Other — 29

Representation Matters	30
Mirrors, Windows, and Sliding Glass Doors	31
Science as a Tool for Advocacy	34
Connecting Initiatives in Science Education Reform and Standards to Equity	37
Equity in the Context of NSTA and NGSS	38
Integrating Standards for Fairness and Agency	39
Chapter Summary	44
Reflection Questions	44

2. Bringing Purpose and Action to Science — 47

How We Do (and Don't Do) Science	48
Science Is a Way of Knowing	49
Scientific Knowledge Assumes an Order of Consistency in Natural Systems	50
Scientific Models, Laws, Mechanisms, and Theories Explain Natural Phenomena	54
What Are Scientific Laws?	57
What Are Scientific Theories?	57
Scientific Knowledge Is Open to Revision in Light of New Evidence	59
What Counts as Science?	62
Who Gets to Do Science?	64
Alternative Science Epistemologies	65
The Value of Community	69
Chapter Summary	71
Reflection Questions	72

PART II: DESIGNING AND IMPLEMENTING SCIENCE LESSONS FOR CRITICAL THINKING AND ACTION — 73

3. Planning Lessons That Matter and Foster Change — 75

Learning About Students	75
Diversity as an Asset	76
Sustaining an Inclusive Environment	78
Establishing Classroom Norms	79
A Framework for Social Justice Science Lessons	80
The Elicit Phase	81
Finding the Phenomena	83
Types of Phenomena	85
Where to Find Sociocultural-Informed Phenomena	89

The Investigate Phase	92
Planning for the Investigate Phase	93
Three-Dimensional Science Teaching	93
Instructional Considerations	94
Focusing on Safety	94
Collaborative Student Groups	95
The Interrogate Phase	96
Structuring Classroom Debates for Critical Thinking	99
Guided Discussion With Claim–Evidence–Reasoning	100
The Act Phase	101
What Does Taking Action Look Like?	102
How Teachers Can Support Student Action	103
Using an Act Menu to Make a Difference	105
Chapter Summary	108
Reflection Questions	108

4. Unit Plans for Critical Thinking and Action — 109

Units in This Chapter	110
Unit Plan 4.1: Water Negotiators	111
Student Page: ELICIT: *Water Negotiators*	121
Student Page: INVESTIGATE: *Water Negotiators*	122
Student Page: INTERROGATE: *Water Negotiators*	124
Student Page: ACT: *Water Negotiators*	126
Teacher Page: INVESTIGATE: *Water Negotiators*	127
Teacher Page: INTERROGATE: *Water Negotiators' Roles*	128
Unit Plan 4.2: Diaper Deserts	129
Student Page: ELICIT: *Diaper Deserts*	135
Student Page: INVESTIGATE: *Diaper Deserts*	136
Student Page: INTERROGATE: *Diaper Deserts*	138
Student Page: ACT: *Diaper Deserts*	140
Unit Plan 4.3: Honorable Harvest	141
Student Page: ELICIT: *Honorable Harvest*	153
Student Page: INVESTIGATE: *Honorable Harvest*	154
Student Page: INTERROGATE: *Honorable Harvest*	155
Student Page: ACT: *Honorable Harvest*	157
Teacher Page: *Mushroom Life Cycle Card Sort*	159
Teacher Page: *General Unit Template*	161
Chapter Summary	162
Reflection Questions	162

5. Grab-and-Go Lessons	163
Lesson 5.1: Accessibility: Inclined Planes	168
Lesson 5.2: Politics and Plastics	178
Lesson 5.3: Invasive Carp	186
Lesson 5.4: Fossil Fuels and Nonrenewable Energy	194
Chapter Summary	205
Reflection Questions	205

PART III: LOOKING AHEAD AND TAKING ACTION — 207

6. Navigating Today's Classrooms With Purpose	209
Knowing Your Purpose, Priorities, and Professional Responsibilities	210
Finding Your People and Sphere of Influence	212
Curating Patience for Growth Opportunities	214
Keeping a Journal to Chronicle Progress	217
Encouraging Growth Mindset	217
Holding on to Hope	220
Chapter Summary	221
Reflection Questions	222
7. Your Call to Action	223
Taking Action in Your Context	223
Revisiting Your Teaching Manifesto	228
Chapter Summary	229
Reflection Questions	230
References	231
Index	235

Foreword

Edna Tan and Angela Calabrese Barton

Elementary school students may not pick up data reports to compare pollution trends across varying geographical locations, but they can undoubtedly make observations in their daily lives and note differences that might not be fair. Can you hear a major roadway from your school's playground? Not all schools can. Can you find shade at a local park? Not all people can.

—Alesia Mickle Moldavan and Bailey Nafziger (2026, p. 28)

A marker of working toward rightful presence is the overall enlargement of who, what, where, when, and for whom that [elementary] school science involves.

—Edna Tan and Angela Calabrese Barton (2023, p. 123)

Young Scientists in Action: Building Critical Thinkers for a Better World lays out accessible on-ramps for elementary school teachers to try out, adapt, and plan standards-aligned, student- and community-focused science lessons rooted in social justice. Drawing from their personal and professional experiences in elementary education, Alesia Mickle Moldavan and Bailey Nafziger delve into three interwoven elements of teaching elementary science in the United States:

1. Young children are inherently curious about the world and deeply value fairness.

2. Science as a discipline has historically been active across cultures with a nature of science that is humanistic and dynamic.

3. Critical scientific literacy is fundamental to empowering and equipping children with the wherewithal to understand and apply scientific content toward more just lives in the here and now, and beyond the walls of the classroom.

Moldavan and Nafziger urge us to teach science toward the all-encompassing wellness of children's whole lives.

In our own work (Calabrese Barton & Tan, 2019, 2020), we have proposed the Rightful Presence framework for justice-oriented teaching. Rightful Presence pushes beyond inclusionary models of equity to orient toward how legitimate participation involves ongoing disruption and restructuring of the powered dynamics that shape participants' opportunities to engage in community with respect and dignity.

Teaching is, and has always been, a political act. When elementary school science is taught as separate from the livelihood of students, especially those most marginalized by schooling and society, students can be positioned as outsiders. The already-present forms of expertise they bring to science learning can be made *invisible*, thereby, too, making children invisible—denying them a Rightful Presence in their learning community.

Working toward Rightful Presence involves disrupting traditional power dynamics and exclusionary norms, aiming to create justice-centered classrooms where students are positioned not just as learners but also as co-constructors of knowledge and community. Students are Rightfully Present in science not because they are good at it, or interested in it, but because their lives—including their pasts, presents, and futures—actively shape what it means to know, do, and become in science.

A core tenet of the Rightful Presence framework is the necessity of allied political struggle, where the ones with more power work with the ones with less power toward shared, justice-oriented goals. One way such allied political struggles manifest is the collective struggle for the right to reauthor rights.

This book offers insights into how elementary school teachers may teach science toward the Rightful Presence of all children.

For example, Moldavan and Nafziger illustrate this right to reauthor rights in the following ways:

- The right to center elementary students as whole children with rich and diverse experiences in their everyday lives as core to the mission of teaching, rather than "covering standards" as a default teaching philosophy
- The right to reclaim time to teach science in the elementary grades, given the high-stakes testing schooling culture that disproportionately elevates literacy and mathematics
- The right to bring everyday observations, concerns, and joyful experiences as legitimate resources for elementary science teaching and learning
- The right to reframe what counts as "phenomena" worthy of scientific study and what counts as sensemaking in relation to these phenomena

- The right to incorporate action-taking that is meaningful to students and communities as powerful and important in science learning
- The right for teachers to ask for and receive help in pausing to reflect, to consider how social justice and science education are inevitably intertwined, and therefore to recognize the power of teaching and learning science toward children and communities experiencing consequential wellness and more just lives—a more Rightful Presence

Working toward Rightful Presence is a collective, social, cultural, and political endeavor. One key starting point, which cuts across the strategies of this text, is finding new ways of making present the lives of children in the everyday learning and work of science. The authors provide a myriad of approaches for disrupting traditional ways of teaching and learning science—the norm of equity as the inclusion model, opening up who and what matters in science class. While working toward Rightful Presence necessitates taking disruptive actions, the authors provide possibilities for how disruption can happen in the pedagogical everyday—such as teachers leveraging sociocultural and sociopolitical phenomena to ground science or centering a dynamic nature of science that extends beyond Western ways of knowing.

Elementary school teachers are professionals doing one of the most important jobs—shaping and equipping young minds and, in doing so, significantly influencing their trajectories. In the United States, elementary school teachers are also some of the most overworked professionals; they are educators who need to be well versed across disciplines, and they are overwhelmingly white, middle class, and female teaching a student demographic that is increasingly diverse, multicultural, and multilingual.

Moldavan and Nafziger take these important factors into consideration. The authors are disarmingly transparent as they reflect on their own learning journeys as white, cis, female elementary school educators and researchers, as well as on their own sensemaking of who they are as people and as elementary teachers, who their students are, and how and why it matters to care deeply for them with and through science teaching for social justice. After laying bare their *whys*, the authors offer concrete suggestions for *hows*, with attention paid to the demands and constraints of varied elementary school contexts. They offer complete adaptable unit plans that are standards aligned, as well as grab-and-go activities for the more time starved, all rooted in social justice.

Together with the authors, we believe unfailingly in the transformative power of science teaching and learning, the noble profession of elementary teaching, and the brilliance of all children. In a world mired in systemic injustices, the elementary classroom, a ubiquitous space that almost all children inhabit almost daily, can be one that attends, mends, empowers, and equips all children, especially children who are negotiating the most challenging circumstances in everyday spaces. "Can you hear a major roadway from your school's playground? Not all schools can. Can you find shade at a local park? Not all people can." Moldavan and Nafziger show us how elementary teachers might begin.

Preface

This work began, like so many meaningful things do, as a simple conversation between the authors, Alesia and Bailey, who quickly realized that they shared the same passion for change. Though our paths into the world of science education were different, we found ourselves walking side by side with a shared goal: to support and inspire elementary science teachers to become *change agents* in their classrooms.

Through ongoing conversations, shared lesson ideas, and moments of "Have you ever tried this?" and "What if we did that?" we realized we weren't just colleagues—we were *critical friends*. We pushed each other to think deeply, to examine our own assumptions and biases, and to constantly reflect on our practices. Our hope is that this spirit of reflection and growth spills off the pages of this book and into your hands, helping you to see your own science classroom as a space for both curiosity and courage.

So, where did this seed of writing a book begin? In 2024, we submitted a session proposal for the National Science Teaching Association's national conference in Denver, Colorado. Our session was titled "Unpacking a Science for Social Justice Toolbox," and the word *toolbox* quickly became more than a session title. It became our metaphor and our mission.

You see, a toolbox isn't just one shiny new idea. It's filled with options. Some tools may be well worn from use, while others may be shiny and new, waiting to be put into use. The toolbox holds resources you reach for when you're stuck, when you're building something new, or when you're simply trying to make something stronger. That's what we wanted to create for you: a science for social justice *toolbox*—one that includes lessons, activities, big ideas, and reflective questions you can use to challenge yourself and your students to think critically about the world around us.

Now, here's where it gets real. While planning that session, we were not only cultivating our professional passion; we were also growing tiny humans at home. Amid research articles and lesson plans were bottles and *lots* of diapers. And—wouldn't you know it?—diapers themselves became a powerful starting point for one of our science lessons.

Ever heard of *diaper deserts*? We hadn't either, until we started to notice that in some communities, including those where our students live and work, access to affordable, high-quality diapers is severely limited. That's a real issue, with real consequences. So, we designed a lesson where we examined the absorbency of various diaper brands at different price points. We had participants inspect diapers up close (yes, really!), make scientific observations, gather data, and then connect these findings to real-world social issues like economic inequality and access to basic care products.

It may sound messy, and it was! But that messiness sparked deep, critical conversations among the teachers in our session—conversations that led to *more* ideas for meaningful, justice-centered science instruction. The diaper lesson wasn't just a quirky activity; it was a seed. And as it turns out, it helped plant another one, too.

In that same session, we met Debbie Hardin, a senior acquisitions editor for Corwin and a powerful advocate for transformative education. She not only recognized the energy in the room and the potential in our approach but also encouraged us to take a bold next step: *write this book*. So, we did.

Now here we are, holding open this metaphorical toolbox for *you*, the passionate, curious, and committed elementary science teacher. We know this work isn't easy and you won't be able to use this framework for every science standard you teach in a year. But just like changing diapers or raising kids, it can be messy. Sometimes it smells. Sometimes you want to hand it off to someone else. But if you stick with it, you get those beautiful, unforgettable moments—the moments when a student *gets it*, or asks a question that makes you stop and think, or sees their own life experience reflected in the science they're learning.

That's the joy we're chasing here. And that's the change we believe (and know) is possible.

We encourage you to use this book not just as a guide but as a conversation starter. You might use this in a professional learning community, in teacher book or study groups, or even in those informal after-school chats at your favorite local spot. Talk with your peers. Ask questions. Try something new. Reflect. Grow.

And remember, just like a child learning to ride a bike, there *will* be bumps, bruises, and skinned knees along the way. But those stumbles are part of the learning journey. They remind us *why* we do this work, and remind us of the need to create classrooms where students don't just learn science but learn to use science to make the world better.

Change begins with you—right there in your classroom, with your students, your stories, and science. The impact you want to see in the world starts with the choices you make and the experiences you create.

Let's open the toolbox and get to work. We're so glad you're here.

—Alesia and Bailey

Acknowledgments

This work is a tribute to the many passionate and dedicated teachers who have inspired us along the way. Your courage to teach with heart, to reflect deeply, and to continually push the boundaries of what science education can be is the very reason this book exists. You are the change agents shaping the next generation of thinkers, problem-solvers, and world-builders. We are grateful to learn from and alongside you.

We owe special thanks to Debbie Hardin, senior acquisitions editor at Corwin, for seeing the spark in our work and giving us the space, encouragement, and support to turn it into something bigger. Your belief in us planted the seed for this project, and your guidance helped it grow.

To our families and friends, thank you for cheering us on and giving us the time and grace to write, reflect, and share our story. Your unwavering love and support made this journey possible.

We also extend our heartfelt gratitude to the reviewers and educators who generously gave feedback on our shared units and grab-and-go lessons. Thank you, Karli Gilbertson, for piloting lessons with your fourth graders and providing valuable feedback. These insights helped shape this book into a practical, thoughtful, and responsive resource for teachers everywhere.

To those in our professional networks who continue to share this work in your classrooms, schools, and communities, thank you. Your commitment to equity, action, and student-centered science helps this work ripple out far beyond these pages.

And finally, to the young scientists who inspire us every single day, you are the reason we do what we do. We encourage you to follow your dreams. Don't be afraid to imagine and use science as a tool to help you achieve those dreams.

With deep appreciation,
Alesia and Bailey

PUBLISHER'S ACKNOWLEDGMENTS

Corwin gratefully acknowledges the contributions of the following reviewers:

Karon Akins
Administrator, Riverside County Office of Education
Redlands, CA

Tamara Daugherty
Third-Grade Teacher, Zellwood Elementary
Orlando, FL

Enya Granados
Life Science Teacher, Clarke Central High School
Athens, GA

Courtney Koestler
Associate Professor
Director, Ohio Center for Equity in Mathematics and Science
Athens, OH

Edralin Pagarigan
Resource Teacher, Adjunct Faculty
Baltimore County Public Schools
University of Maryland Baltimore County
Rosedale, MD

Thomas Roberts
Associate Professor, Bowling Green State University
Waterville, OH

Jennifer Ward
Associate Professor of Early Childhood and Elementary Mathematics
Kennesaw State University
Canton, GA

About the Authors

Alesia Mickle Moldavan, PhD, is an associate professor of elementary mathematics and science education in the College of Education at Georgia Southern University. She received her BSEd in mathematics education at the University of Georgia, her MEd in mathematics education at Georgia State University, and her PhD in teaching and learning in mathematics education at Georgia State University. She specializes in teaching mathematics and science methods courses to both preservice and in-service teachers. With a background that includes teaching in diverse Title I secondary schools in Georgia and facilitating science, technology, engineering, and mathematics (STEM) enrichment programs at the elementary level, Alesia brings a wealth of practical and pedagogical experience to her role. Her teaching cultivates meaningful learning experiences by integrating culturally responsive strategies and preparing teachers to identify students' strengths and areas for growth, nurture positive STEM identities, and become ethical advocates and change agents for all learners.

Her research interests center on equitable and culturally responsive teaching practices, as well as the integration of digital technology in teacher education to enhance accessibility and inclusivity. Rooted in a commitment to social justice, her work examines how systemic inequities affect educational outcomes and explores ways to disrupt inequitable narratives. Her recent scholarship emphasizes the development and implementation of innovative curricula and instructional practices in teacher preparation programs that foster cultural awareness, critically engage with issues of equity, and promote STEM justice-oriented advocacy. By empowering teachers with the tools to recognize and address social injustices in educational settings, her research supports the cultivation of socially conscious teachers who are equipped to enact change within and beyond the classroom.

Bailey Nafziger, EdD, is an assistant professor of elementary science education in the College of Education at Georgia Southern University. She received her BS in elementary education from the College of St. Scholastica in Duluth, Minnesota, her master's in science education from Northern Arizona University, and her educational doctorate from the University of North Dakota.

Bailey spent her first decade in education working as a middle school science teacher and an elementary gifted specialist in southern Arizona. Along with regular teaching responsibilities, Bailey took on teacher-leadership roles including serving as an instructional coach, mentoring new teachers, and leading professional learning communities, as well as designing and facilitating professional development in both science and gifted education at the district and state levels. She also dedicated time to her students by working as a soccer coach, serving as a Student Council advisor, and being an advisor for other various student-led initiatives.

Currently, Bailey teaches elementary science education methods at both the undergraduate and graduate levels. Her classes have a strong theme of asset-based instruction and differentiating to elevate the strengths of each student. Her recent scholarship centers on overlaps between science education, gifted education, and culturally responsive teaching. Her goal is to empower teachers to engage in social justice work in their classrooms while modeling the process to and for their students. Bailey has truly fallen in love with teaching and maintains the goal of preparing teachers for the dedication, passion, and perseverance necessary to succeed in the field today.

Introduction

Science education, at its heart, is about teaching students the methods they'll use to understand the world around them.

—Marilyn Vogel, "Social Justice in Science Class" (2019)

The amount of lesson planning elementary teachers do is extensive—every day, in every subject, and for every student. With reading and mathematics being the most tested subjects, teachers may push science planning and instructional time aside as a form of self-preservation. We get it! You deserve a moment to catch your breath. If you are a teacher who wants to offer more authentic and relevant lessons to your youngest scientists, even with limited time, this book is for you. We aim to support you, as teachers and teacher leaders, to wield science as a force for positive change and ignite passion in your students.

Empowering elementary teachers to create learning environments that foster critical thinking about the broader implications of science is essential. Too often, elementary schools neglect science due to the pressure to prioritize heavily tested skills like reading, writing, and mathematics. This narrow focus can inadvertently overlook science's rich, integrative potential to enhance these skills through inquiry-driven explorations. When given the resources and support to delve into science topics, teachers can help students meaningfully connect scientific concepts to real-world issues, making learning both relevant and purposeful. This approach not only bolsters academic skills across the board but also instills a deeper understanding of how science intersects with and influences various aspects of life.

When science education considers issues pertinent to students' communities, it transforms from a mere academic subject into a powerful tool for social critique and problem-solving. Furthermore, using phenomena-based learning as a catalyst for inquiry lets students see firsthand how they can apply science to address and challenge systems of oppression and injustice in their everyday lives. This approach encourages students to think critically about societal issues and empowers them to use their scientific knowledge to

> *When science education considers issues pertinent to students' communities, it transforms from a mere academic subject into a powerful tool for social critique and problem-solving.*

advocate for change. In addition to fostering critical thinking and analytical skills, teaching science through pedagogical practices rooted in building connections between schools and communities—and, more broadly, the world—cultivates a sense of agency and responsibility in students, which aligns with teaching for social justice. Teachers can use social justice science teaching to equip students with a toolbox to examine social disparities and explore ways they can intervene to seek equity and justice.

As you read and implement the ideas from this book into your classroom, we anticipate that you will see for yourself the benefits of social justice science teaching. These benefits will not only enhance your science teaching but also significantly impact the way your students use science to advocate for themselves and their communities. Specifically, you can expect to do all of the following:

- Gain a deeper understanding of your students, recognizing them as capable science learners and potential social justice advocates.
- See students' diverse assets and experiences as opportunities to amplify their voices and agency within their communities.
- Learn how to connect science to students' lives in meaningful ways through real-world phenomena.
- Ignite students' curiosity and give them the tools to act as scientists and make sense of natural phenomena while improving their science literacy.
- Explore how science can be a tool to address social disparities, empowering students to lead efforts to improve injustices.
- Discover how integrating social justice into your science instruction can advance your professional development and enhance what you are already doing in your classroom.
- Realize that you are not alone in this endeavor and, although the journey may be challenging, it is profoundly rewarding.

WHY THIS BOOK?

> Injustice anywhere is a threat to justice everywhere.
>
> —Martin Luther King Jr.,
> *Letter From a Birmingham Jail* (1963)

Think of justice as a ripple effect and consider how an initial disturbance causes effects that expand outward and influence a broader area. For instance, consider the lack of access to quality science resources and high-quality teachers with the knowledge to teach science at an underfunded school. The lack of funding offered to a school may limit exposure to science activities (during or after school) and the availability of up-to-date curriculum and lab materials to guide student learning opportunities. Students at the school may be less likely to become interested in science and may perform at a lower level than peers at well-funded schools. This ripple effect can reinforce data noting how students from underfunded schools are less likely to pursue science, technology, engineering, and mathematics (STEM) careers. A community with fewer STEM professionals may face economic disparity and shortages in needed STEM fields like health care and technological advancements that impact the quality of life within a community. Furthermore, the underrepresentation of minoritized communities in STEM perpetuates stereotypes and biases, which influences further opportunities for community members, both current and in the future.

Social justice science teaching explores issues of injustice, such as community underfunding, environmental injustice, representation in science, climate change, and food insecurity, just to name a few, integrated into curricula, even at an elementary level. Teachers can play a vital role in helping students understand and address the inequities that exist in science education and the broader community. Your part in teaching science for social justice is needed not only to help break the ripple effect of disadvantage but also to create a more just and equitable society where students, particularly those who identify as Black, Brown, and Latinx,[1] have opportunities to succeed in science and contribute positively to their communities.

> *Teachers can play a vital role in helping students understand and address the inequities that exist in science education and the broader community.*

So, what is the first step in doing this important work in your classroom? Before we jump in, let us take a step back and take a deep breath. Teaching science for social justice is not easy, nor should it be. You may wonder what topics to introduce and how to connect them to the curriculum effectively. You might also question the developmental and age appropriateness of the topics and how to facilitate meaningful conversations on societal issues from varying perspectives, including those of the privileged and the oppressed. Concerns about student reactions and responses from administrators, families, and community members are valid but should not deter you from incorporating social justice into science education. While there may be challenges and risks in engaging in social justice science teaching, especially at a time

---

[1] In this book, we intentionally capitalize *Black* and *Brown* while leaving *white* in lowercase. This language choice honors the cultural, historical, and political identities of these communities. Leaving *white* lowercase pushes back on the idea that whiteness is the default or standard. Language can quietly reinforce systems of privilege, and this small shift is one way we can interrupt that. We also use *Latinx* as a gender-inclusive term for people of Latin American descent, recognizing its intention to include all gender identities and challenge the gender binary embedded in the Spanish language. We use it deliberately and with respect. At the same time, we acknowledge that not everyone in the community embraces the term, and conversations around identity and language are ongoing. We remain committed to using language that strives to be inclusive, even as we stay attentive to how these terms continue to evolve.

when both science and social justice are under partisan attack, the work is essential to humanize education and open the doors of access and opportunity for all, particularly those who have suffered and continue to suffer from unjust practices.

It is also important to challenge the common misconception that young students, such as those in elementary school, are unaware of societal issues. In fact, elementary students are often quick to recognize and articulate instances of unfairness. As a teacher, you can harness this innate awareness to help students examine injustice and understand how they can contribute positively as citizens. We wrote this book to share with you the knowledge, skills, and confidence to undertake this important work. By developing this toolbox, so to speak, you can ensure that children are prepared to make a positive impact on their communities and the world. Throughout the book, we provide practical strategies for teaching science for social justice, empowering students to become agents of change. If the journey gets tough, remember what brought you to this book in the first place—a drive to nurture a generation of informed, empathetic, and proactive individuals through social justice science teaching.

And, while you may have personal reasons for doing this work, research supports several reasons why teaching science for social justice benefits both teachers and students. Teaching science for social justice can do all of the following:

1. Promote Critical Thinking: *Teachers* can enhance their teaching strategies by connecting science content to relevant societal issues to promote inquiry and a deeper understanding of scientific concepts. This approach encourages *students* to question and analyze these issues from a scientific lens, fostering critical thinking and problem-solving skills (Vieira & Tenreiro-Vieira, 2016).

2. Enhance Relevance and Engagement: When *teachers* incorporate students' interests and experiences, they create a dynamic and interactive learning environment where lessons and labs are more impactful and engaging. Making science relevant to *students* increases their engagement and motivation to learn (Shin et al., 2019).

3. Develop Respect and Social Awareness: *Teachers* can foster a more inclusive classroom environment that values diversity and equity. In turn, *students* can understand and respect diverse experiences and perspectives, building social awareness and responsibility.

4. Build Community Connections: *Teachers* can enrich science learning by creating opportunities for community partnerships and collaborative projects. *Students* can use this approach to see how science is applied in their communities to benefit all.

5. Prompt Equity in Education: By framing social justice lessons with equitable teaching practices, *teachers* can create opportunities for larger conversations around equity and how transformative action can bring about positive change both in and out of science classrooms. *Students*, in turn, can explore how social disparities limit participation and voice, learning ways to confront and challenge these disparities through science, thereby striving for social justice (Rodriguez & Morrison, 2019).

6. Empower Advocacy and Agency: *Teachers* can guide students to apply their scientific knowledge to real-world issues. Doing so helps *students* become advocates for change and develops their use of science skills to address social injustices.

7. Prepare Students for Future Problem-Solving: *Teachers* can use innovative educational approaches to ensure students become aware of and responsive to societal needs (Calabrese Barton & Tan, 2019). When equipped with these skills, *students* can tackle complex, real-world problems effectively.

Throughout this book, we will explore these benefits in further detail. We will position these key ideas in the literature guiding science education, three-dimensional science instruction, the Next Generation Science Standards (NGSS), and the initiatives led by professional organizations (e.g., National Science Teaching Association) that strive to promote excellence and innovation in science teaching, including the advancement of science and social justice education. Additionally, in this book we'll build on the work of social justice in science education (e.g., Atwater et al., 2013; Barton, 2003; Hansson & Yacoubian, 2020). We'll also highlight research occurring in other disciplines like mathematics (e.g., Bartell et al., 2023; Berry et al., 2020; Gutstein, 2006; Koestler et al., 2023) and reference the Learning for Justice (2022) standards framing conversations about identity, diversity, justice, and action. These guiding works will provide a solid foundation as we pursue social justice through a science education lens.

OUR LENSES AND BELIEFS FRAMING THIS BOOK

This book reflects our lenses and experiences teaching in K–12 classrooms and teacher education. Our lenses reflect white, middle-class women privileged to experience education, particularly science and STEM education, and continue to seek additional education in postsecondary contexts. We acknowledge that having opportunities to access high-quality education and be raised in families and communities that support this access is a privilege. And, while our experiences reflect that privilege, we also bring experiences teaching and supervising teachers in Title I schools that serve diverse students from low-income families, where a high percentage of our students qualified for free or reduced-price lunches. Our schools used Title I funding in hopes of addressing educational disparities and ensuring students had access to high-quality education; however, the funding initiatives also illuminated the additional supports needed, one of which included offering innovative science curricula that connected to students and their communities and empowered them to seek science as an avenue to disrupt systemic inequities. In the following, we offer a deeper dive into our *whys* for this work and how our partnership gave us the strength to push each other to grow, which includes checking ourselves for blind spots, embracing discomfort, and fighting for students and their communities for whom the system was not built.

My Adaptation and *Why* Motivator: Alesia Mickle Moldavan's Lens

From an early age, I hoped to inspire students as a teacher the same way dedicated teachers inspired me. Growing up in a predominantly white, middle-class neighborhood, I had an expectation to do well in education. This expectation, while family driven, was also supported in my K–12 education. "Onward and upward" and "Raise your hand and participate" rang through my ears every morning as I climbed onto the bus that took me to school from an affluent neighborhood. As I carried my bookbag through the school's halls, I also carried the pressure not to let my family down. This pressure continued in college, being a first-generation college graduate from one side of the family and the first to receive a terminal degree (PhD) on either side.

Another innate pressure that drove my educational pursuit was that of facing education with a chronic illness and the uncertainty that comes with living with a progressive disease that can be camouflaged as an invisible disability. Living with cystic fibrosis (CF) is both a blessing and, well, a blessing. CF is a part of me that makes me unique (a blessing), but it also brings challenges that make me grow stronger (another blessing). The challenges give me insights into a system that was not built for individuals with chronic illnesses to follow their educational dreams, especially given that time works against you and school does not stop when you are absent fighting an infection at home or in the hospital. Without my family and medical support, I would not be where I am today.

I recognize that others do not have this support, which drives me to be the model and cheerleader where I can. I also recognize the privileges of an "invisible disability" and how I can hide my disease and blend in with my surroundings so as not to become seen as a victim, in some instances, to a system where those for whom it was built can continue to flourish and reap the benefits. But even now, I wonder why I disclose this information if I am not hospitalized with an exacerbation, teaching with an IV hidden under my clothes, or fighting an infection with tough antibiotics wreaking havoc on my body. Maybe I am not in these circumstances at the moment, but I never know about tomorrow and the uncertainties and stress that come with that.

When teaching, I saw similar stressors with my students at my Title I magnet high school for science and technology. Some students confided their concerns about being the first Black man or first Latinx woman in their family to do well in mathematics and want to pursue STEM in higher education. Some students did not know when they would eat over a weekend or holiday break, which understandably trumped their concern for how they might finish their trigonometry homework even if I let them borrow one of my classroom calculators. While I could not relate to or even fathom these students' challenges and injustices, I knew being an advocate, whether asked or not, drove my purpose to teach and care for all students in my classroom. Teaching STEM further spurred my drive because of the additional hurdles placed before students in historically marginalized communities who are overlooked or questioned for their pursuits in a space not built for them.

With this book I hope to illuminate the need for students to have access to science and STEM more broadly. I also hope to spark conversations about why injustices exist and how students can explore these injustices, even at an early age. While social justice can be an avenue to generate change and justice for all, it can also be an opportunity for students to self-reflect and see how they can be empowered to confront their life challenges, whatever they may be. With the skills, instructional strategies, and lessons shared in this book, I wish for you to continue to grow into your role as a change agent at your school. Let your difference create a ripple effect in your school and community. Students need strong science teachers who can be their advocates, and I wish to cheer you on since my time in life, and anyone's time in life, is uncertain. So, let us make the difference starting today.

> *Let your difference create a ripple effect in your school and community.*

Looking Back to Move Forward With My *Why*: Bailey Nafziger's Lens

The *whys* for writing this book are the students I had in my first years of teaching. Some of you may hold the same sentiment when reflecting on your first year in the classroom—I just want to apologize to those students! It was not for lack of effort; I worked nights and weekends to plan, grade, and organize class periods and middle school dances. However, I missed the forest for the trees. I did not tune into my students' needs and experiences in the lessons I was planning or the feedback I was providing. Instead, I put my head down and trudged through content without recognizing what my students truly needed from me. *Hint: It was not a lecture on Newton's laws.*

After reflecting, I now know I was not prepared to engage my students *on their terms*. I had the content knowledge and knowledge of "best practices," but it became increasingly clear I was not prepared for *my students and their community*. My students were predominantly Hispanic, and their parents worked long hours as migrant agricultural workers, which was very different from my hometown community, mostly comprising white, middle-class families in North Dakota. My ability to explain Punnett squares was irrelevant to my students' lives. They tuned out, and my frustration grew. I dedicated my time and energy to forcing my students to fit into my idea of what a classroom *should* look like.

> *Capitalizing on student and community strengths puts your students in the driver's seat to steer learning while building stronger relationships, communication skills, and empathy for others.*

As I continued my education and gained more years in the classroom, I learned and experienced how important and meaningful it is to build a classroom *for the students* rather than building the students for the classroom. Capitalizing on student and community strengths puts your students in the driver's seat to steer learning while building stronger relationships, communication skills, and empathy for others. So, my *why* for this book is somewhat of an apology letter to my first classroom and a hope for teachers to see the value in the communities where they work earlier than I did in my career.

We want you to see value in students' communities, cultural backgrounds, traditions, and linguistic strengths and treat these as assets that they bring to the classroom. Recognizing students' assets in the classroom empowers your students to understand and address societal issues, such as fairness, equity, and human rights. This book strives to help you and your students use science as a tool to develop empathy, critical thinking, and a sense of civic responsibility. Whether you identify as a beginning or veteran teacher, our goal should always be to prepare students for our future world, not just academically but also as compassionate and engaged members of society.

A COLLECTIVE PARTNERSHIP

As mentioned in our *whys*, we are white, cisgender females. We are aware of our privileges and see our individual privileges as motivators for why we developed this book. We took on this challenge in response to our personal teaching philosophies and see alignment in how the book reflects our teacher education program initiatives in our College of Education at Georgia Southern University. We both teach elementary science methods courses and collaboratively plan to develop and refine innovative curricula. In our work, we see diverse preservice and in-service teachers with varying levels of science knowledge and confidence in their abilities to teach and learn science.

As part of a student inventory assessment in our elementary science methods courses administered during the first week of class, we ask preservice and in-service teachers to complete a science autobiography to reflect on their relationship with science as both a learner and a teacher. Most of the time, preservice and in-service teachers self-report negative views toward science, often due to past experiences where they struggled with content or found science unengaging. While some of these teachers attribute their negative views to science being an afterthought at the end of a school day and being taught through irrelevant worksheets, others note that they did not see science as something they could do because the content was presented through a list of memorized facts and reflected "scientists" who did not look like them. These negative perceptions impact their self-efficacy in teaching science, meaning they often feel less capable and confident in teaching science effectively.

Those with favorable views toward science recall times when they could ask questions, get hands-on with materials, and explore scientific concepts through meaningful connections and student-centered learning approaches. Having these positive experiences helps to reinforce positive attitudes toward learning science. Furthermore, these types of experiences help to shape teachers' self-image as capable science teachers who can be successful in a science methods course and the field of teaching science.

Given how the beliefs of preservice and in-service teachers about science are multifaceted and influenced by a combination of past experiences, self-efficacy, and instructional methods encountered when learning science, we see a need to provide positive, hands-on experiences with science teaching that can help shift beliefs toward more positive and effective approaches. One such approach is exploring science through a lens of social justice. As teacher educators and past K–12 schoolteachers, we use these experiences as the lens and beliefs driving this work. We are grateful for the opportunity to share this work with you and invite you on the journey.

THE BOOK'S AUDIENCE

We wrote this book for teachers and teacher leaders who are stakeholders in high-quality elementary science education. We envision teachers using this book in professional development contexts and professional learning communities. Even if such a structured space is unavailable, we still encourage you to read the book and see how the guided teaching manifesto and reflection questions prompt individual self-reflection. Furthermore, teachers who read this book may be new to social justice or even on a journey to becoming social justice–focused teachers in elementary schools. Teachers may also be seasoned with years of experience teaching science for social justice in their toolbox. Regardless of where you align in your teaching journey, you do not have to be an expert in social justice or science education to engage in this book.

We also see this book designed for those in leadership working to support science instruction in elementary contexts. For instance, instructional coaches, administrators, consultants, and curriculum designers might find

> *Especially in social justice work, the work of an advocate is never done until there is justice for all. But it takes one to begin the ripple effect in a community, so we hope that is you!*

this book beneficial. Moreover, elementary science teacher educators whose preservice and in-service teachers are developing their understanding of social justice science teaching and see value in using the lessons to inform their practice may benefit. Whatever lens you bring to this book, know you are welcomed and encouraged to use the ideas as stepping stones along your journey. Especially in social justice work, the work of an advocate is never done until there is justice for all. But it takes one to begin the ripple effect in a community, so we hope that is you!

THE BOOK'S ORGANIZATION

The book consists of three parts. At the end of this introduction, you will have an opportunity to pause and reflect, assessing how you see yourself as a social justice science teacher through a teaching manifesto. The manifesto provides a chance to assess your growth in skills and confidence in using science for social justice. You will revisit and revise it as you progress through the book and respond to the end-of-chapter discussion questions. These questions coincide with the chapter's summary and encourage open dialogue for sharing in your professional development or professional learning community, if applicable.

Part I (Chapters 1–2) provides an overview of teaching social justice in science education and why exploring social justice in the context of science is important, especially for children in elementary school. Chapter 1 lays the groundwork for what social justice looks like in science and how teaching through a lens of empathy can help students look beyond their needs and tune in with others. The chapter also discusses why representation matters in the classroom and references recent social justice initiatives in science education reform, including connections to the NGSS and the Learning for Justice (2022) Social Justice Standards. Chapter 2 provides a rationale for bringing purpose and justice into the science classroom. It starts by discussing how we do (and don't do) science, what counts as science, and the value of community connections and support when teaching science for social justice. Additionally, the chapter reviews related literature about ways to advocate using science. Readers who need a foundation for social justice science education will be encouraged to review Part I before looking into Part II (Chapters 3–5), which presents considerations for designing and implementing social justice science lessons.

In Part II, Chapter 3 addresses steps to plan for a social justice science lesson. It notes the importance of learning about students and seeing diversity as an asset. Additionally, it discusses ways to establish an inclusive classroom community to support and sustain social justice exploration. We suggest ways to recognize how diverse voices and perspectives hold value, especially from historically marginalized groups. Classroom norms can be set collaboratively with students to promote respect, active listening, and open dialogue. Students can also ask questions and think critically about social justice issues. The essence of focusing on the foundation of the classroom is to establish a classroom community that values students' experiences, negotiates ethics and morals, and presents opportunities for students to engage in argumentation that builds on evidence-based explanations.

Thereafter, we'll share a framework for social justice science lessons, acknowledging phases that encourage teachers to "elicit," "investigate," "interrogate," and "act." We'll explore discussions pertaining to finding the right phenomena, connecting the phenomena to three-dimensional science learning, and taking action. The lessons are built with reference to phenomena that examine social inequities to promote investigations and debates about fairness and equity. For instance, when considering environmental justice, a phenomenon of interest could be pollution. Making connections between pollution and social justice can open doors to exploring how pollution disproportionately affects marginalized and vulnerable communities. Less affluent communities might live closer to polluting industries or waste disposal sites. These settings frequently experience increased exposure to environmental hazards found in air and water. Connecting the phenomena to three-dimensional science learning in the context of social justice is not easy; thus, we describe ways to hone in on the NGSS content standards and the Learning for Justice (2022) Social Justice Standards in a manner that is responsive to students' learning needs and issues in their communities. We close with manageable steps to meet students where they are as they develop critical consciousness toward social injustice.

Chapter 4 provides three science social justice unit plans. The units are driven by relevant, sociocultural-informed phenomena and explicitly address the three dimensions of high-quality science instruction (i.e., Disciplinary Core Ideas, Science and Engineering Practices, and Crosscutting Concepts) organized using the Elicit–Investigate–Interrogate–Act framework. Students can connect the topics to related issues in their communities and problem-solve ways to take action. The chapter shares the units as examples of ways to teach using the framework and provides additional notes on ways teachers can differentiate and modify the units for similar use in units already implemented in their contexts.

Chapter 5 provides grab-and-go science social justice lessons. These NGSS-aligned lessons reference short case-based scenarios driven by real-life phenomena of social justice issues to prompt individual or collaborative reflection from students. The chapter concludes with reflection questions to identify critical elements of social justice science lessons. The grab-and-go nature of the lessons offers a sample of what students can do in a smaller context, a stand-alone lesson, or a self-guided learning exploration. The lessons are low tech and quick to set up, providing opportunities for students to explore as an enrichment or when there is not enough time in a school day to devote to science planning.

Part III (Chapters 6–7) recommends the next steps for looking ahead and taking action. Chapter 6 suggests ways of teaching social justice in today's climate. We know teaching is political and, thus, can be confrontational. So, ensuring teachers strategize ways to do good for their students and community while protecting themselves is imperative. Consider the oxygen masks on a plane. You must place one on yourself before you can help others. While the actions may seem selfish, the intent is to ensure you have the strength to care for those around you. Your students need you, especially a strong you, to be their advocate. Thus, in this chapter we touch on knowing your purpose, priorities, and professional responsibilities. It's important to find your people and know your sphere of influence. You must also curate patience for missteps and pitfalls and, more importantly, hold on to hope.

To close the book, in Chapter 7 we encourage reflection on ways to take action in your context. We'll reflect on the book and your growth in developing strategies to design and implement social justice science lessons. We'll mention ways to sustain your work through reflection and renewal. We also hope that you reflect on all that you have learned in the book as you revisit and revise your teaching manifesto. You can share this artifact within your learning community or keep it on your desk as a reminder to stay focused on your priorities for doing social justice work.

YOUR TEACHING MANIFESTO

Complete the following statements to reflect on your *why* for doing social justice science education work. Recording your responses allows you to communicate your vision, guide your practice, keep yourself accountable, evolve your motivation, and support your professional growth. You may share your teaching manifesto with others or keep it private. We will also encourage you to revisit it as you progress through this book to see how your thinking has transformed and what goals you have met.

My Teaching Manifesto

My *why* for doing social justice science education entails . . .

_____
_____
_____
_____
_____

When promoting teaching science for social justice,

- I will be intentional about . . .

  _____
  _____
  _____
  _____
  _____

- I will keep the focus on . . .

  _____
  _____
  _____
  _____
  _____

- I will provide opportunities for . . .

  _____
  _____
  _____
  _____
  _____

- I will be thoughtful in my lesson planning by . . .

  _____
  _____
  _____
  _____
  _____

- I will teach . . .

  _____
  _____
  _____
  _____
  _____

- I promise to . . .

  _____
  _____
  _____
  _____
  _____

- I will view students as . . .

  _____
  _____
  _____
  _____
  _____

- I will view the community as . . .

  _____
  _____
  _____
  _____
  _____

PART I

Using Science to Solve Problems

Where Do We Begin?

CHAPTER 1

Connecting Minds and Hearts Through Critical Thinking and Engagement in Science

Science makes people reach selflessly for truth and objectivity; it teaches people to accept reality, with wonder and admiration, not to mention the deep awe and delight that the natural order of things brings to the true scientist.

—Lise Meitner, 20th-century physicist

Teachers are undeniably busy, and we truly appreciate you taking the time to explore our book! Whether teaching science makes you break out into a cold sweat or it's the highlight of your week, we're thrilled you're here to expand your perspective on how elementary students can use science to benefit their communities.

As educators, we have the unique opportunity to create environments where students collaboratively address issues of fairness, respect, and social responsibility—both in their classrooms and beyond. This book aims to provide practical strategies, thoughtful discussions, and valuable insights to help you foster a classroom atmosphere where every student feels valued and empowered to make a positive impact.

So, before you start thinking about the next stack of papers to grade, let's dive in!

> *As educators, we have the unique opportunity to create environments where students collaboratively address issues of fairness, respect, and social responsibility.*

SOURCE: iStock.com/wundervisuals

BUILDING CRITICAL THINKERS

Think about where you see and use the phrase *critical thinking* at school. It might appear on your classroom bulletin board, in the school's mission statements, on standardized assessment rubrics, and in countless educational frameworks. But what does it *really* mean to nurture critical thinkers in our classrooms, and how often are students *truly* positioned to think critically rather than just complete tasks?

In today's fast-moving, information-rich world, the ability to analyze, evaluate, and synthesize information is not just a skill—it's a necessity. For students, becoming critical thinkers means moving beyond rote memorization and passive learning to actively questioning assumptions, identifying patterns, evaluating evidence, and making informed decisions. It means *how* to think, not just *what* to think. This shift requires intentional instructional design and classroom practices that invite inquiry, encourage debate, and celebrate diverse perspectives. As teachers, we must consistently reflect on how our teaching either supports or stifles these habits of mind.

When posed with the same question—*Where do you see critical thinking at school?*—more than 100 science teachers from around the nation contributed to this word cloud:

From kindergarten through graduate school, critical thinking is a key objective outlined in standards, textbooks, and curriculum expectations. Given its prevalence in our field, it should be safe to assume we all know exactly what it is. Right?

Wrong.

Teachers and researchers have yet to agree on a concrete definition and are left with a "sticky thicket" of literature full of differing definitions and developmental models (Nilson, 2021, p. 15). Table 1.1 is a summary of some of the definitions and developmental trajectories researchers have published. What similarities and differences do you notice?

SOURCE: iStock.com/Ed Williams

TABLE 1.1 Definitions of Critical Thinking

DEFINITIONS OF CRITICAL THINKING	DEVELOPMENTAL MODELS OF CRITICAL THINKING

Brookfield's (2012) Assumption-Based Approach
• Three types of assumptions in five different traditions that occur in three interrelated phases:
  ○ (1) discovering the assumptions, (2) checking the accuracy, and (3) taking informed decisions
	Perry's (1968) Theory of Undergraduate Cognitive Development
	• Four stages:
	  ○ Stage 1 (Dualism) to Stage 4 (Commitment)

(Continued)

(Continued)

DEFINITIONS OF CRITICAL THINKING	DEVELOPMENTAL MODELS OF CRITICAL THINKING

Halpern's (2014) Cognitive Psychology Approach
 	
• Six critical thinking skills:
  ○ (1) verbal reasoning, (2) argument analysis, (3) scientific reasoning, (4) statistical reasoning, (5) decision-making, and (6) problem-solving
	Paul and Elder's (2010) Foundation for Critical Thinking
	
	• Six stages:
	  ○ Stage 1 (Unreflective Thinker) to Stage 6 (Accomplished Thinkers)
	• Nine intellectual traits:
	  ○ (1) humility, (2) autonomy, (3) integrity, (4) courage, (5) perseverance, (6) curiosity, (7) empathy, (8) fair-mindedness, and (9) confidence in reason

Facione's (2023) Skills and Dispositions
 	
• Eight skills:
  ○ (1) interpretation, (2) explanation, (3) analysis, (4) inference, (5) evaluation, (6) deduction, (7) induction, and (8) numeracy
• Seven dispositions:
  ○ (1) systematic, (2) inquisitive, (3) judicious, (4) truthseeking, (5) analytical, (6) open-minded, and (7) confident in reasoning
	Wolcott's (1999) Steps for Better Thinking
	
	• Five stages
	  ○ Stage 0 (Confused Fact-Finder) to Stage 4 (Strategic Revisioner)

SMALL STEPS FOR BIG IMPACT: Define What It Means to Analyze and Evaluate

▶ We often ask students to *analyze* a passage or *evaluate* items, but do they know what that means? What is the process they should follow to *analyze* or *evaluate* something? Poll your students and collaboratively define what those words mean. Students need to be able to understand and speak the vocabulary of critical thinking to be successful.

While there are many perspectives on what critical thinking is and how it develops, certain aspects are widely agreed on by researchers and educators. With numerous studies dedicated to establishing a standardized developmental trajectory, we know that critical thinking can indeed be taught and learned. However, it requires intentional and explicit integration into our objectives, questions, and assessments.

Critical thinking doesn't always come easily or naturally to our students, and that's OK! It can be a real challenge because it asks students to engage in self-regulation and using metacognition to manage one's emotions and thoughts when working with others toward a shared goal. As teachers, we should be ready to step in and gently prompt students to consider alternative perspectives that might contradict their beliefs, biases, and misconceptions. Critical thinking isn't just about skills like analyzing and evaluating; it also depends on personal dispositions, like being curious, open-minded, and willing to be empathetic when seeing things from someone else's perspective.

Critical thinking is an intentional process of analyzing, evaluating, and synthesizing information to make reasoned decisions, solve complex problems, and engage thoughtfully with diverse perspectives. It involves questioning assumptions, using evidence, and applying logic in ways that are active, reflective, and contextually responsive.

As teachers, we should be ready to step in and gently prompt students to consider alternative perspectives that might contradict their beliefs, biases, and misconceptions.

Throughout this book, we center the teaching of science on critical thinking because developing thoughtful, informed learners is just as important as building scientific knowledge. The activities in both the units (Chapter 4) and the grab-and-go lessons (Chapter 5) follow a consistent structure designed to give your students explicit practice with critical thinking. Each lesson begins with a phenomenon to spark curiosity, followed by opportunities to explore primary or secondary data, and includes structured ways for students to engage in discussion, argumentation, and reflection. These components work together to build the cognitive skills and dispositions necessary for critical thinkers (see Figure 1.1). Better yet, students will practice these skills as they explore complex, real-world problems—learning to think deeply and act responsibly in ways that can create a better world.

EMPATHY IN SCIENCE

One of the intellectual traits of a critical thinker identified by Paul and Elder (2010) is *intellectual empathy*. At first glance, this might seem like an unusual fit for science lessons. After all, empathy is often associated with personal emotions and human connection, while science is traditionally viewed as objective and impersonal, focused on facts, data, and universal truths. Empathetic individuals build relationships, seek to understand other's perspectives, and engage emotionally. Scientists, on the other hand, are often (mis)portrayed as detached, overly rational, and indifferent to social or emotional concerns. These stereotypes, reinforced by popular media, have shaped how the public tends to view scientific work and those who pursue it.

FIGURE 1.1 Purposeful Integration of Critical Thinking in Our Units and Lessons

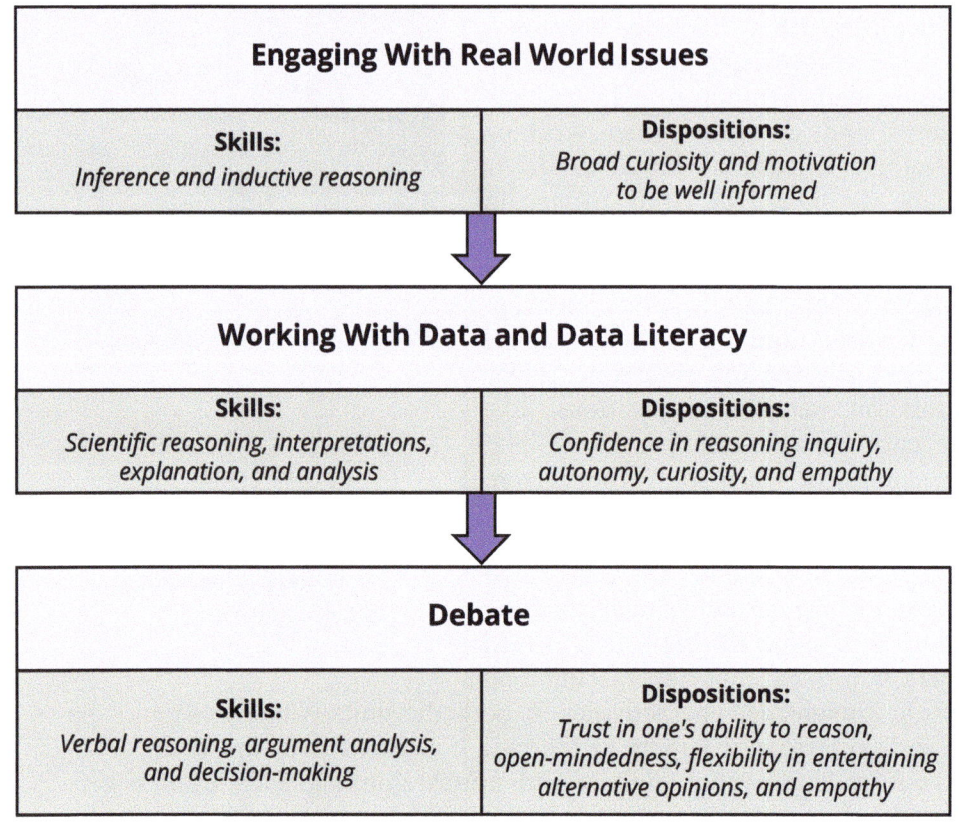

However, at its core, science is a *human endeavor* driven by curiosity, creativity, collaboration, and, yes, empathy. In this book, we emphasize the importance of recognizing that human traits, including empathy, are not separate from science but integral to how it is practiced and understood. Encouraging intellectual empathy in science classrooms helps students connect with diverse perspectives, appreciate the social dimensions of scientific issues, and engage more thoughtfully in the world around them.

> *At its core, science is a* **human endeavor** *driven by curiosity, creativity, collaboration, and, yes, empathy.*

SCIENCE AS A HUMAN AND SOCIAL ENDEAVOR

Science thrives on human curiosity, creativity, innovation, and perseverance. These are not optional add-ons to the scientific process; they are the driving forces behind every breakthrough, every discovery, and every question that has ever reshaped how we understand our world. At the heart of every scientific advancement is a person, or a team of people, who followed their genuine curiosity, asked meaningful questions, and used their creativity to imagine possibilities and design ways to explore them.

Consider the discovery of penicillin. In 1928, Alexander Fleming noticed something unusual: A mold contaminating one of his petri dishes seemed to be killing nearby bacteria. Rather than discarding the petri dish and moving on, he paused, questioned what he was seeing, and pursued a line of inquiry that would eventually revolutionize medicine. Nearly a century later, two high school students in California identified two previously unknown species of scorpion (Jain et al., 2022). These examples, though separated by time, geography, and scale, share a common thread: an insatiable curiosity that's at the very foundation of critical thinking. Asking "Why?" and "What if?" is where science begins. By nurturing these questions in our students, we're not just teaching them facts or formulas. We're helping them develop the key disposition for critical thinkers. In doing so, we position them not only as learners of science but as potential contributors to it.

> *Asking "Why?" and "What if?" is where science begins. By nurturing these questions in our students, we're not just teaching them facts or formulas. We're helping them develop the key disposition for critical thinkers.*

SOURCE: iStock.com/PeopleImages

Science is fundamentally a social endeavor. Discoveries rarely happen in isolation, for they emerge through collaboration, communication, and shared curiosity. Take, for example, Prakrit Jain and Harper Forbes, the teenage scorpion savants mentioned earlier. Their work didn't occur in a vacuum.

Instead, they used the online social platform iNaturalist (www.inaturalist.org) to share their observations and connect with a broader community of scientists and enthusiasts. This virtual collaboration led them to Dr. Lauren Esposito, an arachnologist at the California Academy of Sciences, who joined them in formally studying and documenting the species.

> *Without collaborative actions, whether through digital platforms, lab teams, or scholarly publication, novel ideas and discoveries cannot be considered scientific facts.*

Together, the trio began the lengthy process of publishing their findings in a scientific journal so others would continually reference and build on their novel discovery. Without collaborative actions, whether through digital platforms, lab teams, or scholarly publication, novel ideas and discoveries cannot be considered scientific facts.

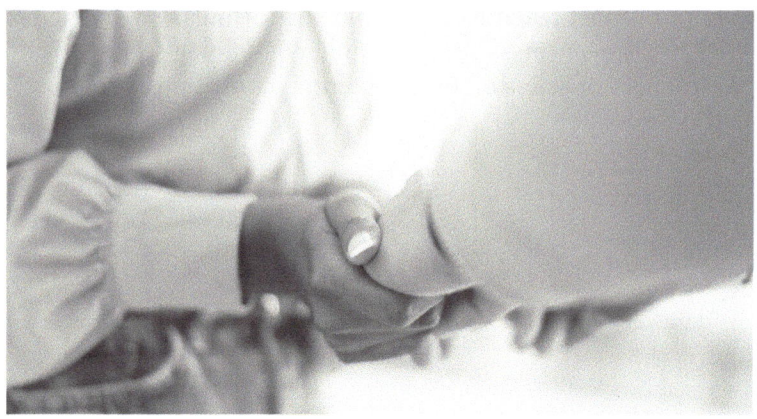

SOURCE: iStock.com/Jacob Wackerhausen

Without a healthy balance of empathy, science has the potential to do more harm than good. For example, embedded racism, sexism, and other forms of prejudice have played a role in the development of scientific knowledge. Scientists with biased agendas have cloaked their work in "scientific facts" and engaged in unethical research to advance flawed ideas and beliefs. For example, up until 1972, the U.S. Public Health Service conducted a study on Black men in Tuskegee, Alabama, to observe the natural progression of untreated syphilis. Another example of scientists failing to practice emotional empathy is the case of Henrietta Lacks, whose stem cells, taken in 1951, later became instrumental in medical research. Neither Lacks nor her family received any compensation, credit, or even information on how the immortal HeLa cells led to immeasurable benefits in the fields of cancer research, human genomics, and virology, and even in the development of polio and COVID-19 vaccines (Johns Hopkins Medicine, n.d.). With science being a pathway some take to capitalize on humanity's strengths or weaknesses, it's important we empower our students with the tools to use science for good and allow them to practice critical thinking and empathy. Their future, and our future, depends on it.

> *With science being a pathway some take to capitalize on humanity's strengths or weaknesses, it's important we empower our students with the tools to use science for good and allow them to practice critical thinking and empathy.*

Tracing Pedagogical Approaches, Illuminating Students' Assets and Communities

If you have completed a teacher preparation program in the past 20 years, you've likely encountered culturally relevant pedagogy. Gloria Ladson-Billings's (1995) work transformed pedagogical thinking by urging teachers to intentionally connect with their students' cultures and experiences, giving voice to those often marginalized. While new terms have emerged since, the pedagogies share a common goal: to leverage students' cultural backgrounds as valuable assets that enrich their learning and promote student success (see Figure 1.2).

FIGURE 1.2 Progression of Culturally Relevant Pedagogy Informing Teaching for Social Justice

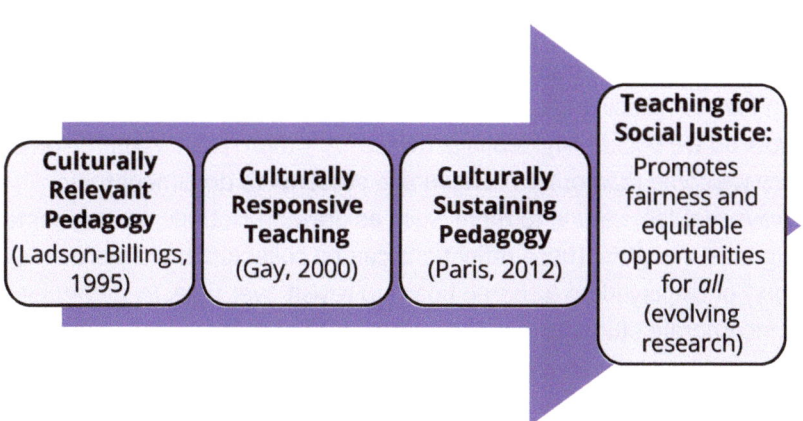

When teaching science for social justice, it is important to note that we are building on culturally relevant pedagogy (Ladson-Billings, 1995), culturally responsive teaching (Gay, 2000), and culturally sustaining pedagogy (Paris, 2012) by focusing on *action*. We are asking our students not just to recognize and reflect on social inequalities but to *act* for themselves, their classmates, and their communities to make the world a better place—a tall order for elementary students, you might say. It is. However, elementary students are capable and ready for the challenge. It's up to us, as teachers, to provide the tools and scaffolding.

Remember the child who came to your desk the other day lamenting about something unfair? Your student's issue may have been about something trivial, such as who gets to be the line leader, but it serves as evidence that they are capable and willing to identify inequitable issues. They may also have identified larger issues, such as food disparity or gender stereotypes in mathematics classrooms, but not yet have the words to communicate or take action. Elementary school students are naturally observant and notice issues of fairness and justice around them. These observations are important opportunities for us to notice as fellow teachers to guide students toward empathy, fairness, and a deeper understanding of social justice. In this book, we'll discuss the small steps and quick activities you can take in your classroom today to help prepare your students to think critically and use science *and* empathy for good tomorrow.

SMALL STEPS FOR BIG IMPACT:
Create a Fairness Inventory

▶ Creating an inclusive and just classroom environment begins with empowering young learners to recognize and address fairness. Even small moments of inequity—such as some classmates always getting to use the newest lab supplies first or certain voices being heard more often during discussions—can serve as powerful entry points for conversations about fairness. By guiding children to observe and articulate these experiences, teachers can help foster a sense of agency and responsibility in their students.

To start, invite students to look around their classroom or school and identify something that doesn't seem fair. Ask probing questions; for example, *Who gets to use certain materials first? How do we decide who leads activities? Are there places where some students feel more welcome than others?* Encourage students to document their observations in ways that feel natural to them, such as drawing pictures, writing sentences, or verbally sharing their thoughts. These reflections can be collected in a classroom "Fairness Inventory" or displayed on a shared board to revisit over time. By gathering these insights, you can incorporate students' concerns into your future lessons, demonstrating that small steps toward fairness can create meaningful change in their learning community.

Using Science to Explore Fairness

> *Young children have a strong sense of fairness—they notice when something isn't right and aren't afraid to speak up about it.*

Young children have a strong sense of fairness—they notice when something isn't right and aren't afraid to speak up about it. In a science lesson, for example, a teacher might set up an experiment where students observe how plants grow under different conditions. One plant gets plenty of sunlight and water, while another is left in the shade with little care. When students see the struggling plant, it's a perfect opportunity to ask, "What happens when some people don't have the same resources as others? How does that affect their ability to grow and succeed?" Even young children show an understanding of fairness—think about how toddlers react when a friend gets more crackers or when they see someone being left out of a game. These everyday moments remind us that fairness isn't something we have to teach from scratch—it's already there. Our job is to help students connect it to the bigger picture.

At its heart, science is about asking questions and making sense of the world. Social justice works the same way—it's about understanding how society functions, advocating for access and equity, and recognizing that fairness is not about treating everyone the same but about ensuring everyone gets what they need. When we weave science and social justice together in the classroom, especially in elementary science, we give students the tools to think critically, ask tough questions, and become not just better scientists but also more thoughtful, responsible citizens. By nurturing their curiosity, we help them see that learning isn't just about understanding the world—it's about finding ways to make it better.

> *Social justice works the same way—it's about understanding how society functions, advocating for access and equity, and recognizing that fairness is not about treating everyone the same but about ensuring everyone gets what they need.*

SOURCE: iStock.com/Andrii Yalanskyi

One way to think about science and social justice is by considering how scientific discoveries impact different communities, at both local and global levels. For example, consider environmental science and the issue of pollution. Low-income communities and communities populated largely by people of color often face the brunt of environmental issues like air and water pollution (Valencia et al., 2023). Elementary school students may not pick up data reports to compare pollution trends across varying geographical locations, but they can undoubtedly make observations in their daily lives and note differences that might not be fair. Can you hear a major roadway from your school's playground? Not all schools can. Can you find shade when you are at a local park? Not all people can.

Marginalized communities comprising predominantly people of color within 100 meters of major roadways are exposed to up to 15% more fine particle matter and nitrogen oxide (air pollutants) than white, affluent communities from traffic-related air pollution (Valencia et al., 2023). When children are on the swings, the air can feel thick, making breathing hard, and sometimes it makes them cough. Suppose they visit other playgrounds in different parts of town. They might notice the discrepancies in the cleanliness of the playground, including trash scattered around, strange-tasting water from the fountains, or the hazy sky overhead. These differences in the environmental conditions can stand out, especially when they start to affect how much fun children have or how safe they feel. This kind of pollution, seen through children's eyes, is just one example discussed later in the book. These lessons highlight how students engage with and "do" science, as well as how they can use science to tackle real-world problems.

Empowering students to recognize and critique inequities sets a crucial foundation for their engagement with larger societal issues, fostering both awareness and agency. When students are encouraged to observe and question the world around them, they begin to develop a lens for understanding systemic injustices. The approach allows children to identify inequities and pushes them to envision ways to advocate for change based on their own experiences. By studying real-world issues, such as environmental pollution, students can witness firsthand how science uncovers and explains injustices, especially in marginalized communities.

> *Empowering students to recognize and critique inequities sets a crucial foundation for their engagement with larger societal issues, fostering both awareness and agency.*

By deepening students' understanding of the causes and effects of injustices, teachers can foster student empathy for the communities most at risk. Teachers can plant seeds of inquiry to grow students' inspiration to think critically about solutions and recognize their role in bringing these solutions to life. Whether through technology, policy, or community action, students can advocate for justice, both in their local communities and on a broader scale. Empowering students to connect science with social awareness cultivates a generation of critical thinkers who see themselves as active participants capable of solving real-world challenges.

SOURCE: iStock.com/Muhammad Labib Adilah

SMALL STEPS FOR BIG IMPACT: Establish a Classroom Care Council

▶ One simple yet powerful way to foster agency in young children is through a "Classroom Care Council." This can start as a weekly discussion where students identify something in their environment that could be improved—perhaps the classroom supplies aren't shared equally, or a quiet student isn't getting a turn to lead an activity. After identifying an issue, guide students in brainstorming solutions. Maybe they will decide to create a sign-up system for shared materials or a buddy system to ensure everyone gets a turn. Small actions like these help children see that their voices matter and that they have the power to make changes, even in their own classroom. By modeling this process and celebrating their efforts, teachers help children develop the confidence and problem-solving skills they need to take meaningful action beyond the classroom.

Understanding Our World and Each Other

As a way to empower students to connect science to their own lives, we want to discover how our students imagine scientists. But first, let's take a moment to reflect on our own perceptions. In the space provided, take two minutes to jot down the names of any scientists that come to mind. Don't overthink it—just write. Once you have your list, consider the following questions to guide your reflection.

_____

_____

_____

_____

_____

Reflect

1. What do you notice about the scientists you listed?
2. Are there any patterns related to gender or race among the scientists you thought of?
3. Did you mention any of your students as scientists? If not, why do you think that is?
4. How do these patterns reflect broader societal ideas of who "gets to" be a scientist?
5. How can we expand our view of what a scientist looks like, and how might that influence the way we teach science in our classrooms?

REPRESENTATION MATTERS

Use your reflections as a powerful entry point to introduce more diverse representations of scientists in your classrooms, which will help your students see themselves as active members of the scientific community. While it is true that largely white, Western men have historically shaped the historical image of science (at least in North America), it is essential to recognize the systems that have privileged certain voices while marginalizing (and obscuring) others. At its core, science is about curiosity, discovery, and making sense of the world. It is a humanized practice, driven by the experiences, observations, and cultures of people from all walks of life.

> *We must proactively challenge our own and our students' perceptions of who gets to do science.*

We must proactively challenge our own and our students' perceptions of who gets to *do science*. Integrating social justice into science education is one approach. Students need to see that science is not just for one group of people or defined by one set of ideas. In Chapter 2, we will dive deeper into this idea of who gets to participate in science. So often, what we teach in schools focuses on Westernized views of science, but a whole world of knowledge exists outside of that lens. Encouraging students to explore different perspectives creates more inclusive and meaningful learning experiences. It also invites students to see that *anyone* can contribute to science, not just those in a white lab coat. When students recognize that science is diverse and is shaped by many cultures, they can begin to appreciate how valuable their ideas and backgrounds are in scientific spaces, making science more accessible and relevant to them. This broadening of what "counts" as science encourages deeper conversations and more flexible mindsets, where many voices can be heard, respected, and valued.

SOURCE: iStock.com/zeljkosantrac

Mirrors, Windows, and Sliding Glass Doors

So, how can teachers deepen students' understanding of the importance of diverse representation in science? We can draw on Bishop's (1990) concept of "mirrors, windows, and sliding glass doors" to ensure students have varied learning experiences that challenge them to reflect on their scientific identities. Bishop's metaphor helps us critique how the stories and perspectives we present in the classroom either reflect students' own experiences (mirrors), provide glimpses into the lives of others (windows), or allow them to step into new worlds and experiences (sliding glass doors). Applying these concepts in science education helps students see themselves and others within the scientific community.

SOURCE: iStock.com/supersizer

When we provide scientific "mirrors," we offer students, especially those from marginalized groups, the opportunity to see themselves as scientists, something they may not have traditionally encountered in science curricula. These mirrors help students connect their personal experiences and cultural backgrounds to science, reinforcing the idea that their ways of knowing and understanding the world have a place in the scientific community. For example, a Hispanic student learning about Ellen Ochoa, the first Hispanic woman astronaut (NASA, 2023), might recognize their own potential and cultural heritage in a field they previously thought was out of reach—or just never considered.

SOURCE: iStock.com/brizmaker

At the same time, students need access to "windows" into the diverse lives and perspectives of others. Science is a global practice shaped by people from all walks of life. By introducing students to scientists from different backgrounds, such as Indigenous scientists like Dr. Robin Wall Kimmerer (2020), teachers open windows that allow students to learn about alternative methods of approaching and solving problems. These windows offer students the chance to appreciate that science is better because of the diversity of experiences and viewpoints people bring. For instance, studying Indigenous ecological knowledge can give students new perspectives on sustainability and conservation, broadening their understanding of environmental science and environmental appreciation.

Finally, "sliding glass doors" allow students to step into new perspectives and experiences, expanding their sense of what is possible for themselves

SOURCE: iStock.com/ufukvural

and the world. When students engage with stories of scientists who have overcome barriers, challenged the status quo, and made groundbreaking discoveries, they begin to see science not just as a set of facts but as a field where they, too, can contribute and innovate. Sliding glass doors invite students to imagine themselves walking into the world of science, realizing they have the agency to change the field, just as others have done before them.

By incorporating Bishop's (1990) idea of "mirrors, windows, and sliding glass doors" into science education, teachers can humanize science and create a more inclusive, equitable learning environment. This approach presents science as a dynamic, human-driven field that belongs to everyone and emphasizes the value of diverse perspectives in scientific inquiry. When students understand that science is shaped by many voices and lived experiences, they are more likely to ask questions, explore new ideas, and actively participate in scientific inquiry. In doing so, they become part of the ongoing story of discovery and innovation. We must value diverse scientific contributions not just to diversify the history of science—but to reshape its future by inspiring the next generation of problem-solvers.

> *When students understand that science is shaped by many voices and lived experiences, they are more likely to ask questions, explore new ideas, and actively participate in scientific inquiry.*

SMALL STEPS FOR BIG IMPACT: Bring Mirrors, Windows, and Sliding Glass Doors Into Your Classroom

▶ You can bring Bishop's (1990) framework into your science classroom by guiding students through intentional reflections and actions connected to real-world issues. Start by choosing a relevant science topic, such as ecosystems, weather patterns, or human impact on the environment, and frame discussions using mirrors, windows, and sliding glass doors. For example, if you're exploring water pollution, begin with mirrors by asking students to reflect on their own experiences: *Have you ever seen litter in a nearby stream or pond? How did it make you feel? Where does the water you drink come from, and how do you use it every day?* Next, provide windows into other communities by sharing a book, video, or news story about places where water pollution affects wildlife and people's health: *How might a polluted river impact the animals and people who rely on it? What do scientists do to help solve these problems?* Finally, create opportunities for sliding glass doors, where students take action based on what they've learned: *What can we do to keep our water clean? Can we organize a school-wide cleanup, design posters to raise awareness, or write letters to community leaders?*

By weaving these prompts into your science lessons, you help students move beyond learning about a topic to actively engaging with it. Mirrors help them connect science to their own lives, windows broaden their perspectives, and sliding glass doors give them an entry point to take meaningful action. Whether it's through classroom discussions, hands-on projects, or small community efforts, these steps empower students to see themselves as scientists and changemakers, reinforcing the idea that learning is not just about understanding the world—it's about shaping it for the better.

Science as a Tool for Advocacy

One of the most impactful ways science connects with social justice is through advocacy. Science gives us the tools to understand problems and develop evidence-based solutions. When students realize that science is not just a collection of facts but a way to solve real-world problems, they start to see its potential to address the issues that matter most to *them* and their communities. Students who learn how to engage in scientific inquiry and critical thinking can advocate for change in their schools, neighborhoods, and beyond. This shifts the focus of learning science from being based on historical facts to being a tool for action in the present—something that can directly improve their lives and the lives of others.

> *When students realize that science is not just a collection of facts but a way to solve real-world problems, they start to see its potential to address the issues that matter most to* **them** *and their communities.*

For example, students might explore environmental concerns in their community by conducting research that supports healthier, greener spaces. They could gather data on the benefits of planting trees around their school, showing that shaded areas lead to cooler playground temperatures, making recess more comfortable and safer during warmer months. Alternatively, they could test air quality in areas with and without trees and use their findings to advocate for more green spaces in their neighborhoods. In Bailey's teaching career, this type of work led to the school's student council hosting a garage sale to purchase five Fan Tex ash trees, which they planted near the softball fields for shade. Actionable work empowers students, showing them that science can create meaningful change, even on a local level.

SOURCE: iStock.com/InCommunicado

SMALL STEPS FOR BIG IMPACT: Explore Shade Equity

▶ Would you like to try a similar activity? Maybe planting trees isn't an option, but there are plenty of other ways students can make a difference in their school environment—starting with the playground! Encourage your students to investigate how temperature varies in different areas, such as shaded versus nonshaded spots. They can measure playground temperatures at different times of the day and across seasons to see how heat levels change. To take it a step further, have students collect and organize survey results from classmates about how comfortable they feel during recess in different weather conditions. Do they notice a difference when playing in the shade versus direct sunlight?

Once students organize and analyze their data, they can use their findings to advocate for a solution—like installing shade structures. Have them draft a persuasive letter or create a presentation to share with school leaders. Along the way, guide their thinking with questions like these: *Where would shade structures make the biggest impact? How can we show others that adding shade benefits everyone? What's the best way to share our findings with the school community?* By leading students through the process of researching, analyzing, and advocating for change, you're helping them see how small steps—like collecting data and sharing their ideas—can lead to meaningful improvements in their school and beyond.

Science advocacy projects also provide a way to address equity by encouraging students to examine disparities in their communities (there is a reason the trees were planted near the softball fields and not the baseball fields, as there were more spectators and sponsors for baseball). Students might analyze the number of trees or green spaces in different parts of their town and connect those findings to issues of socioeconomic status. They might find wealthier neighborhoods have more parks and shaded areas, while lower-income neighborhoods have fewer. Armed with these data, students can make a compelling case for why their community deserves investment in green spaces, arguing that access to clean air and cool outdoor spaces should not be tied to income levels. In this way, science becomes more than just a tool for understanding the world—it becomes a means to fight inequality and improve the quality of life for all.

> *Science becomes more than just a tool for understanding the world—it becomes a means to fight inequality and improve the quality of life for all.*

Teachers play a critical role in guiding students through these processes. By fostering a classroom environment where students feel empowered to explore issues that matter to them, teachers can help students see how science intersects with justice and equity. Encouraging students to ask questions like "Who benefits from this solution?" or "Whose voices are missing from this conversation?" can spark critical discussions about how science can highlight inequities and help advocate for underrepresented communities. Students learn that science is not just for answering large, intangible questions but for creating local, positive change.

SOURCE: iStock.com/monkeybusinessimages

Ultimately, when students see how science can be a tool for advocacy, they begin to understand its full potential—not just as a subject they study but as a means of shaping the world. Whether they advocate for safer playgrounds, cleaner air, or healthier food options, they learn that they can use evidence to effect change. This reinforces the idea that science belongs to everyone and that, regardless of their background or identity, they have a role in using science for the greater good. By engaging students in projects that connect scientific inquiry with advocacy, we can inspire a new generation of scientists and leaders who see science as a field of study and a path toward justice and equity.

> *Connecting science with social justice is not just about teaching facts—we are helping students see the people represented by the facts.*

Connecting science with social justice is not just about teaching facts—we are helping students see the people represented by the facts. This approach shows students that science can help make the world a better place. It also shows students that science is not just something that happens in a lab—it is something that happens in their communities and something that they should be a part of. Furthermore, integrating social justice into science lessons builds critical thinking skills and encourages students to ask deeper questions. It is not just about the "what" or the "how" of science but also the "why" and the "who." Why are certain communities more affected by environmental issues? Who benefits from scientific discoveries? Who might be left out? These are the kinds of questions that will help students grow into thoughtful, informed citizens who understand how to use science for positive change.

SOURCE: iStock.com/Sergey Khakimullin

CONNECTING INITIATIVES IN SCIENCE EDUCATION REFORM AND STANDARDS TO EQUITY

Remember, you are not alone in this endeavor! National associations are advocating for science education that promotes social justice. Both the National Science Teaching Association (NSTA) and the Next Generation Science Standards (NGSS) have increasingly emphasized the need to teach science through a lens of equity. This focus stems from recognizing that access to high-quality science education is not universally available and that teaching for social justice plays a critical role in shaping the opportunities available to all students. When teaching is approached through a social justice lens, it incorporates equitable access by addressing and challenging systemic inequalities and biases within the curriculum. NSTA and NGSS call for educators to use equity and social justice principles when designing curriculum and instruction to create more inclusive learning environments that empower students to engage critically with societal issues and contribute to a more just society (NSTA, 2020).

Equity in the Context of NSTA and NGSS

NSTA emphasizes that "equity is at the heart of science and teaching, and education is a beacon of light for our students" (NSTA, 2020, para. 3). Furthermore, NSTA has written that science teachers have the responsibility to involve culturally diverse students in science, technology, engineering, and mathematics (STEM) fields by using instructional strategies that recognize and respect the cultural differences students bring to the classroom (NSTA, 2000). More recently, NSTA has expanded its commitment beyond equity to focus on social justice, urging teachers to design lessons around real-world scenarios and help students ask critical questions; for example, *Who made these decisions? Who benefits? Who suffers? Whose voices were silenced?* (MacKenzie et al., 2020).

SOURCE: iStock.com/Delmaine Donson

The NGSS place a strong emphasis on the responsibility of teachers to provide equitable educational opportunities for all students, especially those from non-dominant groups. This includes economically disadvantaged students, students from historically marginalized racial and ethnic backgrounds, students with disabilities, students in rural contexts, and English learners. The NGSS (see NGSS Lead States, 2013) also highlight the need for purposeful instructional planning for *all* students regardless of their sexual orientation, placement in alternative education programs, or learning needs (e.g., neurodivergent, gifted and talented). The standards call on teachers to intentionally design learning experiences that ensure equitable participation in science, recognizing the diverse needs and strengths each student brings to the classroom.

NGSS Appendix D, titled "All Standards, All Students," urges teachers to use equity-based practices for students to "develop agency in science" (NGSS Lead States, 2013, p. 366), which aligns with a social justice approach. Teaching for equity and agency means ensuring that all students, regardless of background or ability, have access to high-quality science instruction and the support they need to succeed. It also means recognizing the systemic barriers that have traditionally kept nondominant groups from fully participating in STEM fields and working to dismantle those barriers within the classroom. When science becomes accessible and relevant to students' lives, interests, and communities, it fosters a sense of **agency**, which refers to a student's capacity to act independently and make choices in their learning. Students who develop agency in science are empowered to explore, ask questions, and engage deeply with scientific concepts. Teachers who cultivate agency help students see themselves as active participants in science, capable of contributing to the scientific community and using science to solve problems that matter most to them.

> **Agency** is a student's capacity to act independently and make choices in their learning.

SOURCE: iStock.com/Yutthana Gaetgeaw

Integrating Standards for Fairness and Agency

In addition to the NGSS, there are other standards that support teachers in fostering agency through a social justice lens. One set of standards that we find informative and easy to adapt to different grade bands is the Learning for Justice (2022) Social Justice Standards. The standards, formally known as the Teaching Tolerance Social Justice Standards, were developed by Learning for Justice, a project of the Southern Poverty Law Center that focuses on educational initiatives to promote equity, inclusion, and justice across schools in the United States. The standards were first introduced in 2016 to equip teachers with the tools to create learning environments that challenge prejudice, support diversity, and encourage student engagement in social justice causes. The project was renamed from "Teaching Tolerance" to "Learning for Justice" to recognize that there is more to teaching tolerance, for teachers must actively engage students in the work of equity and justice.

The standards are organized into four domains (see Figure 1.3):

- Identity
- Diversity
- Justice
- Action

Each domain comprises five anchor standards (see Figure 1.4) that help students learn about themselves and others while also empowering them to recognize and challenge bias, oppression, and inequality.

FIGURE 1.3 Four Domains of the Learning for Justice (2022) Social Justice Standards

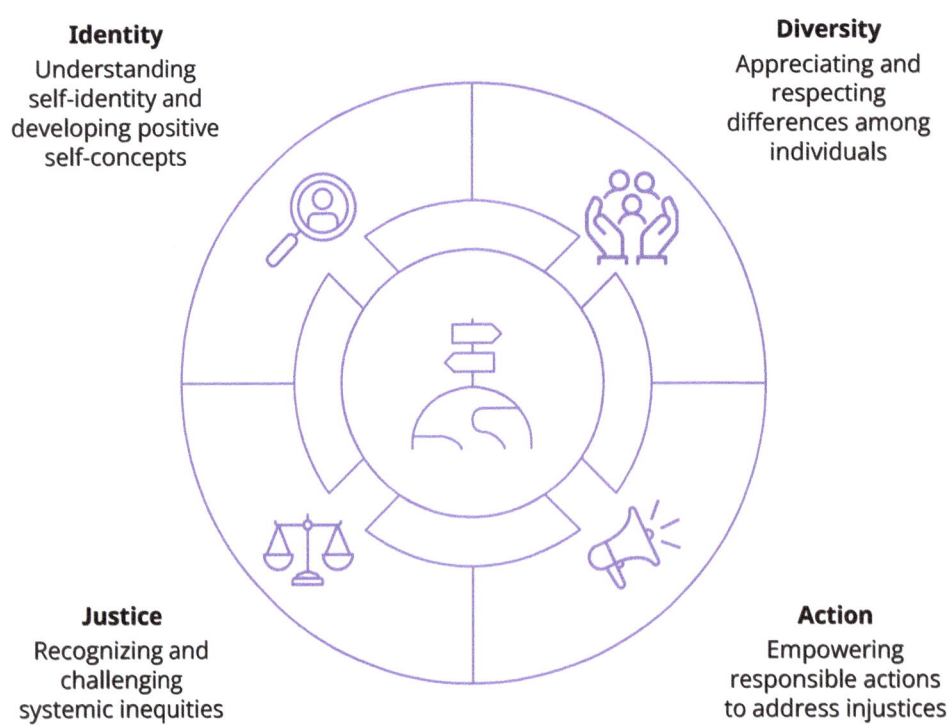

SOURCE: magnifying glass by Istock.com/myvector, hands icon by Istock.com/FishCoolish, scales icon by Istock.com/Stock Ninja Studios, megaphone icon by Istock.com/Serhii Brvko

FIGURE 1.4   Five Anchor Standards for Each Domain of the Learning for Justice (2022) Social Justice Standards

Social Justice Standards

 Identity **Diversity**  **Justice** **Action**

Identity	Diversity	Justice	Action
1. Students will develop positive social identities based on their membership in multiple groups in society. 2. Students will develop language and historical and cultural knowledge that affirm and accurately describe their membership in multiple identity groups. 3. Students will recognize that people's multiple identities interact and create unique and complex individuals. 4. Students will express pride, confidence and healthy self-esteem without denying the value and dignity of other people. 5. Students will recognize traits of the dominant culture, their home culture and other cultures and understand how they negotiate their own identity in multiple spaces.	6. Students will express comfort with people who are both similar to and different from them and engage respectfully with all people. 7. Students will develop language and knowledge to accurately and respectfully describe how people (including themselves) are both similar to and different from each other and others in their identity groups. 8. Students will respectfully express curiosity about the history and lived experiences of others and will exchange ideas and beliefs in an open-minded way. 9. Students will respond to diversity by building empathy, respect, understanding and connection. 10. Students will examine diversity in social, cultural, political and historical contexts rather than in ways that are superficial or oversimplified.	11. Students will recognize stereotypes and relate to people as individuals rather than representatives of groups. 12. Students will recognize unfairness on the individual level (e.g., biased speech) and injustice at the institutional or systemic level (e.g., discrimination). 13. Students will analyze the harmful impact of bias and injustice on the world, historically and today. 14. Students will recognize that power and privilege influence relationships on interpersonal, intergroup and institutional levels and consider how they have been affected by those dynamics. 15. Students will identify figures, groups, events and a variety of strategies and philosophies relevant to the history of social justice around the world.	16. Students will express empathy when people are excluded or mistreated because of their identities and concern when they themselves experience bias. 17. Students will recognize their own responsibility to stand up to exclusion, prejudice and injustice. 18. Students will speak up with courage and respect when they or someone else has been hurt or wronged by bias. 19. Students will make principled decisions about when and how to take a stand against bias and injustice in their everyday lives and will do so despite negative peer or group pressure. 20. Students will plan and carry out collective action against bias and injustice in the world and will evaluate what strategies are most effective.

SOURCE: Social Justice Standards (Learning for Justice, 2022, p. 3)

IMAGE SOURCE: magnifying glass by Istock.com/myvector, hands icon by Istock.com/FishCoolish, scales icon by Istock.com/Stock Ninja Studios, megaphone icon by Istock.com/Serhii Brvko

The Social Justice Standards offer teachers a way to weave social justice principles into various disciplines by building on culturally responsive teaching. They emphasize the importance of acknowledging students' identities, assets, and experiences as part of their learning journey. These standards also align with broader movements in antiracist teaching, aiming to dismantle systemic inequities in schools. Teachers can use these standards to create lesson plans, classroom discussions, and even school policies that foster *critical consciousness* and *student agency*. While it might seem like an extra set of learning targets, these standards are not meant to be treated as an add-on to the curriculum. Instead, they serve as a suggested framework for integrating social justice themes into the content you are already teaching. For example, they can guide classroom conversations on identity in science or lead to an exploration of the environmental impact of policies.

SMALL STEPS FOR BIG IMPACT: Foster Agency

Helping students see themselves as scientists starts with recognizing that science is all around them—it's not just something that happens in a lab. A great way to explore their science identity while fostering agency is through a meaningful activity: "Me as a Scientist." Ask students to think about a time when they investigated, explored, or solved a problem in their daily lives. Maybe they experimented with mixing ingredients while cooking, observed insects outside, or figured out why a toy wasn't working. Then, have them draw a picture of themselves as a scientist, showing what they're doing, where they are, and what tools they might be using. For students who prefer writing, they can describe a time they engaged in science, explaining what they did and what they learned. If technology is available, students can even record a short video demonstrating or explaining something science-related they do at home or school. To deepen their critical consciousness, encourage students to also consider how science helps communities solve real-world problems, such as finding ways to reduce waste at school.

As students work, ask guiding questions to help them reflect on their role as scientists and problem-solvers: *What does a scientist look like? Do they have to wear a lab coat, or can they be someone like you? Have you ever asked a question and tested different answers? What happened? What kinds of problems do scientists solve, and what kinds of problems have you solved? How can science help us understand and improve our community?* Prompts like these help students recognize that science isn't just about memorizing facts—it's about curiosity, problem-solving, and taking action to make the world better. Once students finish, create a classroom display or have a share-out session where they present their drawings, writings, or videos. To extend their agency, invite them to brainstorm a small science-based action project to address an issue they care about, such as reducing food waste in the cafeteria. Seeing how their ideas connect to real-world change builds confidence in their ability to use science as a tool for advocacy, helping them recognize that they are not just learners but active contributors to their communities.

Furthermore, the Learning for Justice (2022) Social Justice Standards are designed for different grade levels, with specific outcomes noted for K–2, 3–5, 6–8, and 9–12, along with example scenarios. For elementary science, they provide a foundation for helping young students learn more about themselves, their community, and the broader world. They help students see science as a tool for understanding and promoting equity and social change. By learning to think critically and engaging in civic activities that use science for the common good, students develop important life skills.

Take the Identity domain, for instance. The standards help students see that anyone can be a scientist, regardless of their background. Teachers can introduce diverse role models from the world of science while encouraging students to explore scientific concepts that directly relate to their lives and communities. This helps students see that science isn't something distant—it is happening all around them and involves people just like them.

The Diversity domain highlights that scientific discovery is a global, multicultural effort that belongs to everyone. By creating collaborative learning opportunities, teachers can show students how different perspectives enhance scientific inquiry. Group projects that involve teamwork teach students that diverse viewpoints can lead to innovative solutions.

Regarding Justice, the standards encourage students to explore environmental or social issues that affect marginalized communities. Students can discuss the ethical implications of scientific advancements, such as who benefits from certain technologies and who might be left out. These conversations help students identify inequities and recognize the importance of working toward fairness.

The Action domain is all about empowering students to use their scientific knowledge for social good. Whether they are advocating for change in their communities or designing projects to tackle real-world problems, students learn how to apply science in meaningful ways. They might explore issues like renewable energy or water conservation and use their knowledge to suggest solutions or raise awareness.

SOURCE: iStock.com/priyanka gupta

Establishing a classroom culture that promotes critical thinking and student agency takes time and thoughtful effort. However, the rewards are immense. By using these standards to guide students in taking ownership of their learning, teachers help cultivate lifelong learners and creative

> *Science education becomes about acquiring knowledge and developing students' confidence and capacity to make meaningful contributions to their communities and the world.*

problem-solvers. These students gain confidence in their ability to experiment, think critically, and work collaboratively with others. In this way, science education becomes about acquiring knowledge and developing students' confidence and capacity to make meaningful contributions to their communities and the world.

CHAPTER SUMMARY

- Integrating social justice into elementary science education fosters critical thinking and empowers students as agents of change.
- Frameworks and resources like the Learning for Justice (2022) Social Justice Standards and NGSS can support teachers in creating learning environments that emphasize equitable, inclusive, and real-world relevance.
- Highlighting diverse role models and fostering collaboration helps students see science as a tool for advocacy and problem-solving.
- Exploring environmental and social justice issues transforms science from an academic subject into a means for civic engagement and social change.
- Teachers play a critical role in student empowerment by creating engaging, safe, and student-driven learning opportunities to grow as learners and leaders.
- Whether you are a first-year or veteran educator, making a commitment to equity in science education benefits students, families, and communities.
- Making science relevant, actionable, and equitable inspires a new generation of thinkers who understand their role in shaping a more just and inclusive world.

REFLECTION QUESTIONS

1. As a student, did you learn science as facts or as a human endeavor? How did that shape your relationship with the field?
2. What scientists do you currently teach in your classroom? Could the list be more diverse?

3. What have you learned about the role empathy has in science?
4. Brainstorm a list of potential issues in your local community that you can use as a teaching moment in your classroom.
5. What steps can you take to ensure all students, especially those from nondominant and underrepresented groups, feel empowered, confident, and excited to dive into scientific inquiry and make their own discoveries?

CHAPTER 2

Bringing Purpose and Action to Science

Isn't it astonishing that all these secrets have been preserved for so many years just so that we could discover them!!

—Letter from Orville Wright to
George A. Spratt (June 7, 1903)

Picture yourself at the teacher supply store looking at that one wall with all the 17 × 22 posters. What is the first poster you see in the science section? (*Hint:* It was the first poster Bailey bought for her classroom, as it seemed mandatory for any science teacher.) You guessed it: the tried-and-true scientific method poster—primary colors, beakers, the big question mark, and all. You may even have it hanging on your wall right now! The linear checklist has served as an anchor chart to guide many students through cookbook labs and maybe even a science fair project or two. Observe, question, research, experiment, conclusion, and—*boom*—science!

SOURCE: iStock.com/Roman Bykhalets

But here's a fascinating twist: Did you know this method dates back more than 100 years? That's right! John Dewey first shared it in his 1910 book, *How We Think*, to simplify the process so that it would fit neatly in a textbook. That means we're still teaching students to think as scientists did in an era without the internet, antibiotics, insulin, airplanes, or even sliced bread! What else are we still using in our classrooms from more than 100 years ago? Go ahead and put that outdated poster on the table in the teacher's workroom where supplies go to die.

HOW WE DO (AND DON'T DO) SCIENCE

As science evolves, so should our approach to teaching and learning it. To help modern classrooms better reflect the complexity of what *is* and *is not* science, researchers have outlined the culture of creating science knowledge, known as the **Nature of Science (NOS)**. While the scientific method describes one structured approach to investigation, NOS portrays science as a dynamic, iterative process shaped by evidence-based reasoning, creativity, and collaboration. NOS deepens our understanding by examining how scientific knowledge is developed, validated, and revised over time, highlighting science as a way of thinking as well as a body of knowledge. Advocates for NOS emphasize that diverse perspectives, methodologies, and contexts all contribute to scientific processes, allowing students to appreciate the broader, interconnected landscape of scientific exploration. The Next Generation Science Standards (NGSS Lead States, 2013) embrace NOS, defining key traits that shape a scientifically literate

> The **Nature of Science (NOS)** is an evolving, evidence-based process that combines reasoning, creativity, and collaboration to develop and refine scientific knowledge over time. NOS highlights science as both a way of thinking and an interconnected exploration shaped by diverse perspectives and methodologies.

FIGURE 2.1 The Nature of Science and NGSS

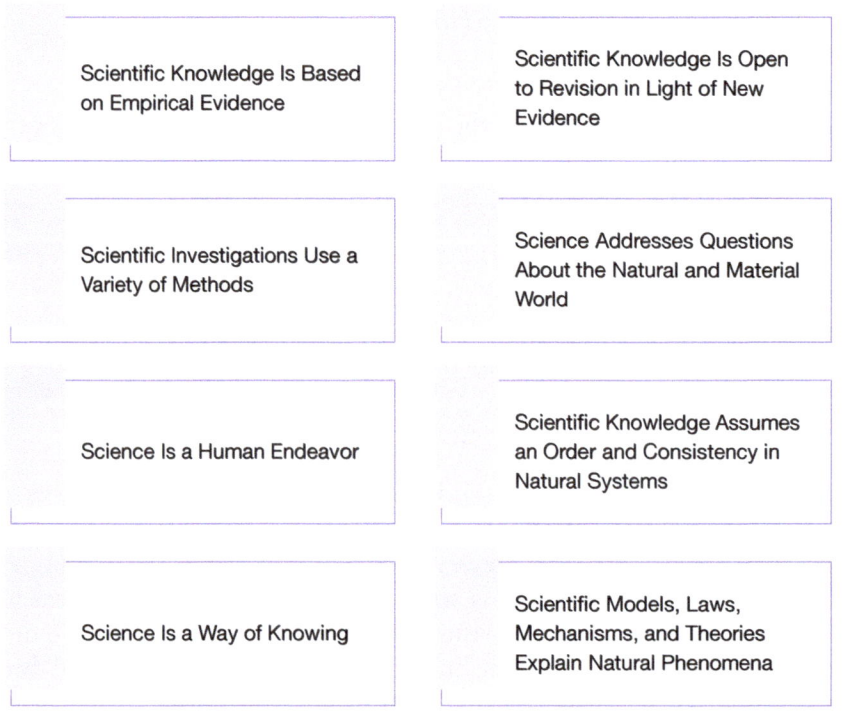

Scientific Knowledge Is Based on Empirical Evidence	Scientific Knowledge Is Open to Revision in Light of New Evidence
Scientific Investigations Use a Variety of Methods	Science Addresses Questions About the Natural and Material World
Science Is a Human Endeavor	Scientific Knowledge Assumes an Order and Consistency in Natural Systems
Science Is a Way of Knowing	Scientific Models, Laws, Mechanisms, and Theories Explain Natural Phenomena

SOURCE: Information adapted from NGSS Lead States, 2013, p. 431

person's understanding of science today. In Figure 2.1, discover the important aspects that the NGSS authors believed students need to understand about the evolving nature of scientific inquiry and discovery.

While we will not take the time to dissect each component of NOS thoroughly, we will touch on the most relevant highlights. If you would like more information on what this might look like at your grade level or how to teach these abstract concepts explicitly, see Appendix H of the NGSS (NGSS Lead States, 2013, p. 430).

Science Is a Way of Knowing

To foster scientifically literate students, we must first delve into what it truly means to be "scientifically literate." **Scientific literacy** is not merely about memorizing facts or following lab protocols. Instead, it's about a powerful way of engaging with the world—a method of knowing, questioning, and understanding, which has been shaped and refined by countless people across many generations and cultures. Unfortunately, many of our past school science experiences take us back to desk work reading about seemingly irrelevant science discoveries made by others. Now it's time to rewrite history for school science and get students hands-on and knee-high in relevant inquiry to continuously push the boundaries of what we know about science and how it can be used to transform the world.

> **Scientific literacy** is the ability to critically question, interpret, and apply scientific knowledge to understand the world and make informed decisions. It is both a method of knowing, rooted in evidence-based inquiry, and a way of thinking that fosters curiosity, skepticism, and problem-solving to evaluate information and understand science's role in society.

> *Now it's time to rewrite history for school science and get students hands-on and knee-high in relevant inquiry to continuously push the boundaries of what we know about science and how it can be used to transform the world.*

At its core, science is built on the collection and examination of empirical data reflecting observations and measurements that we can repeatedly test and confirm. These data fuel our search for explanations for the natural world, helping us find patterns, build theories, and uncover principles linking events or phenomena. But just as science seeks to answer the questions of "how" and "why" in the natural world, it also cannot answer *every* question, and those with high scientific literacy understand that. Aesthetic inquiries are for artists asking questions like "What is beauty?" and "How many shades of gray is too much gray?" Furthermore, questions about morals or supernatural entities like "Why are we here?" and "How should we live?" are answered by philosophers and religious leaders. Rightfully so, these realms belong to art, philosophy, and religion. That leaves science firmly focused on testable questions that can

SOURCE: iStock.com/Qvasimodo

be explored through observation and answered with empirical evidence and evidence-based reasoning.

In science, ideas are not static truths but dynamic concepts subject to challenge and revision. Every theory, principle, and discovery is open to questioning and scrutiny. The newest ideas must withstand rigorous testing. Those that can't meet the demands of the empirical validation that inherently comes with science get rejected, and we move on. This process helps science advance while also building a culture of critical thinking and skepticism. As science teachers, we aim to develop scientific literacy in our students and equip them with the tools to be critical consumers of science. Pseudoscience lurks around every corner of the internet, so our job is to prepare students to spot misinformation, make informed decisions, and foster innovation. The first step in modeling and teaching scientific literacy is knowing what science is and is not. See Figure 2.2 for some defining features of the culture of science—the soft stuff that helps us appreciate the field of science.

Scientific Knowledge Assumes an Order and Consistency in Natural Systems

Science is rooted in patterns, and its progress relies on the assumption that natural systems behave consistently over time. These patterns are the foundations of our understanding, allowing us to observe, predict, and explain the world around us. When we say science depends on patterns, we mean that we trust

FIGURE 2.2 The Real Process of Science

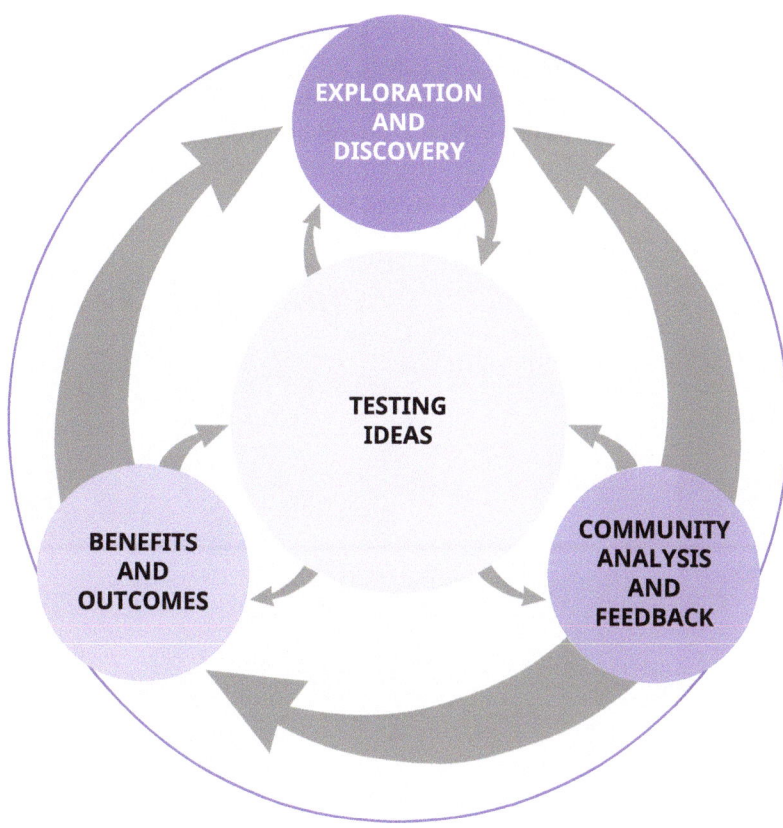

SOURCE: University of California Museum of Paleontology, 2022

in a natural order—a set of rules governing how things work in the past, present, and future. For instance, we must assume that an apple with the same mass and dropped from the same height will fall the same today as it would have 1,000 years ago. We must assume it will do the same thing 1,000 years from now, as long as the conditions remain unchanged. Such regularities help us create what we call **laws of nature**, but these laws aren't just rigid rules; they're guidelines built on observed evidence, repeated tests, and patterns that emerge from countless observations.

> **Laws of nature** are fundamental principles that describe consistent and observable patterns in the natural world. They are based on empirical evidence, tested through experimentation, and are universally applicable under specific conditions, providing a framework for understanding how the universe operates.

Documenting these patterns is critical, because well-documented patterns based on measurements and observations allow us to raise an eyebrow when something different occurs (e.g., the concept of gravity on Earth and in space). For this reason, a science notebook is a fantastic tool for students—not just to take notes but to actively observe, record, and personalize their understanding of these patterns in nature. By writing down observations, students can begin to notice how natural events align or deviate from expectations, shaping their ability to see and question the world through a scientific lens.

SOURCE: iStock.com/peepo

SMALL STEPS FOR BIG IMPACT: Keep a Science Notebook

▶ A personalized science notebook can be a powerful tool for students to explore, reflect, and take ownership of their learning. By using it as a space to record observations, ask questions, and track their thinking over time, students develop a deeper connection to science as an active, inquiry-driven process. Start your year by guiding students in setting up their science notebooks with sections for predictions, investigations, data collection, and reflections. Encourage them to personalize their science notebooks with drawings, diagrams, and written observations to make their learning visible. This structure not only helps students organize their curiosity but also provides a valuable resource for discussions during parent–teacher conferences, showcasing their growth as scientific thinkers.

To foster engagement, prompt students with questions that spark curiosity and encourage deeper reflection:

- *What do you notice? What do you wonder?*
- *How has your thinking changed since you started this investigation?*

- *What patterns do you see in your data?*
- *How does this connect to something you've experienced outside of school?*
- *What new questions do you have after today's experiment?*

By consistently using scientific notebooks to document reflection, students develop a habit of documenting and revisiting their ideas, strengthening their ability to think critically, make connections, and communicate their reasoning—key skills that will serve them well beyond the science classroom.

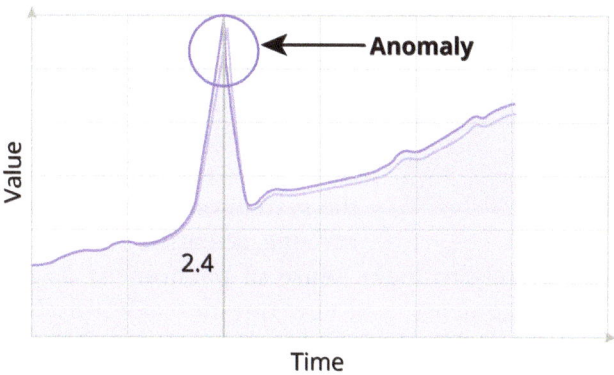

SOURCE: iStock.com/Alexey Bezrodny

Now, patterns are about more than what happens most of the time. In science, anomalies—or exceptions to the pattern—are often even more valuable because they invite us to ask questions. Anomalies open doors to discovery, driving us to wonder. Plus, they are one reason scientists get to work! Questions begin to flow, leading us to investigate, hypothesize, and sometimes even discover a whole new layer of understanding. It's all making sense why science is so complex!

> *As students learn to recognize and trust patterns, they also develop the ability to question and investigate when the natural order seems to break—a skill at the heart of scientific inquiry.*

Let's revisit the apple scenario. What if the apple *did* fall differently today than it did 1,000 years ago? If we begin to question how apples are falling, we might ask, "Why did the apple fall differently? What changed? What can it tell us?" These questions excite scientists, and your students will be excited, too. So, as students learn to recognize and trust patterns, they also develop the ability to question and investigate when the natural order seems to break—a skill at the

SOURCE: iStock.com/Bismillah_bd

heart of scientific inquiry. Exceptions to established laws mean there are unanswered questions, the fuel to scientific curiosity. And, if there is one thing that curious minds love, it's unanswered questions waiting to be answered! Oh, the thrill of the aha moments!

Scientific Models, Laws, Mechanisms, and Theories Explain Natural Phenomena

Before we dive into these important terms, let's try an activity designed to encourage reflection through modeling to explore (and explain) the relationship between the terms *law* and *theory* in science. A scientific **model** represents a phenomenon or system. Such models may appear as drawings, diagrams, flowcharts, equations, graphs, simulations, or physical replicas. They include only features that are important to understand the system or phenomenon. Creating and revising scientific models are done publicly and collaboratively to make sense of phenomena as students reason about ideas, data, arguments, and new questions (Windschitl et al., 2008, 2020). Your model may be a quick sketch, a labeled flowchart, or even a visual metaphor that shows how these terms work together to communicate scientific knowledge.

> **Models** can be used to create representations of a system or concept for purposes of making abstract or complex ideas more concrete and accessible.

To engage in this activity, grab some colored pencils or markers to get your creative juices flowing. Before drawing your model, consider:

- What *connections, labels, or arrows* could you use to show how theories and laws relate?

- How does your model capture the role of *evidence, testing, and refining ideas* in science?

Now, draw your model in the space on the next page. Create a labeled diagram that visually represents the relationship between theories and laws. You may wish to annotate or write a short explanation of your drawing so you can recall your thought process when you share or revisit your model later.

Optional: If you are reading this book with others, consider partnering with a colleague to explain your model to one another. To guide your discussion, consider the following questions:

- How are your models similar or different?
- What aspects of your models best illustrate the role of evidence and refinement in scientific understanding?

Reflecting through a model allows you to actively think about how scientific laws and theories work together to form a comprehensive view of natural phenomena. A key idea to remember about models, and science, is that they are subject to change over time (Windschitl et al., 2020). Therefore, as you continue reading this section, exercise your chance to think like a scientist and refine your understanding of these foundational concepts. You may choose to make your revisions in another color, add sticky notes, or create a "before and after." Just please *do not erase your initial ideas*—these initial ideas are valuable for tracing how and when your thinking evolved. We recognize that it can be difficult to revise ideas you've put a lot of effort into developing. And remember, your students will likely experience the same struggle!

SMALL STEPS FOR BIG IMPACT: Use Sticky Notes to Show Changes in Thinking

▶ Using color-coded sticky notes or different-colored writing utensils (e.g., highlighters, pens) can be helpful to track changing ideas. The visual impact of using different colors can help depict different types of changes in one's thinking without asking students to "mess up" their initial work.

First, introduce the phenomenon. Facilitate whole-group conversations for students to share observations, past experiences, and questions. Then, ask students to collaboratively draw their model (e.g., through labeled *before*, *during*, and *after* pictures) to show the process that explains the phenomenon. This is their *starting idea*.

Throughout the course of the lesson or unit, revisit your students' initial ideas. What do they wish to change with their new knowledge gained? Assign different colors of sticky notes to depict changes in thinking:

- Yellow sticky notes—ideas that have been added (new knowledge or thoughts)
- Blue sticky notes—ideas that have been revised (modified or adjusted thinking)
- Orange sticky notes—ideas that have been removed (thoughts no longer held or reconsidered)
- Pink sticky notes—questions or things students are still wondering or unsure about

To encourage students to reflect on how their thinking has shifted, have them choose one of their sticky notes to write a short explanation about how their understanding has changed and why.

SOURCE: iStock.com/South_agency

What Are Scientific Laws?

To build a better understanding, let's recall how **scientific laws** describe phenomena that consistently occur under specific conditions. They are often expressed mathematically and predict the outcome of certain events based on empirical data (i.e., numbers). For example, Newton's law of universal gravitation mathematically describes the gravitational force between two masses. As we discussed earlier, scientific laws are generally considered to be universally applicable within their scope, but *they do not explain why* the phenomena occurred; they simply describe the relationship observed.

What Are Scientific Theories?

In contrast, **scientific theories** offer comprehensive explanations for a wide range of phenomena. Grounded in substantial

> A **scientific law** describes a statement or mathematical equation that consistently explains a natural phenomenon based on repeated observations and empirical evidence. Scientific laws describe what happens under certain conditions but do not explain why it happens.

> A **scientific theory** is a well-substantiated explanation of a natural phenomenon, supported by a vast body of evidence and multiple lines of inquiry. Scientific theories explain why something occurs, are testable and falsifiable, and can be refined as new evidence emerges.

evidence, they often encompass laws, hypotheses, and established facts. Theories are developed through extensive testing and validation and are subject to revision as new evidence emerges. For instance, the theory of evolution explains the "why" behind facts like the law of natural selection, principles such as the Hardy–Weinberg principle, and empirical evidence found in the fossil record. Unlike scientific laws, which describe observable patterns, theories seek to explain the underlying mechanism and reasons behind those patterns.

So, when you hear somebody say, "It's just a theory," when discussing science, they are misusing the word. Or, when they say, "I have a theory that my neighbor is stealing my newspaper," they're being imprecise in that they are not using *theory* in a scientific sense—that is, unless they have a significant amount of quantitative and qualitative evidence that can be used to create a universally accepted scientific law to support their theory that *all* neighbors steal newspapers, while also explaining the underlying mechanisms. Be kind when you correct them, but please do correct them!

With a better understanding of these key ideas, let's revisit your model. What did you draw to visually represent the relationship between theories and laws? Maybe you drew a puzzle, where scientific laws are like the shapes of the puzzle pieces where consistent and predictable patterns determine if they fit together, and a theory was represented by the picture on the puzzle box explaining why the pieces fit together.

Let's take a look at some other models created by teachers to represent the relationship between scientific laws and theories (see Table 2.1). To help guide your critique of their thinking, see the prompts in the right-hand column. Of the examples provided, which model do you believe is the most accurate at describing the relationship between scientific laws and scientific theories? After reviewing, go back to your initial model and consider any revisions that might better illustrate the connection between these foundational scientific terms.

TABLE 2.1 Example Models of Scientific Laws and Theories

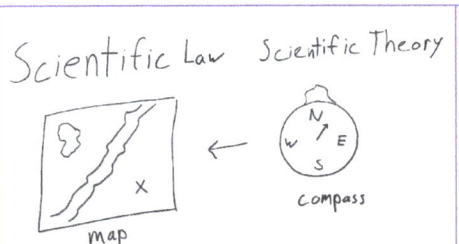 This teacher represented a scientific law as a map and a scientific theory as a compass.	What observed strengths do you see in this representation? What observed weaknesses do you see in this representation?

Scientific Law	Scientific Theory
Recipe	Guide
~~Revised~~ Speed Limit Sign	A Traffic Report

This teacher revised their thinking after learning more about the topic. First, they compared a law to a recipe and a theory to a guide. After learning more, they compared a speed limit sign to a law and a traffic report to a scientific theory.

How did the teacher's model become more accurate after learning more about scientific laws and theories?

Scientific Knowledge Is Open to Revision in Light of New Evidence

Scientific facts, laws, and theories *change*. We love this aspect of science! Generally, accepted laws and theories are durable, but as technology advances, so does our understanding of science. This sort of change in thinking makes sense to you, I'm sure. But remember that thick textbook of scientific facts you once lugged around in your backpack? It didn't necessarily model the true process of science. A misconception many people hold is that those textbooks *are* science—rigid, heavy, and seemingly impervious to change.

> *Scientific facts, laws, and theories change.*

Scientific facts often refer to observations or statements that are consistently supported by empirical evidence. When such observations can be repeatedly measured and verified, they become widely accepted within the scientific community. However, these facts are not immutable, as they can evolve with new data, improved interpretations, or advances in technology. For example, the belief that Earth is round emerged only after new evidence challenged earlier assumptions that it was flat. (Of course, some still cling to the flat Earth belief—but that's a conversation for another day.)

In addition, the invention of the microscope around 1590 completely changed how we viewed the world. Before then, people believed mice spontaneously emerged from piles of grain, bacterial infections came from bad air, and somebody who was sick had an imbalance of their "humors" (blood,

> *Context matters!*

phlegm, black bile, and yellow bile). Being able to observe cells changed the field of science. It is also necessary to recognize that facts in science depend on the conditions under which they are observed. Context matters! The boiling point of water changes with altitude, temperature changes the rate of most chemical reactions, and the pull of gravity is stronger at the poles than at the equator. Or take the case of poor Pluto, which in 2006 was demoted from the ninth planet from the Sun to a dwarf planet after more sophisticated technology identified anomalies in its orbit, causing astronomers to question the established definition of a planet.

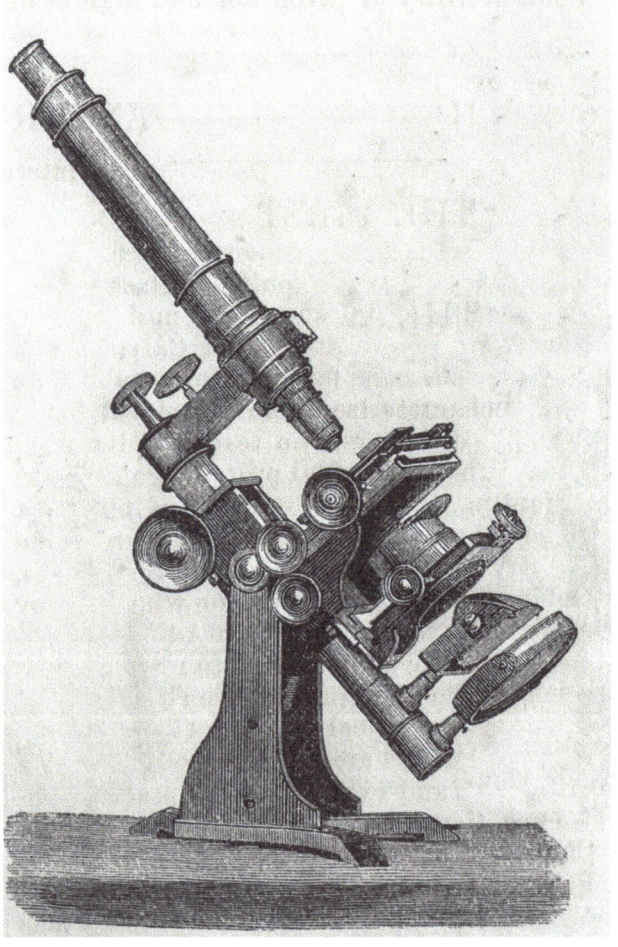

SOURCE: iStock.com/KenWiedemann

Great science thrives on a healthy dose of debate and doubt. It's all about questioning new or revised ideas to see if they have the chops to stage a scientific coup. This relentless skepticism and the quest for even better, evidence-backed solutions keep science sharp and on its toes. It is our job, as science teachers, to teach students how to be skeptical of data, flexible in their thoughts to entertain others' ideas, and open to changing their minds if data no longer support long-believed facts.

> *It is our job, as science teachers, to teach students how to be skeptical of data, flexible in their thoughts to entertain others' ideas, and open to changing their minds if data no longer support once-believed facts.*

SMALL STEPS FOR BIG IMPACT: Create a Timeline That Shows Progression of Scientific Understanding

▶ You can help students understand that scientific knowledge evolves over time. For example, let's look at an activity that can be shared with your students that focuses on the issue of lead in drinking water. Start by discussing the problem of lead in drinking water, focusing on communities where this issue has disproportionately affected low-income and minoritized populations. You might refer to the Flint, Michigan, water crisis as an example, where elevated levels of lead were found in drinking water, impacting thousands of residents, especially children (Masten et al., 2016).

Share how, for many years, it was believed that lead pipes were safe and that lead contamination wasn't a widespread concern. Over time, however, new research and the discovery of lead in drinking water in cities like Flint shifted scientific understanding of the risks of lead exposure. This illustrates how science evolves as new evidence, testing, and public outcry bring attention to overlooked issues.

Have students use chart paper to create a timeline that traces the evolving scientific understanding of lead in drinking water. Provide resources that highlight how scientists, public health professionals, and advocacy organizations have contributed to raising awareness and developing solutions over time. For example:

- Early belief that lead pipes and water systems were safe
- Discovery of lead contamination in water supplies (e.g., in Flint in 2014)
- Scientific studies linking lead exposure to health issues, particularly in children
- Action taken by communities, governments, and scientists to address lead contamination

To close the activity, have students engage in a discussion sharing their insights on how scientific understanding of lead contamination evolved. Teacher prompts might include the following:

(Continued)

(Continued)

- How did new evidence change the way people understood the dangers of lead exposure?
- Why do you think it took so long for scientists and communities to recognize the issue of lead contamination?
- How did social justice and activism play a role in addressing the lead contamination crisis?
- What steps are being taken today to prevent further exposure to lead in water, especially in marginalized communities?
- What can we do as a class or community to ensure clean, safe water for everyone?

WHAT COUNTS AS SCIENCE?

While science is often about quantifying facts, this perspective alone can limit our understanding of what counts as valid scientific knowledge. You might recall from Chapter 1 how science is a human endeavor. This means that science is a cumulative effort among diverse people, cultures, and social contexts. The values and biases of the scientific community influence what questions are asked and what knowledge is prioritized. This leads to the discussion about whose knowledge is elevated and whose is often placed on the back burner or, worst of all, silenced.

Traditional Western science is just one leg of the broader journey. Many other perspectives and systems of knowledge, such as Indigenous wisdom, Eastern philosophies, and traditional practices, contribute valuable insight. Each offers unique approaches and solutions to the challenges we, as humans, face. For instance, Indigenous ecological practices offer deep scientific understandings of environmental sustainability but are often dismissed by Western scientists as anecdotal, spiritual, or unscientific. In Ndebele villages, primarily located in southern Africa, the villagers have rich traditions in architecture, crafts, agriculture, and environmental practices. Alesia had the opportunity to visit a Ndebele village in South Africa and experience firsthand how villagers engage in sustainable practices (see Figures 2.3 and 2.4). Ndebele farmers used weather patterns and natural signs, like changes in animal behavior, to determine planting, harvesting, and crop rotation. They practiced **agrobiodiversity** and

> **Agrobiodiversity** refers to the variety and variability of living organisms within agricultural systems. It includes the diversity of plants, animals, and microorganisms used for food, livestock, and other agricultural products, as well as the diversity of ecosystems in which they are found. Agrobiodiversity is critical for maintaining the resilience of food systems, supporting sustainable agriculture, and ensuring food security, as it helps maintain ecosystem services such as soil fertility, pest control, and pollination.

water harvesting to protect natural resources. In medicine, healers use Indigenous plants to heal wounds. Plant knowledge was verbally handed down through generations and tied to empirical observations and cultural practices. Thus, the Indigenous knowledge systems, rooted in cultural practices and traditions, exemplify what counts as science.

FIGURE 2.3 Ndebele Village in South Africa, Where Alesia Visited

SOURCE: Alesia Mickle Moldavan

FIGURE 2.4 More of the Ndebele Village in South Africa

SOURCE: Alesia Mickle Moldavan

SMALL STEPS FOR BIG IMPACT: Share Stories to Explore Diverse Viewpoints

▶ If you're looking to introduce students to different ways of thinking about science beyond the Western tradition, children's books are a great place to start (Moldavan & Gupta, 2024). Books like Singh's (2020) *111 Trees: How One Village Celebrates the Birth of Every Girl* and Maillard's (2019) *Fry Bread: A Native American Family Story* can offer a window into cultural perspectives on nature, environmental stewardship, and scientific concepts. These stories help connect cultural traditions with science in a way that's engaging and accessible for young learners. Additionally, you might consider collaborating with local communities or cultural organizations to learn about traditional ecological knowledge. Bringing in guest speakers or taking field trips can provide students with firsthand insights into how science is practiced in different cultural contexts, whether it's about sustainable agriculture, water conservation, or medicine (Aragaki & Milks, 2026).

Another way to explore diverse scientific viewpoints is by sharing stories of scientific contributions from other cultures. For example, you could introduce students to the astronomical observations made by ancient Chinese civilizations or the advanced irrigation practices of Indigenous cultures. By comparing these practices with modern science, students can reflect on the different ways people approach problem-solving and communicate innovation. It's also helpful to discuss global environmental challenges and how various cultures use traditional knowledge to address them. By weaving these diverse perspectives into your lessons, you'll help students appreciate science as a global endeavor and encourage critical thinking about how different ways of knowing can shape our understanding of the world.

Science isn't just about knowledge acquisition; it's a tool for solving real-world problems. Studying science through theoretical models and experiments positions science inside the margins of traditional science laboratories and textbooks. Yet, science extends beyond the traditional, Western boundaries to address community needs, social justice issues, and environmental challenges. Don't be intimidated to take the lead in community initiatives using science just because you don't have a lab coat. All of us, including our students, can and should contribute valuable knowledge. Let's continue exploring this idea.

WHO GETS TO DO SCIENCE?

In addition to critiquing what science is, we must challenge the notion of who gets to do science. By questioning who has access to scientific spaces, we can better understand the biases and limitations

> *By questioning who has access to scientific spaces, we can better understand the biases and limitations that have shaped our knowledge.*

that have shaped our knowledge. Moreover, we can ensure that science is inclusive, particularly for certain groups—often based on race, gender, or socioeconomic status—who have been historically excluded from scientific discovery and innovation.

Alternative Science Epistemologies

When Bailey first started teaching middle school science, the state standards explicitly listed the names of "must-know" scientists students were expected to memorize for standardized tests. Alfred Wegener, Niels Bohr, Gregor Mendel, and Charles Darwin were some of the figures deemed important enough to mandate adolescents memorize. Bailey diligently printed pictures of each scientist, tacked them on cardstock, and proudly displayed them on her classroom walls. Laminated, of course!

However, in her southern Arizona classroom, where over half the students identified as Hispanic, the message unintentionally conveyed that the most influential scientists were all white, European men.

> *The message unintentionally conveyed that the most influential scientists were all white, European men.*

This approach was a misstep. Thankfully, the standards have since been revised, but there is still work to be done to ensure that all students see themselves represented in the scientific community. Teachers can support this effort by critically examining whose scientific contributions they highlight in the classroom, ensuring that students learn about groundbreaking discoveries made by scientists from diverse backgrounds. For example, Marie Curie, a Polish French physicist, made pioneering contributions to radioactivity, and she is one of the few women regularly mentioned in science curricula. Expanding beyond this, teachers can introduce Katherine Johnson, the Black mathematician whose calculations were critical to NASA's space missions; Chien-Shiung Wu, a Chinese American physicist who made fundamental discoveries in nuclear physics; and Julio Palacios, a Mexican physicist known for his work in thermodynamics and crystallography. Additionally, Salim Ali, an Indian ornithologist, revolutionized the study of birds in India, while Tu Youyou, a Chinese pharmaceutical chemist, developed a groundbreaking malaria treatment that has saved millions of lives.

The history of science is a fascinating topic, yet it is often framed as an individualistic pursuit led by a small group of white, European men rather than as a cumulative and collaborative endeavor shaped by diverse cultures and communities across the world. This narrow portrayal not only distorts the reality of scientific progress but also has lasting consequences for students' perceptions of who belongs in science, technology, engineering, and mathematics (STEM) fields. The adverse effects of this exclusion can last a lifetime. For instance, middle school Black girls have been shown to have the weakest identification with STEM careers in basic biology, basic physical science, and applied physical science when compared to Latina, white, and multiracial peers (Kang et al., 2019). This weak identification does not emerge in isolation—it is shaped by multiple, interconnected factors, including a lack of representation in curricula, societal stereotypes about who is naturally "good" at science, and limited access to mentorship and role models who share their backgrounds.

In a similar context, American Indian/Native American was the only racial group that did not see a drastic increase in enrollment in medical school between 1997 and 2017, and it is estimated that it will take more than 100 years to reach equitable representation at current rates without systematic change (Lopez-Carmen et al., 2023). One layer of those systematic changes should include modifying practices to value Indigenous ways of knowing and lived experiences. For example, Indigenous cultures hold strong traditional beliefs about death. The deceased are sacred; therefore, remains are treated with utmost respect, and burial grounds should be left undisturbed. However, requiring medical students to work in cadaver labs throughout their education is common practice in medical schools throughout the Western world. American Indian/Native American students are forced to choose either pursuing a career in medicine or following the traditions of which they were raised.

SOURCE: iStock.com/Frazao Studio Latino

When students view science as something reserved for a select few, it's easy to feel disconnected and excluded, especially if the scientific figures they encounter don't reflect their identities, backgrounds, or experiences. Recall Bishop's (1990) metaphor of "mirrors, windows, and sliding glass doors." Science, after all, is meant to be a universal pursuit—a collective endeavor in which diverse perspectives enrich our understanding of the world. When science education incorporates mirrors, windows, and sliding glass doors, it reshapes students' perspectives, building a sense of belonging in the field. Students learn that science isn't a rigid field bound by tradition and only the contributions of famous white men. Rather, it's a dynamic community that thrives on innovation, diverse perspectives, and novel ideas.

This approach offers students opportunities to see themselves not as passive recipients of scientific knowledge but as valuable contributors to a field that impacts their lives and communities. Furthermore, this approach not only strengthens students' scientific literacy but also fosters their self-efficacy and resilience, empowering them to see that science is not just for "others"; it is a space where everyone has a role in making meaningful contributions to the world.

Science is also about community, collaboration, and using knowledge to improve society. By highlighting the work of diverse scientists from different races, genders, cultures, and backgrounds, we do more than diversify our content; we help students connect with the human side of science. Science is a collective endeavor, shaped and redefined by people across the globe, each bringing unique insights and perspectives. As teachers, it's our role to open the "sliding glass door" and invite *all students* to join the conversation.

> *Science is a collective endeavor, shaped and redefined by people across the globe, each bringing unique insights and perspectives.*

SOURCE: iStock.com/izusek

SMALL STEPS FOR BIG IMPACT: Connect With Science Happening in Your Community

▶ You can help students explore how science is used in their local community by helping them identify individuals and initiatives that contribute to scientific progress. The following can be used as a quick way to brainstorm ideas with your students. Begin by asking students:

- Where do you see science happening in our community? Why do you think scientific work is important for our community?
- Who are the people using science to make our community a better place?
- What are some problems in our community that science could help solve?

To support students in their brainstorming, you may wish to look into local health, technology, agriculture, environmental conservation, and engineering initiatives. It might be helpful to obtain printed or digital community resources and pull images of local scientific contributions (e.g., community gardens, technology centers, medical research centers, historical contributions).

As students work to investigate local science initiatives, ask them the following questions:

- Whose voices and ideas are shaping the way science is used here?
- Are there people in our community who have great ideas but may not have access to resources to implement them?
- What can we do to help more people in our community get involved in science?
- If you could work on a science project to help our community, what would it be?

Through this activity, students will have opportunities to identify issues of representation and break down barriers of who they might envision engaging in science.

Ultimately, equitable science education is about more than just access to the same curriculum—it is about ensuring that every student can fully participate, succeed, and see themselves reflected in the subject matter. By using equity-based practices and creating high-quality learning experiences for *all students*, teachers are not just meeting standards but empowering students to become active agents in their learning and contributions to society. This is where the intersection of science and social justice becomes critical, as it provides the foundation for students to use science as a tool for advocacy and change in their communities.

The Value of Community

Without a doubt, community is the backbone of any meaningful movement for social justice. When people come together, they create more than a collection of voices—they build a collective strength that can drive change, challenge the status quo, and advocate for a cause. Whether focused on equity, environmental sustainability, or public health, social justice is rooted in the idea that the world can be made fairer, more inclusive, and more resilient. But achieving these changes requires the power of community to share knowledge and work toward solutions that benefit everyone.

At the elementary level, students must see the strengths of their community. As previously stressed, each student in your classroom has an important role, and the collaborative effort of each person pushing into their assets builds a unified front. So, in the classroom, students must see how their community and community members all play essential roles in addressing current issues and developing innovative solutions. One way to demonstrate this is by exploring how scientists, engineers, and problem-solvers often work in teams to tackle challenges, such as doctors and researchers collaborating to develop vaccines or local environmental groups working together to restore ecosystems. Students can also investigate how traditional knowledge from Indigenous communities has contributed to scientific discoveries, like sustainable agricultural practices or herbal medicine. By engaging in hands-on projects, such as a classroom experiment that requires teamwork, they can experience firsthand how collaboration leads to meaningful advancements.

SOURCE: iStock.com/FatCamera

> *When science and community unite, they become a powerful force for social change.*

Let's consider climate change. Scientists worldwide are sounding the alarm, but when communities rally together, solutions start to take root. From advocating for renewable energy in local governments to organizing cleanup efforts, community action brings scientific data to life. When there is limited shade in a green space, how can a school community unite to make a change? One student's voiced concern will echo through the halls when friends and classrooms rally together to broadcast the message louder. When science and community unite, they become a powerful force for social change.

SMALL STEPS FOR BIG IMPACT: Brainstorm About Collective Action

▶ To help your students begin thinking about collective action, have them brainstorm stories about how communities have come together to solve problems, such as disaster relief efforts, environmental cleanups, or fundraising initiatives for a community project. When an example has been identified, ask students the following questions:

- What does it mean to work together as a community?
- How do different people in our community like firefighters, doctors, teachers, and shop owners work together to make life better for everyone?
- If you could change one thing in your community to make it better, what would it be? How could we work together to do that?
- What is one small action we could take as a class that would make a big difference in our school or neighborhood?

These questions can help students see the power of collective action both in their immediate communities and beyond.

Science itself thrives on diverse perspectives and shared knowledge, much like a strong community. In fields like environmental science, for example, scientists partner with communities disproportionately affected by pollution to document health impacts and push for regulations. Together, they don't just make data points; they create stories, which, when shared and amplified, can influence policy and inspire others to act. This community-driven approach to science emphasizes that we don't just *do* science in a vacuum; we use it as a tool to solve problems that affect real people.

Building a strong community around social justice in science also means creating spaces where everyone feels valued and empowered to contribute. Some uncomfortable conversations may need to occur for our students to feel like they truly belong in science class and are not just guests who must follow the rules established by the dominant discourse (e.g., privileging traditional Western science epistemologies; Calabrese Barton & Tan, 2020). We must go beyond discussing problems and take action on solutions. Students, teachers, scientists, and community members can come together to address relevant issues that affect our everyday lives, whether it's access to clean water, healthy food, or safe schools. When we commit to building inclusive communities, we encourage a sense of responsibility and ownership—everyone has a stake and must play a part in improving the world.

Ultimately, the value of community in social justice lies in its ability to amplify individual voices, pool knowledge and resources, and drive impactful change. When we come together as a community, we do more than raise awareness; we lay the groundwork for fundamental, systemic shifts. Science can be essential to that journey, giving us the data and methods to understand complex issues. But it's community—people rallying together, supporting one another, and taking a stand—that moves us from knowledge to action. First, though, we as teachers must work to bring societal issues and historical injustices to the forefront and problematize them critically (Calabrese Barton & Tan, 2020).

> *When we come together as a community, we do more than raise awareness; we lay the groundwork for fundamental, systemic shifts.*

CHAPTER SUMMARY

- The traditional, static view of the scientific method is outdated. Instead, the act of doing science should be portrayed and communicated to students as a fluid, ongoing, collaborative, and creative endeavor.

- Science cannot answer all questions. Science questions are testable and answered with empirical evidence. When new data do not fit within well-documented patterns, scientists work to find out why.

- A scientific law describes a consistent, universal observation about the natural world, often expressed mathematically, like Newton's laws of motion. A scientific theory explains the underlying reasoning for those observations, providing a well-substantiated explanation based on empirical evidence, such as the theory of evolution.

- As technology evolves and we ask better questions, our understanding of scientific facts changes.

- Science thrives on high-quality, evidence-based argumentation.

- Science is too often taught solely through a Western perspective. We must intentionally incorporate alternative epistemologies to ensure that all students see themselves reflected in science and that historically overlooked contributions are recognized and valued.

- Every student should have the opportunity to see themself as a scientist.
- Teaching for social justice depends on students feeling like they belong. Valuing the local community and context empowers your students to question and take action for equity.

REFLECTION QUESTIONS

1. How is the scientific method you learned in school similar to and/or different from what you learned in this chapter?
2. Create an example and nonexample of how to use the term *theory* in science. Think about why your nonexample is incorrect.
3. When you think back to your own science education, do you recall learning about scientists from nondominant or historically marginalized groups? How well did those individuals represent the diversity you now see in your own classroom?
4. How are you currently challenging systemic inequalities in your classroom to ensure all students feel valued, heard, and empowered?

PART II

Designing and Implementing Science Lessons for Critical Thinking and Action

CHAPTER 3

Planning Lessons That Matter and Foster Change

We will not march back to what was. We will move to what shall be.

—Amanda Gorman

Before planning for social justice science lessons, teachers must establish a strong classroom community to support social justice work in elementary science classrooms. Such a community fosters inclusivity, belonging, and equity by valuing and leveraging students' diverse **funds of knowledge**—the skills, experiences, and cultural insights that students bring to the learning environment (Moll et al., 1992). Capitalizing on students' backgrounds, interests, and sociocultural contexts requires intentional effort and sustained engagement. This raises an important question: How can teachers effectively tap into students' funds of knowledge to cultivate a classroom community that empowers students to critically examine societal issues and take informed action? Since this is a critical question to set the stage for designing science lessons that advance social justice work, let's take a closer look.

> **Funds of knowledge** include the skills, experiences, and cultural insights that students bring to the learning environment.

LEARNING ABOUT STUDENTS

We all know that the first day of school is an important one. It's the first day teachers see their new students all in the same room, looking back at them. Excitement, and maybe a little angst, is palpable from both teachers and students as everyone is curious about what's in store for the new academic year.

In addition to learning the curriculum, students want to learn about their teacher, and, hopefully, their teacher wants to learn about them.

Learning about students begins on the first day of school and must remain an ongoing endeavor throughout the academic year. Students' stories are intricately woven, forming a rich tapestry of experiences, cultural traditions, and personal challenges. Each thread of this tapestry contributes to students' unique ways of knowing and engaging with the world. For teachers, identifying these threads requires intentionality and sensitivity, as it involves recognizing, valuing, and affirming the diverse assets students bring to the classroom.

> *Students' stories are intricately woven, forming a rich tapestry of experiences, cultural traditions, and personal challenges.*

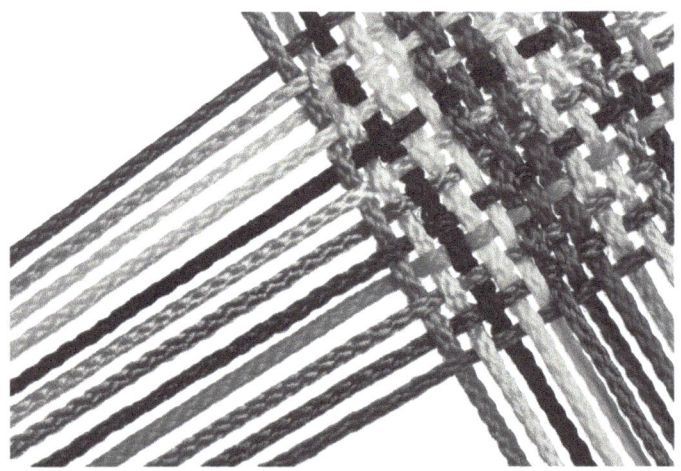

SOURCE: iStock.com/JamesBrey

Now, as a teacher, you don't need to "untangle" these threads. For one, who is to judge that the threads are tangled? Also, the beauty of how the threads weave in and out of patterns and designs depicts the story of each student and their community. Thus, a teacher's role is to holistically look at the threads and understand how students' threads can be woven into the classroom's tapestry. This approach illuminates students' assets as paramount factors that must be considered.

Diversity as an Asset

You don't need us to tell you that diversity is an asset rather than a deficit. When teachers see the richness of their students' cultural backgrounds and personal experiences as a strength, they engage in an **asset-based approach** to teaching that transforms the classroom into a vibrant and inclusive community of learners. Such an approach affirms students' identities and enables them to see themselves and their peers as capable scientists, thinkers, and problem-solvers. By recognizing students' contributions to the scientific discourse, teachers position students as active participants in science learning, promoting equitable engagement and opportunities to succeed.

> **An asset-based approach** to teaching focuses on recognizing, valuing, and building upon existing strengths, experiences, cultural backgrounds, and knowledge that students bring to the classroom.

SOURCE: iStock.com/FG Trade

Creating an inclusive environment through an asset-based approach to teaching begins with small but meaningful practices. For instance, engaging students in casual conversations about their interests and productive storytelling about their experiences can help teachers weave connections between students' lives and scientific concepts. As students share, teachers gain insights into their funds of knowledge (Moll et al., 1992) and can design culturally relevant and personally meaningful science instruction. This approach supports the development of positive science identities and fosters a sense of belonging, which is critical for sustained engagement in the content.

SMALL STEPS FOR BIG IMPACT: Chronicle Student Interest

▶ Before the first day of school, create a form—either digital or on paper—with a list of your students' names. Leave space to jot down notes about each student's family structure, interests, learning preferences, and strengths. Throughout the first few weeks, engage students in conversations, informal activities, and interest surveys to gather insights about them. Listen carefully during class discussions, student-to-student interactions, and group work to update your form with information about students' hobbies, cultural backgrounds, and academic strengths.

Keep this document easily accessible and continue adjusting it throughout the year. Use it as a reference when planning lessons, forming collaborative groups, or differentiating instruction. For example, if you know a student loves storytelling, you might encourage them to demonstrate their understanding of a science concept through a creative narrative. If another student likes to draw, you can incorporate more opportunities to communicate their understanding through illustrations and models. By consistently updating and using this form, you'll create a more personalized and inclusive learning environment where students feel valued. Over time, it will become an invaluable tool for fostering meaningful connections and ensuring that instruction aligns with students' strengths and needs.

Sustaining an Inclusive Environment

To sustain this inclusive environment, teachers must also consider the evolving nature of their students' stories. Students grow and change over time, even across a month, and their experiences inside and outside school continue to shape their understanding of the world. The students who walked into your room on the first day of school are not the same people come May! Or maybe we are just reflecting on our children, who are busy growing up every day. Where has the time gone?

The process of learning about students is dynamic, requiring teachers to remain observant, reflective, and responsive. By continuously seeking to understand the many threads that make up each student's tapestry, teachers can create learning experiences that resonate deeply, helping students see themselves as valued members of the scientific community. This ongoing effort not only nurtures empathy and mutual respect but also equips students with the confidence and skills to contribute meaningfully to discussions and collaborations, ensuring that the tapestry of the classroom reflects the diverse assets of all its members.

> *The process of learning about students is dynamic, requiring teachers to remain observant, reflective, and responsive.*

SOURCE: iStock.com/monkeybusinessimages

Establishing Classroom Norms

Establishing classroom norms can be an effective practice for sustaining an inclusive environment and one that is open to critical conversations about societal issues. Classroom norms can be seen as guidelines and expectations. Unlike classroom rules, which are often communicated as explicit directives indicating what is allowed and prohibited in the classroom, classroom norms should be shared expectations for behavior and interactions collectively agreed upon by the class community. For classroom norms, the focus is on relationships rather than compliance and creates a positive classroom culture that fosters mutual respect.

We recommend that teachers collaborate with students to co-create classroom norms. This way, students can recognize their ideas and have a sense of ownership of what it means to create a supportive, respectful, and collaborative learning environment. Allowing students to contribute to the decision-making process also reinforces their role as active participants and cultivates a sense of shared responsibility. Some classroom norms might include the following:

1. **Respect All Voices:** Treat everyone respectfully, listen when others talk, and remember that all ideas are important.

2. **Be Curious and Ask Questions:** Ask questions, explore ideas, and make mistakes—that's how we learn.

3. **Work Together:** Teamwork is important. Share jobs and help each other when working in groups.
4. **Use Friendly Words:** Be kind with your words so everyone feels welcome.
5. **Actively Participate:** Take part in activities and have fun learning.
6. **Help Each Other Learn:** Everyone learns in their own way. Be patient and support your peers when they need help.
7. **Take Care of Materials:** Be gentle with tools and supplies so everyone can use them. Help clean up when done.

In your classroom, you can reinforce classroom norms by consistently modeling the guidelines and providing appropriate verbal praise. Additionally, you can engage in pedagogical practices that prioritize student-centered learning, fostering active engagement and collaboration. For instance, well-designed strategies like think-pair-share and inquiry-based learning promote discussion and argumentation, enabling students to develop critical thinking skills while engaging in meaningful discourse. Equally important is being intentional about wait time—both after posing a question and after a student responds—as this allows students to reflect on their peers' ideas and thoughtfully articulate their own. By integrating these approaches, you can cultivate a classroom culture where all voices are respected and diverse perspectives are valued, ultimately enriching learning experiences and deepening students' understanding of scientific concepts. Through these efforts, you can nurture a learning environment that fosters the development of strong science identities among your students and sets the stage for effective learning through social justice science lessons.

A FRAMEWORK FOR SOCIAL JUSTICE SCIENCE LESSONS

Once we've established expectations for an inclusive classroom community, we can shift our focus to planning social justice science lessons. We will use a four-phase framework as a guide to support this process. The framework is informed by commonly used science frameworks, such as the Biological Sciences Curriculum Study led in 1987 by Rodger Bybee, who developed the BSCS 5E Instructional Model (i.e., Engage, Explore, Explain, Elaborate, and Evaluate; Bybee, 2015), the GRC framework (i.e., Gather, Reason, Communicate; Moulding & Bybee, 2017), and Ambitious Science Teaching (Windschitl et al., 2020)—all stressing the need for students to *Explore before Explain*. When considering ways to *Elaborate* and *Reason* in the context of societal issues and injustices, we consider ways for students to *Interrogate* and *Act*. Thus, we reconceptualized the Elaborate phase to involve the critical examination of science content, practices, and societal implications.

Students can then be empowered to use their scientific understanding to address inequities and promote positive change. As shown in Figure 3.1, the Elicit–Investigate–Interrogate–Act framework used to inform social justice science lessons includes the steps Elicit, Investigate, Interrogate, and Act. These steps are explored in greater detail in the descriptions provided in Figure 3.1.

FIGURE 3.1 Planning a Social Justice Science Lesson

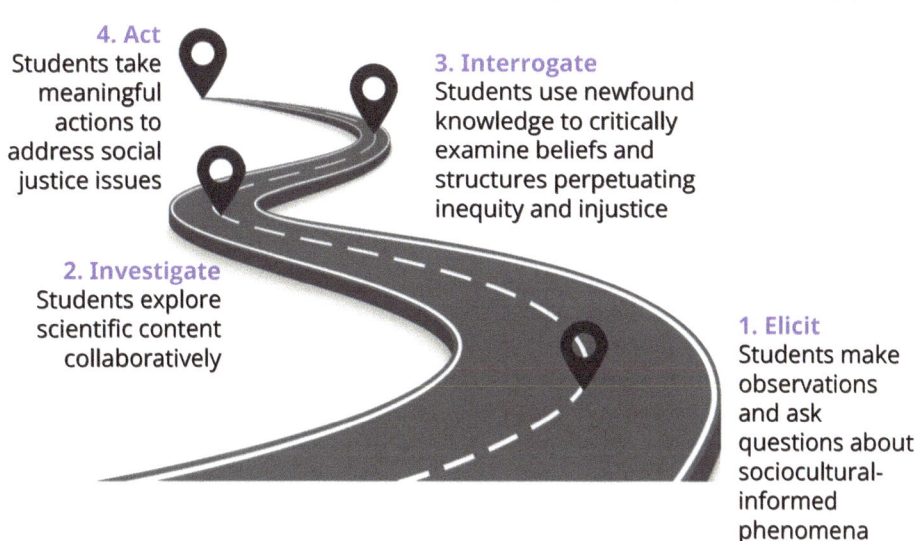

SOURCE: Image from iStock.com/sanchesnet1; iStock.com/Design Circle

NOTE: Each lesson follows one storyline rather than a variety of unrelated activities. Using a storyline engages students with real-world connections, engages them in scientific thinking, and empowers them to unravel the story through a coherent progression.

The Elicit Phase

First, we must understand how **phenomena** (plural of *phenomenon*), or anchoring events (Windschitl et al., 2020), can be used to elicit students' understanding of the natural world through scientific inquiry. The Elicit phase serves as a preassessment and springboard for students to dive into solving real-world problems. Phenomenon-based science teaching is not brand new. Its roots are in constructivist education theories (Matthews, 2024), based on work by researchers like Piaget (1970, 1972), Vygotsky (1962, 1978), and Maria Montessori (1917), who advocated for active, student-centered learning environments. The approach to learning depends

> **Phenomena** are observable events or occurrences in the natural world that are complex and intriguing and can be explained through scientific inquiry.

on students facing situations that may challenge their existing beliefs and urge them to

- reconsider alternative conceptions,
- construct new understandings based on their experiences,
- apply new knowledge,
- reflect, and
- perhaps undergo a conceptual change.

You may already be using a phenomenon to generate curiosity in your students and focus your lessons on exploring real-world problems—great work! Now, since you are here, let's extend your practice. Thomas Kuhn, famous for revolutionizing how we understand the process of science, introduced the idea of *paradigm shifts* (Kuhn, 1962). A paradigm shift occurs when anomalies (i.e., observations that cannot be explained by current understanding) become significant. As a result, a new paradigm, a framework of theories, methods, or standards, must emerge. For example, Western science believed the Earth revolved around the Sun, just as Aristotle proposed for many, many years. As time and technology advanced, Copernicus, Galileo, Brahe, and Kepler found flaws in the model and provided alternative claims and evidence until ultimately, with pushback and banned books, the heliocentric model of our solar system was accepted (Bowler & Morus, 2005). The new framework marked a paradigm shift because it fundamentally altered how humanity understood the universe and challenged established scientific and religious beliefs.

While Kuhn used his work to define scientific revolutions for Western civilization, the same pattern occurs when phenomena are used to introduce science content to elementary students. A well-chosen phenomenon (as further discussed in the next section) causes students to ask questions and find evidence that challenges their current understanding of scientific concepts. With scaffolding from the teacher and time to reflect, a conceptual change occurs, shown in students' model revisions, leading to a more profound and lasting understanding of science.

When teaching science for empathy and social justice, we use phenomena similarly; we just frame what we are looking for a bit differently. This next section focuses on where to find phenomena and how to use them to frame your unit or lessons.

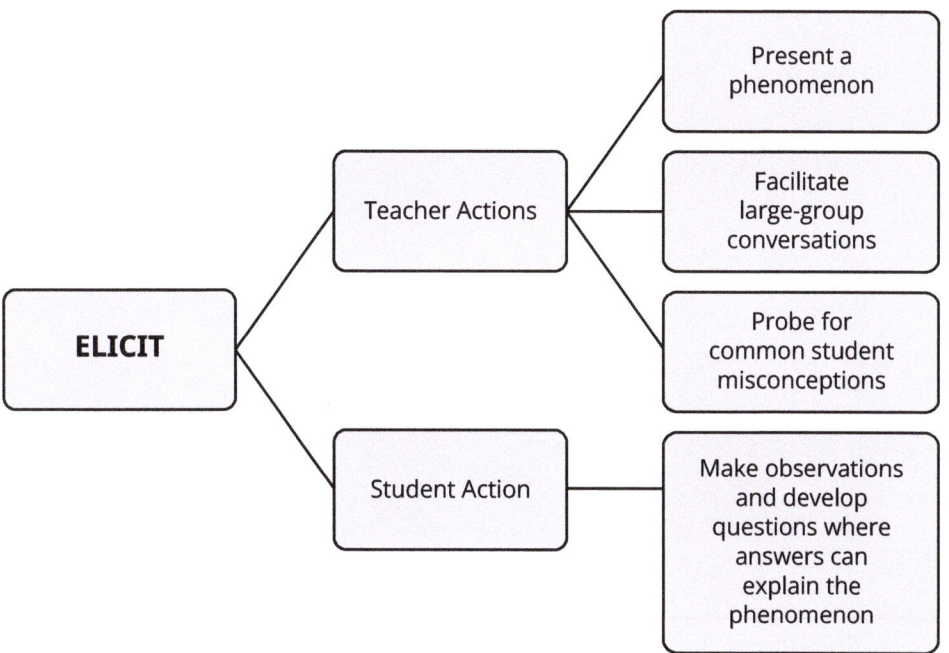

Finding the Phenomena

In three-dimensional science teaching, the role of a phenomenon is paramount. A phenomenon should be introduced to students at the beginning of a science lesson or unit to pique students' curiosity, generate puzzling questions, and help teachers preassess students' misconceptions through real-world scenarios. By the end of your lesson or unit, students should walk away with an accurate explanation of why and how the phenomenon occurred.

Let's look at a common phenomenon that you might find in an elementary science classroom. Consider the photo of boiling water that could be used to teach about phases of matter. A typical phenomenon-informed lesson would start by showing the students the photo or, better yet, using a demonstration to elicit student observations and questions. Without providing answers or vocabulary *yet*, this gives students time to make observations and develop questions to help them find the words and reasoning behind the boiling water.

SOURCE: iStock.com/Diy13

Students may notice the bubbles or condensation on the top of the pitcher. Some students may share their experiences with electric kettles and talk about the heat source or setups for boiling water. Your students probably can observe the bubbles, but their current knowledge cannot explain why the process happens. You have found an anomaly! They may know the word *evaporation*, but can they draw a model of the process? Your students have a new bit of information they may never have thought of: Something is happening to that water molecule when it changes, but what does it look like? Why, how, and what is next? Your students need a new paradigm to answer their questions!

By the end of this lesson or unit, students will be able to draw, write, or verbalize that the electrical energy is converted to thermal energy, which raises the water temperature until it reaches its boiling point (100°C or 212°F), causing the water molecules to move faster until transitioning from a liquid to a gas (steam). However, at this stage, it is your role to determine which students know what and to use the information gleaned from discussion about the phenomenon to inform future instruction.

You will notice that phenomena do not always have to be phenomenal! If a phenomenon is visible to your students and the content knowledge you want your students to learn describes what is happening, you have a good phenomenon. If you find a good phenomenon to guide instruction, your students' questions and observations guide instruction and provide a reason for learning. At the same time, they practice the dispositions

> *Phenomena do not always have to be phenomenal!*

and skills of authentic scientists. As a result, students take ownership of their learning and naturally explore content at a deeper level. Thus, more effective learning outcomes are achieved.

Types of Phenomena

While all phenomena must be observable and testable, different *types* of phenomena can be used for different purposes. The electric kettle is an example of a **high-interest phenomenon**. Students might be interested in an electric kettle because it is a common, relatable object. They might even go home after school and be inclined to describe the process to whoever is making pasta that night!

> **High-interest phenomena** describe observable, interesting, and complex events.

While a high-interest phenomenon does get a conversation going, you may also choose to use the same lesson plan about phases of matter but introduce the topic by using a pothole of water that disappears when the sun comes out on the school's playground (i.e., a **physical location phenomenon**). In this case, students can connect the phenomenon to a specific location or environment they are familiar and interact with. Students may be able to observe, measure, or experience the phenomenon in their setting occurring naturally or influenced by human activity.

> **Physical location phenomena** describe observable, interesting, and complex events that occur in a space accessible to students, such as the playground or a school's cafeteria.

SOURCE: iStock.com/olaser

> **Culture** is a shared set of beliefs, values, customs, or behaviors that characterize a group of people.

> **Culturally important phenomena** describe observable, interesting, and complex events that are purposefully selected to connect with students' cultural backgrounds.

However, what if we wanted to adapt the same lesson plan on phases of matter to connect with your students' **culture**? For example, a **culturally important phenomenon** for those of us in the South could be the process of making grits, a dish made from corn, specifically hominy, that is boiled with water or milk until it reaches a creamy, porridge-like consistency. We could introduce the lesson by making a pot of grits to share with the class or discussing what was served in the cafeteria for breakfast. And, if grits aren't on the menu, students could use the same idea of boiling water and connect it to other foods like rice or pasta. Connecting cultural foods with scientific terms, such as *evaporation* and *absorption*, as students try to work out where all the water goes during the cooking process can foster an appreciation for how science and human activity intersect with the natural world.

SOURCE: iStock.com/xavierarnau

You'll notice that the use of phenomena as a tool for instruction does not mean completely revamping your teaching style. Rather, instead of using examples to confirm a directly taught concept, a phenomenon-based science lesson uses the phenomenon as a preassessment to elicit students' thinking, questioning, and intrigue before digging into the content. The phenomenon is then reintroduced at the end of the lesson to close the storyline and as an assessment for students to use their new knowledge of concepts and vocabulary words to explain what is happening.

The use of phenomena as a tool for instruction does not mean completely revamping your teaching style.

When we typically think of phenomena, it is easy to choose observable events in nature, such as rainbows, leaves changing color, or poison dart frogs. These three phenomena are relatively safe, considering they are accessible and relevant—who can be offended by rainbows and frogs? We are asking you to rethink the purpose of a phenomenon and center people as a method to build empathy *and* critical thinking in elementary scientists. We are proposing selecting phenomena that, when explored and questioned, empower students to make a difference. Considering people at the core of topics, we must investigate social and cultural dynamics. Next, we will discuss the type of phenomenon we will focus on throughout this book: sociocultural-informed phenomena, as seen in Table 3.1.

We are asking you to rethink the purpose of a phenomenon and center people as a method to build empathy and critical thinking in elementary scientists.

SOURCE: iStock.com/jacoblund

TABLE 3.1 Types of Phenomena Informing Student Perspectives

TYPE OF PHENOMENON	STUDENT PERSPECTIVE	EXAMPLES
High-interest	Important or interesting to *me*	• Blue crab physical adaptations
Physical or geographical location	Relevant to my *physical place*	• Video of a blue crab interacting with its local salt marsh ecosystem
Culturally important	Relevant to my *culture*	• Engineering nets to catch blue crabs that mimic traditional fishing practices of the Gullah Geechee communities in the Georgia salt marsh
Sociocultural-informed	Real-world events with potential social, environmental, or political implications for *people and cultures*	• Observing and questioning implications to the Gullah Geechee communities' food sources (e.g., blue crab) when commercial overfishing impacts the ecosystem's food webs

SOURCE: Image from iStock.com/Martina Birnbaum

> **Sociocultural-informed phenomena** are centered on people and anchored in real-world events with significant social, environmental, cultural, or political implications.

Sociocultural-informed phenomena are centered on people and anchored in real-world events with significant social, environmental, cultural, or political implications. Sociocultural-informed phenomena emphasize the inclusion of diverse people and their perspectives, thus asking our students to practice extending empathy and creative problem-solving to address real-world problems. These types of phenomena help students recognize the value of the cultural and linguistic backgrounds of others and question issues of power and equity within the classroom and society. We are encouraging (and expecting) students to critically reflect on how scientific knowledge and practices can be used to either perpetuate or challenge social inequities. Choosing to anchor your science instruction with sociocultural-informed phenomena involves connecting science learning to local community issues or environmental justice. Table 3.1 provides a scaffolded example suggesting ways to focus a "high-interest" phenomenon into one that is "sociocultural-informed" to inform social justice science lessons.

Where to Find Sociocultural-Informed Phenomena

Here comes the tricky part—finding the right phenomenon and visual to spark your students' interest, give them something to question, and act as the North Star for your lesson's storyline. A good first place to look is at your classroom tapestry, including all students' assets and their community. When you take the time to learn about your students, you have a great entry point into what's important to them and their community.

Look at students' community events and societal challenges that have scientific dimensions. Is there a local water system that is or is not frequently polluted? Which areas of town have more or fewer parks? How far away from major highways are the schools in your district—is there a pattern? Engage with your students and your community members to help identify potential local environmental concerns, traditional ecological knowledge, or community health issues. If you think these topics may sound too complex for elementary students, you may be surprised at their capabilities.

You may also wish to consider your students' cultural backgrounds and experiences. Utilizing culturally relevant pedagogy helps make science more relatable and meaningful for *everyone* in the class, including traditionally underrepresented students in your classroom. Using a polluted local stream as a phenomenon will raise some different questions from your students if

> *Using your students' cultural beliefs and practices as assets will lead to your students responding to scientific content in a way that is unique to your students, school, and community.*

teaching through the Indigenous perspective of the Cherokee people, who would see the polluted stream as a concern to both the environment and spirituality. To the Cherokee people, water is a sacred element essential to well-being and central to many spiritual celebrations and rituals. Using your students' cultural beliefs and practices as assets will lead to your students responding to scientific content in a way that is unique to your students, school, and community.

However, we still need to find methods to help our students visualize the science content and related sociocultural-informed phenomena. Table 3.2 shows a potential sociocultural-informed phenomenon that can be used to investigate so-called diaper deserts—areas where access to affordable diapers is limited—in the United States. This example, while far from an electric kettle boiling water, provides a context for introducing a phenomenon that reflects and is shaped by broader social, cultural, and economic systems. Diaper deserts arise from and perpetuate systemic inequities, reflect societal norms about caregiving, and disproportionately affect marginalized communities. Diapers can also be used to teach physical changes and unit rates! Thus, they provide another example of ways to conceptualize sociocultural-informed phenomena.

TABLE 3.2 Observing a Sociocultural-Informed Phenomenon

WAYS TO OBSERVE A SOCIOCULTURAL-INFORMED PHENOMENON	EXAMPLE: DIAPER DESERTS
Maps	Using online maps, type in the zip code of a low-income area in your state. • How far away is the nearest supermarket in town? • How far away is the large warehouse store in town?
Data tables or graphs	High-Poverty Zip Code in Georgia in the United States: |	DISTANCE AWAY	DIAPERS: SIZE 1	COST OF 1 DIAPER
---	---	---	---
Sam's Club	88 Miles	176 pack = $26.48	$0.15
Walmart	18 Miles	148 Pack = $39.97	$0.27
Dollar General	In Town	32 Pack = $11.00	$0.34	
Pictures or infographics	**DIAPER DESERTS: NEIGHBORHOOD CHARACTERISTICS** "Priority" areas are identified by the need for diaper access based on average median income and low access to stores that sold most common diaper sizes. **72%** — THE NUMBER OF PRIORITY NEIGHBORHOODS MADE UP OF RENTER-OCCUPIED HOUSING. **67%** — DEMOGRAPHICS OF PRIORITY NEIGHBORHOODS Of the priority areas, 67% of the neighborhoods' inhabitants identify as Black, African American, Hispanic, or Latino. Massengale, K. E., Jones, M. A., Liao, J., Park, C., & Old, M. (2022). Priority areas for child diaper access: Low-income neighborhoods with limited retail access to the basic need of diapers. *Health Equity, 6*(1), 767–776. https://doi.org/10.1089/heq.2021.0192

WAYS TO OBSERVE A SOCIOCULTURAL-INFORMED PHENOMENON	EXAMPLE: DIAPER DESERTS
Reputable news articles or links	**National Diaper Bank** qrs.ly/1kgr444 National Diaper Bank Network. (2024). *What is diaper need?* https://nationaldiaperbanknetwork.org/the-need/

After presenting your students with the phenomenon, giving them time to wrestle with the ideas is important. Keep your students on track! We are not asking them to make inferences or explain things here. Focus on the facts. What do they notice? What do they wonder? Anticipating the questions your students may have is important. You will use these questions in the next step—when planning, list the questions you want your students to ask. It will help you steer the whole-group conversation.

In the context of the diaper desert example, your students may wonder about online retailers like Amazon or even consider cloth diapers. You may gently steer the conversation toward the effects of needing throwaway diapers to meet specific requests, like that of a day care that might expect caregivers

SMALL STEPS FOR BIG IMPACT: Restate the Idea

▶ When a student shares an observation or asks a question that closely aligns with a key concept you plan to address, use revoicing as a strategy to refine and clarify their thinking. Instead of simply answering or redirecting, restate their idea using precise academic language while ensuring they remain the owner of their thought.

For example, if a student says, "It looks like the object is moving faster because the ramp is steeper," you might respond with "That's an interesting observation! Are you saying that the object's speed increases as the slope gets steeper? Is it OK if we write it that way?"

Or if a student asks, "Why does the shadow move like that?" you could respond with "That's a great question! Are you wondering how the position of the light source changes the shadow's direction?"

By pausing to ask for the student's approval—such as "Is it OK if we say it this way?"—you empower them to take ownership of their ideas while also reinforcing correct terminology and clarity in scientific discourse.

to provide a full week's worth of disposable diapers at the start of every week, or shipping and membership costs associated with online retailers. This leads nicely to the next step of the lesson: Investigate. For an extended look into how this example of a sociocultural-informed phenomenon can be used to drive a social justice science unit, see Chapter 4 (Unit Plan 4.2). Now, let's get back to our boiling electric kettle and investigate!

The Investigate Phase

Whether or not your state has formally adopted the Next Generation Science Standards (NGSS), there is a good chance your state standards have been redesigned to align with *A Framework for K–12 Science Education* (National Research Council, 2012). The biggest shift in science education these standards and framework have brought about has been that students are expected to learn science content knowledge by practicing working scientists' skills and dispositions. It makes sense, right? Teaching our students science solely through reading a textbook would be like expecting a pilot to learn how to fly an airplane with just an instructional manual. Finding a related reading (or worksheet) may be easier, but it does not lead to relevant and authentic science learning. We want our students to understand how scientists work—and have worked—to answer scientific questions. As previously mentioned, there is more than one way to "do" science. Therefore, our students need multiple experiences to truly understand the intricacies of science as a whole. In this section, we explore the Investigate phase in the framework for planning social justice science lessons. Students should be working hands-on to collect data and answer their own questions.

> *We want our students to understand how scientists work—and have worked—to answer scientific questions.*

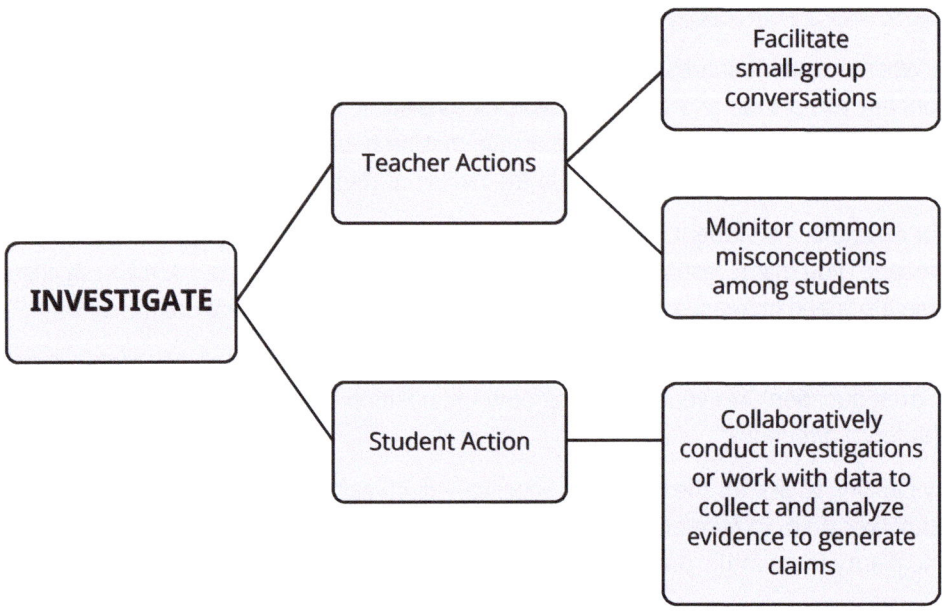

Planning for the Investigate Phase

Before you can plan *how* your students will investigate, you first need to know *what* they will investigate. As the teacher, you must articulate the subsequent phases of the storyline. What key details of the phenomenon do your students need to explore? In the Elicit phase, what content did students hold the most misconceptions about? The storyline should include *why* the observable events happened and factors that your students cannot see, such as how the water molecules in the electric kettle move with differing amounts of thermal energy (Windschitl et al., 2020). Your storyline may be told through a labeled drawing, written paragraph, or flowchart. Better yet, create multiple modalities to give your students options for their turn to communicate what they have observed and learned. Once you have the "final answer" on paper, choosing how your students will investigate the phenomenon becomes much more manageable.

For example, we prompted generative artificial intelligence (AI) to "create an explanation for why water boils in an electric kettle, including processes that we cannot see with our eyes." The following is an example of a provided AI-generated output. Can you picture how your students may investigate, record data, and use the results to better explain the phenomenon? Let's reference three-dimensional science teaching to help us generate some ideas.

> *When you turn on an electric kettle, electricity heats a metal coil at the bottom, which transfers heat to the water through conduction. As the water molecules absorb this heat, they move faster, an invisible increase in kinetic energy, until they have enough energy to break free from the liquid and form gas bubbles. These bubbles form at the water's surface, rise to the top of the kettle, and release steam as they burst. This process continues until the water reaches its boiling point, where the vapor pressure equals atmospheric pressure, and the kettle typically shuts off automatically (OpenAI, 2025).*

Three-Dimensional Science Teaching

While considering how the students will investigate and collect data, it is paramount to explicitly include the Science and Engineering Practices (SEPs) and the Crosscutting Concepts (CCCs). The SEPs are a set of skills that students will use to investigate the phenomenon. A key idea here is the word *practice*. We can't expect students to be able to ask testable scientific questions intuitively, but we can help them practice! The CCCs are overarching themes that serve as bridges across the various domains of science. When content in science class can jump from moss to black holes, explicitly using the CCCs to help students see connections across fields is vital. Including the SEPs and CCCs and *telling students* what they are practicing and how they should be thinking are non-negotiable in three-dimensional science teaching and learning (Table 3.3). For more information, see the NGSS website (www.nextgenscience.org/resources/ngss-appendices), Appendix F (SEPs; NGSS Lead States, 2013, p. 382) and Appendix G (CCCs; NGSS Lead States, 2013, p. 413).

TABLE 3.3 Exploring the Science and Engineering Practices and Crosscutting Concepts

SCIENCE AND ENGINEERING PRACTICES (SEPs)	CROSSCUTTING CONCEPTS (CCCs)
• Asking questions and defining problems* ○ *The students are the ones to ask scientific questions. This is not just answering teacher-posed questions.* • Developing and using models • Planning and carrying out investigations • Analyzing and interpreting data • Using mathematics and computational thinking • Constructing explanations and designing solutions • Engaging in argument from evidence • Obtaining, evaluating, and communicating information	• Patterns • Cause and effect • Scale, proportion, and quantity • Systems and system models • Energy and matter • Structure and function • Stability and change

Instructional Considerations

In addition to familiarizing yourself with the associated SEPs and CCCs to guide your investigation, you must consider effective instructional practices in science education. If you are well versed in science education literature, you will notice there is nothing in this section that strongly deviates from the BSCS 5E method (Bybee, 2015) calling on students to *Explore before Explain*. The following are some tips and tricks to help make the most of instructional time and help ensure your classroom is student-centered, collaborative, and safe when conducting investigations.

Focusing on Safety

Safety in the science classroom is paramount and starts in your planning phase. For an investigation, you must identify the materials needed and how they will be distributed. With our boiling water investigation, it may be easier and quicker to do one demonstration for students while they actively work to collect and organize the data individually. When planning, always anticipate what safety issues may arise, how best to address students' learning needs, and how you will prepare your students to effectively engage.

Students must also know how to properly collect and dispose of materials after an investigation. While chemicals and supplies in elementary science are typically found around the house, it is still important to be prepared. For example, flour should not be handled or used around students with celiac disease, but gluten-free alternatives will allow students to still engage in the activity. Or, when using sand from the playground to investigate erosion, be sure to have students wash their hands after the investigation and be on the lookout for cat poop!

We have provided a short list of safety procedures, but encourage you to refer to the American Chemical Society's top-notch reference *Safety in the Elementary Science Classroom*, summarized as follows (Committee on Chemical Safety, 2011):

1. Plan time for your students to wash their hands after completing an experiment or activity, including when they have worked with seeds, plants, and animals.
2. Wear properly fitting goggles while working or observing others working with chemicals, hot liquids, or flying objects.
3. Remind students to keep science materials away from their mouths, noses, and eyes throughout the activity.
4. Read the labels of all household chemicals to learn the hazards and warnings.
5. Always store chemicals and solutions in labeled containers.
6. Dispose of chemicals properly. Check the MSDS (Material Safety Data Sheet) for any questions.
7. Store dry ice in an open container so carbon dioxide gas can escape.
8. Try to precut materials for students as often as possible to avoid injury.
9. Dispose of corroded batteries in a community hazardous waste recycling collection.
10. Prohibit students from using thermometers as stirring rods.

Collaborative Student Groups

There are several ways to group students for an investigation. For example, if students are exploring what happens to water temperature as it boils, they might begin by predicting whether the temperature will increase, decrease, or remain constant. Based on these predictions, you can thoughtfully organize student groups to promote meaningful engagement with the task.

1. Heterogeneous Student Grouping

   During investigations, consider using heterogeneous groupings where students are assigned specific roles and responsibilities. Grouping students with varying abilities, backgrounds, and experiences encourages a rich exchange of ideas and skills. For example, some students may be more comfortable tinkering with hands-on tasks, while others may be more adept at analyzing data. Alternatively, you can group students based on shared interests. Regardless of the approach, it's important to leverage students' diverse strengths by assigning roles such as facilitator, recorder, communicator, timekeeper, or reporter. This ensures that *all* students participate in ways that support their assets and interests. Additionally, this strategy supports differentiation through student choice, fostering a sense of ownership and deeper engagement in the learning process. By clearly defining roles, you can help your students understand their responsibilities, which promotes accountability and collaboration within the group, and also provide structured ways to participate, offering valuable scaffolding for students who may be more reserved or introverted.

   To further foster peer collaboration, especially for students who might benefit from multimodal communication, allow students to write or draw their thoughts before speaking. Digital tools can also be leveraged for students to contribute ideas in writing before discussing them verbally. Sentence frames (e.g., "I think ____ because ____" or "I would like to add to what ____ said by ____") can be used to prepare for conversations.

2. Flexible, Homogeneous Grouping

   If you wish to group students by their readiness levels, you might consider flexible, homogeneous grouping. Grouping students with similar levels of understanding and verbal reasoning skills allows for targeted differentiation, enabling more focused instruction and discussions with peers. The effectiveness of homogeneous grouping lies in keeping the groups flexible and continuously assessing student progress to regroup students as their learning progresses. A student's initial placement at the start of a unit may need to be adjusted after a few lessons to reflect growth or changing needs. This dynamic approach keeps instruction responsive and ensures that all students remain engaged in learning experiences tailored to their evolving readiness. Additionally, flexible grouping encourages teachers to continuously observe and respond to students' strengths and interests, making instructional decisions that support each learner's development.

The Interrogate Phase

After students have brainstormed initial ideas in the Elicit phase and found new evidence in the Investigate phase, it is time to Interrogate. In this phase, students will apply their newfound knowledge to determine *who* is being impacted and the potential implications of the phenomenon. So far, we have used the example of an electric kettle boiling water. Although it is a high-interest phenomenon, is there anything your students can interrogate?

Are there any ethical considerations to elicit creative problem-solving and empathy from your students? As previously shared, the electric kettle is an example of a high-interest phenomenon rather than a sociocultural-informed phenomenon. While the high-interest phenomenon leads to student-centered learning, it falls short of helping our students understand that science is not void of human actions, beliefs, or biases. Implications, both good and bad, occur because of science in the real world.

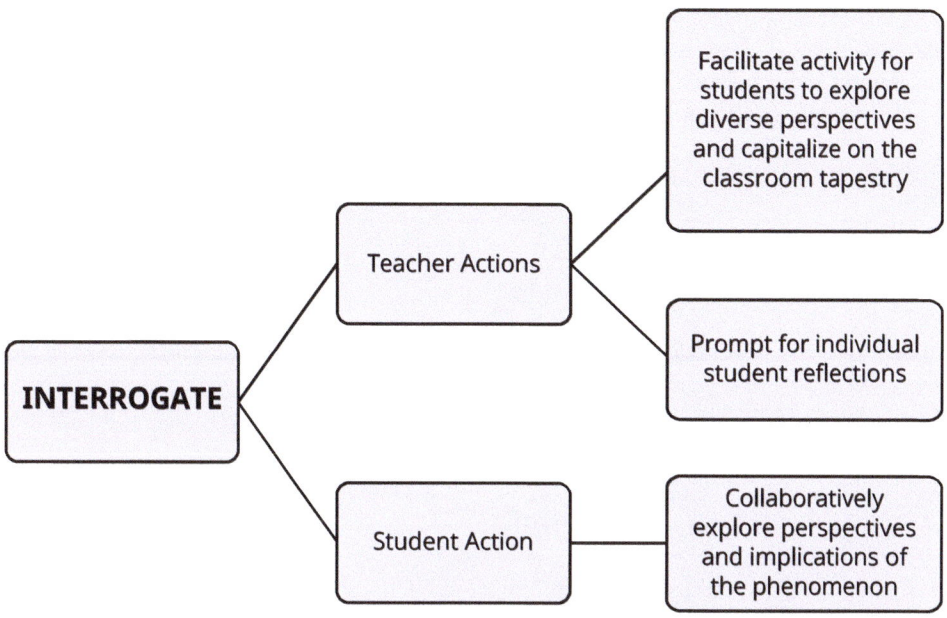

In the following two sections, we are deviating from our electric kettle of boiling water but approaching *the same content* through the lens of a sociocultural-informed phenomenon. So now, let's make the connection and fill in some details on how to get to a powerful interrogation!

SOURCE: iStock.com/adventtr

While you will see this whole unit on the phases of matter through the lens of a sociocultural-informed phenomenon in the next chapter (see Unit Plan 4.1), what follows is a summary to reorient us and to see why the Interrogate phase benefits our students as scientists and humans (Table 3.4).

TABLE 3.4   Example: States of Matter Lesson

Science Content: States of Matter	
Lesson Objective: Apply concepts of phase changes to analyze and evaluate the implications of rising global temperatures and population density affecting water scarcity in the southwestern United States.	
Elicit *Introduce the sociocultural-informed phenomenon*	Lake Mead and Hoover Dam 2001:  SOURCE: Istock.com/ LPETTET • What do you notice? • What do you wonder?
Investigate	How do rising global temperatures and population density affect water scarcity in the southwestern United States? • Students track temperature data and water amount while the teacher demonstrates with a pot of boiling water. • Students use a Colorado PhET simulation on the states of matter, investigating how adjusting the temperature affects the water molecules' motion (PhET Simulations, 2018).

Interrogate	Students investigate who is most impacted by diminishing water levels in the Colorado River.
	• Who is being impacted the most?
	• What are some other causes?
	• What are the implications?

SOURCE: Image from iStock.com/LPETTET; Advisory Committee on Water Information Open Water Data Initiative. (n.d.). *Drought in the Colorado River basin.* Developed by the Department of Interior, U.S. Geological Survey, and U.S. Bureau of Reclamation, with contributions from the U.S. Environmental Protection Agency, Oregon State University, and the Western States Water Council. https://labs.waterdata.usgs.gov/visualizations/OWDI-drought/en/index.html

The use of sociocultural-informed phenomena at the beginning of the lesson's storyline positions our instruction for students to interrogate and, ultimately, act. Within this context, students now have the knowledge to interrogate what global climate change is doing to our water here on Earth and, therefore, us. For example, more heat (i.e., thermal energy) means more evaporation. More evaporation means more water vapor in the atmosphere, contributing to storms' frequency and intensity. The rising global temperatures lead to more evaporation, disproportionately affecting marginalized communities' access to clean water (Leap et al., 2024; Levy & Patz, 2015; Parsons et al., 2024). Thus, in the Interrogate phase, students are positioned with evidence from their investigation to rationalize: *Who is impacted? What are the implications?*

Structuring Classroom Debates for Critical Thinking

There are various methods for having students interrogate outside of having them passively sit at a computer and do "research." As previously discussed, collaborative learning is necessary to capitalize on the classroom's tapestry of backgrounds and ideas while modeling how to respect differing viewpoints. Incorporating stories, experiences, and perspectives from people and cultures affected is particularly impactful for building empathy. Having students role-play different stakeholders in an issue allows students to better understand diverse perspectives and the importance of equitable solutions. Structuring classroom debates is one of the most engaging tactics that build students' critical thinking ability. Debates can be conducted as large- or small-group discussions, inviting students to articulate and defend their positions while engaging with diverse perspectives. Always ensure there is appropriate time for students to independently write their thoughts *before and after* the debate. Reflections are a powerful metacognitive tool to use for classroom discussion and independent processing. Here are some suggestions of formats for structuring debates:

> *Collaborative learning is necessary to capitalize on the classroom's tapestry of backgrounds and ideas while modeling how to respect differing viewpoints.*

- **Point–Counterpoint** (Silberman, 1996): Issues presented must have multiple positions. Small groups are each assigned a different position to represent. Research can be done in class or as homework. Before the debate, small groups should coordinate arguments and assign numbers to group members. During the debate, all #1s present their argument, followed by #2s, and so on. After each student has provided their argument, a whole-group discussion is conducted to compare and evaluate the differing positions.

- **Change-Your-Mind Debates** (Nilson, 2021): Designate opposite sides of the classroom as agreeing or disagreeing with a statement and include an "undecided" middle ground. Before and during the debate, students are allowed to physically move when their position changes. At the conclusion, students reflect on what perspectives caused them to change their viewpoints with those students lingering in the "neutral zone" and give their analysis of the debate overall. Additional scaffolds, such as talking chips or "three-before-me," can be used to ensure a variety of voices are heard. We encourage you to implement these scaffolds at your discretion.

- **Structured Controversy** (Johnson et al., 1991): For a more structured challenge, assign students a position to defend within small groups of about four students. Assign half of each small group one side of a two-sided debate. After the initial small-group debates, the partners switch sides and debate for the opposing side. Lastly, students reconcile or synthesize the opposing sides.

Guided Discussion With Claim–Evidence–Reasoning

At the conclusion of the Interrogate phase, it is imperative to provide structured time for students to independently process their thinking and determine why their thoughts changed (or did *not* change) based on their peers' comments and stakeholders' needs. This self-reflection can reinforce the role of critical thinking and being open-minded throughout scientific discussion.

A common framework used in science classrooms to guide scientific discussion is Claim–Evidence–Reasoning (CER; McNeill & Krajcik, 2011). While CERs have been used to explain scientific phenomena through scientific principles, we argue that adding a sociocultural-informed layer to the practice leads students to higher levels of thinking and, most importantly, makes the content relevant to our students. When collecting data, observed scientific concepts are essential to support evidence of the claim.

We argue that it is also important for students to consider data that contribute to understanding the social and cultural factors at play within a specific community or population. Guiding questions for the added sociocultural-informed layer of a CER can always be "Who is being impacted? What are the implications, and how do we know?" Evidence built on scientific concepts and sociocultural implications can then be used to establish reasoning justified with scientific and societal issues in mind. Students should be able to distinguish between facts, research findings, and speculations in their explanations. Furthermore, they should be able to detail where they received their evidence and how it meets the criteria and constraints of the problem. A model for the phenomenon or a solution to the problem can also be used to support or refute an explanation.

> **SMALL STEPS FOR BIG IMPACT: Use English Language Arts to Support Science**
>
> ▶ A quick search on the internet will provide you with multiple options for CER graphic organizers. Being intentional about using similar language prompts as you do in English language arts is a great way to capitalize on the limited amount of instruction time you have and lean into transdisciplinary teaching.

At the elementary level, students will need scaffolded support to consider ways of collecting data that are culturally sensitive and appropriate for the context. That support can come from you or involve community members. Either way, seeking data through participatory approaches can help students gain valuable insights and build trust, particularly in the communities for which they wish to make sense of the data. After students have questioned, investigated, and interrogated, it is time for action.

The Act Phase

After students have empowered themselves with evidence and reasoning to interrogate the sociocultural-informed phenomenon, it's now time for them to act. In the Act phase, students reflect on their stance in the CER to inform them what they plan to do about the issue. Students may reflect back on who is being impacted and what they can do to elevate the voices of those affected. So, how do we get students to take action, and what type of action are we talking about? To begin this conversation, let's define what it means to take action.

As an elementary student, taking action or being a **change agent** means recognizing that even young students can make meaningful contributions to their communities by addressing challenges, raising awareness, and fostering positive change. For elementary students, this involves understanding real-world problems, identifying ways they can help, and participating in activities that reflect their capacity to influence the world around them.

> A **change agent** is a person who actively contributes to positive transformations within their classroom, school, or community—taking initiative in problem-solving, advocating for themselves and others, making sure everyone's voices are heard, and taking action to make meaningful contributions.

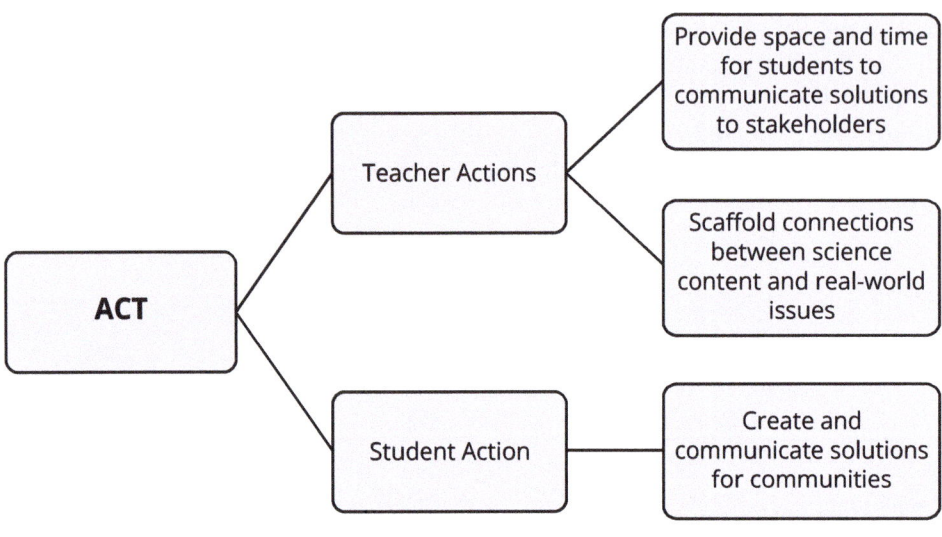

What Does Taking Action Look Like?

When students take action, their engagement may vary from raising awareness to participating in hands-on projects and collaborating with others to amplify their impact. The time and resources that are available to you and your students may impact the type of action your students take. However, we see all actions, no matter how big or small, that identify a problem, propose an evidence-based solution, and have students take responsibility as equally important.

1. **Raising Awareness:** Students can use their voices to educate others by sharing their knowledge of scientific concepts through presentations, demonstrations, newsletters, pamphlets, or videos. For example, students might wish to create a campaign to conserve water by explaining the water cycle and how wasteful practices impact communities. Students may not have a solution per se, as the problem is global, but even identifying the issue allows students to learn about their community and notice problems. They can also begin to brainstorm ideas for change or share the identified issue with others who might be able to connect their ideas to conceptualize a project.

2. **Hands-On Projects:** Students might also participate in hands-on initiatives at local, regional, national, or global levels. The projects may evolve from scratch or reflect other projects in the works. Students may wish to plant a garden to combat food deserts, organize a diaper drive, add data to a citizen science project, create posters to promote recycling, or organize an event for litter pickup at a local park. While students may come to class with projects of their own, teachers might also need some ideas on projects that are feasible given the constraints of the school (e.g., funds, time). Nevertheless, teachers are encouraged

to provide students with opportunities for developing projects that allow students to make decisions, problem-solve, and reflect on their actions. You may be surprised with what they can accomplish!

3. **Collaborating With Others:** Recognizing the power of collaboration and teamwork is important when considering making an impact. Turning to family members, school stakeholders, and community organizations can be helpful to put ideas into action. Networking with others who do advocacy work or can influence the work of others doing this important work can help students see how collective effort amplifies their impact. Thus, students might act by generating ideas, connecting with others, and seeing how their ideas bloom in an authentic context.

How Teachers Can Support Student Action

Teachers can support students in taking action by providing the tools, guidance, and opportunities to connect scientific inquiry with meaningful real-world issues. At other times, supporting student action may look like simply releasing the reins and stepping back to allow students the opportunity to problem-solve. After teachers help students cultivate awareness of social justice issues, they can encourage students to explore how these issues affect their communities or those they identify with, making the issue personal and fostering a deeper connection and motivation to take action.

Using evidence gathered from the Investigate phase and reasoning explored in the Interrogate phase, teachers can use the Act phase to facilitate solution-oriented discussions. As a teacher, you can support students by proposing ways to address the issue. We also encourage you, when doing this work, to consider the impact of the proposed solutions. Model problem-solving discussions where collaboration can be used to demonstrate how scientists and advocates approach challenges systematically.

SMALL STEPS FOR BIG IMPACT: Use Problem-Solving Methods of Scientists

▶ You can help guide students in engaging in structured, respectful discussions to address social issues, using the problem-solving methods of scientists and advocates. Let's start with posing the following scenario:

> Today, we are going to practice talking and working together like scientists and advocates! Scientists ask questions, investigate problems, and find solutions based on evidence. Advocates speak up for people and ideas to make things better. When we put these together, we can work as a team to solve important problems in our classroom, school, and community. Let's try it together!

(Continued)

(Continued)

To support student thinking, you might provide the following prompts:

Step 1: Identify the Problem

- What is something in our classroom, school, or community that we could make better?
- Scientists and advocates might ask, "Why is this happening? What do we need to learn more about?" Let's investigate.

Step 2: Gather Information and Brainstorm Ideas

- Great observations! Scientists and advocates also collect information. How could we find out more about this problem?
- We're gathering evidence like scientists. Now, let's think like advocates. What can we do to help?

Step 3: Propose Solutions and Discuss Impact

- These are great ideas! Scientists test solutions, and advocates make sure ideas are fair and helpful. What might happen if we try these ideas?
- Good question! Advocates think about challenges. What could we do to make sure everyone feels comfortable and/or able to benefit?

Step 4: Take Action and Reflect

- Now that we have a plan, what do scientists and advocates do next?
- Great idea! Scientists and advocates always reflect and improve their ideas.

To close the conversation and encourage future problem-solvers, you could consider saying the following:

> You all just worked like scientists and advocates to solve a problem together! You asked questions, collected ideas, thought of solutions, and planned ways to help. These are skills you can use in and out of school to make the world better.

Teachers are also encouraged to support students in breaking down the proposed action into manageable steps, modeling flexibility and helping students navigate from planning to executing solutions while modeling and teaching invaluable problem-solving skills. Teachers can scaffold instruction to help students communicate their findings and proposals to stakeholders, such as writing letters to local officials or presenting their suggested work at school or community events. Reconnecting with community members whom students communicated with to acquire evidence in prior steps can also help initiate co-planning ideas. This way, the community members have direct input into the impact of a solution and ensure any advocacy work is grounded in the community's context and reflects authentic concerns. We have learned in our previous work with community members that building a mutually beneficial relationship with them is imperative. Reciprocal support recognizes how all in the relationship can learn from and assist one another. It also values the role of shared decision-making, ensuring all voices are heard, and fostering trust. Furthermore, collaboration can provoke sustained support, creating a long-lasting impact through collective and reciprocal efforts.

> *Collaboration can provoke sustained support, creating a long-lasting impact through collective and reciprocal efforts.*

We now turn our attention to an Act Menu that can serve as a helpful tool teachers can use to support learners with brainstorming ways your students can take action.

Using an Act Menu to Make a Difference

Teachers can help students use the scientific evidence and reasoning gathered during their investigation to take meaningful action. The Act Menu (Table 3.5) can be used to support students in sharing their new knowledge and helping them address the issue. Pulling only some of the ideas or adapting them to fit your school context, time constraints, and students' grade levels may be necessary. Additionally, scaffolding to explicitly connect science content with solution ideas takes intentional planning. Alongside the student choice options, we encourage you to address expectations for using vocabulary words related to the targeted standards and lesson objectives. Working with students to generate a list of key vocabulary words that must be used in the final product keeps the task student-centered while allowing you to assess the content standard.

TABLE 3.5 An Act Menu to Guide Meaningful Action

ACT MENU	
1. Educate others	• Design an educational poster, infographic, or brochure to teach others about the issue and what you can do to help.
	• Create a video, song, or presentation to share your findings and inspire action.
2. Advocate for change	• Write a persuasive letter to a local leader, organization, or community group, explaining the issue and suggesting how you can help.
	• Create a petition or advocacy group to raise awareness and gather support for a solution.

(Continued)

(Continued)

ACT MENU	
3. Plan a community event	• Organize an event or awareness walk to engage others in solving the problem.
4. Promote community collaboration	• Host a "teach-in" where community members can learn about the issue and brainstorm solutions. • Partner with a local organization, expert, or group to co-design a project that addresses the issue.
5. Create a solution	• Develop a prototype, model, or experiment that could help solve the problem. • Use writing or art to propose creative solutions (e.g., storybook, website) about the problem and how to fix it.
6. Show gratitude and support	• Write thank-you letters to people working to address the issue, letting them know you appreciate their efforts. • Create a kindness or appreciation campaign to support those affected by the problem.
7. Consider other ideas	• Invite creative ideas or modifications from the ones above to design a unique way to act.

To conceptualize how this Act Menu might be used in relation to our states of matter lesson (see Unit Plan 4.1), we might ask students to think of a way to show gratitude and support for communities supporting sustainable water use. For example, students might wish to write thank-you letters to Indigenous groups acknowledging what initiatives they are doing in the Colorado River basin (see www.waterandtribes.org). As part of the letter, students may wish to include facts they've learned about both the Indigenous communities' sustainable practices and the science of evaporation, demonstrating respect and engagement. They can accompany their letter with an illustrated model depicting the cause, effects, and process of evaporation along the Colorado River.

As a form of scaffolding support in response to students' interest in writing thank-you letters, you can offer sentence starters to guide their writing. Example sentence starters include the following:

Thank you for your work in protecting the Colorado River.

- **Recognition of Effort:** We learned about your efforts to use water sustainably, which include . . .
- **Connection to Science Content:** We learned that evaporation is important to the water cycle. Your method helps keep water in the river by . . .

- **Examples of Sustainable Practices and Solutions:** We admire how you use traditional knowledge to conserve water, such as . . .
- **Connection to Local Impact:** Your work helps ensure enough water for everyone who uses the river to do . . .
- **Actions Inspiring Work:** We're starting a project at our school about saving water and how evaporation works. We plan to . . .
- **Ongoing Support:** We hope to share your story about your efforts with our community to learn from your example. We want our community to know . . .

Along with the student-drawn models highlighting key science vocabulary and scientific processes, students can include reflections on how learning from the Indigenous communities has deepened their appreciation for traditional knowledge. Moreover, they may choose to include a statement of solidarity detailing their effort to support similar practices. By taking action, students show gratitude while communicating their scientific knowledge and respect for advocacy efforts.

> *By taking action, students show gratitude while communicating their scientific knowledge and respect for advocacy efforts.*

Empowering students to see themselves as change agents is crucial in helping them shift from feeling overwhelmed by issues to recognizing their capacity to make a difference. Rather than stewing in anxieties about societal challenges, students can be encouraged to focus on their strengths—their creativity with technology, their ability to write compellingly, or their talent for engaging others through verbal presentations. By providing opportunities to act, teachers help students learn that their voices, ideas, and actions matter, and they begin to see themselves as part of the solution. This not only fosters a sense of agency and hope but also equips them with the skills and confidence to navigate and positively impact a complex world. When students understand they have the tools to act, they are empowered to turn their knowledge into meaningful action, inspiring change in their communities and beyond.

> *Empowering students to see themselves as change agents is crucial in helping them shift from feeling overwhelmed by issues to recognizing their capacity to make a difference.*

CHAPTER SUMMARY

- Recognizing, valuing, and affirming your students' *funds of knowledge* in planning and instruction creates an inclusive and empowering environment for your students.

- Establishing *classroom norms* is a powerful way to foster an inclusive environment that encourages open and critical discussions about societal issues.

- The Elicit phase allows teachers to use *sociocultural-informed phenomena* to preassess students' content knowledge, encourage students to ask relevant questions, and use the information to plan future instruction.

- The Investigate phase requires teachers to intentionally embed the Crosscutting Concepts (CCCs) and the Science and Engineering Practices (SEPs) for students to mimic authentic science inquiry while working to answer questions students generated on a phenomenon.

- The Interrogate phase encourages students to explore and evaluate who is affected by societal issues and to consider their implications, fostering reasoning that integrates scientific principles with social considerations.

- In the Act phase, students are encouraged to apply their sensemaking to take meaningful action. These actions, whether small or large in scale, provide valuable opportunities for students to recognize that their voices, ideas, and efforts matter, empowering them to see themselves as active contributors to solutions.

REFLECTION QUESTIONS

1. What cultural and community assets do your students bring to the classroom?

2. How can you continually enforce classroom norms and hold students accountable throughout the school year?

3. How can you design opportunities for students to share their initial beliefs and understandings about sociocultural-informed phenomena in ways that promote curiosity and questioning?

4. What CCCs and SEPs are you most confident in, and how can you use them in an upcoming lesson?

5. What meaningful action opportunities can you provide to help students connect their learning to community impact and see themselves as capable contributors to solutions?

CHAPTER 4

Unit Plans for Critical Thinking and Action

When students-as-scientists have authentic, relevant opportunities to actively make sense of the world and beyond—what we call sensemaking—science learning becomes engaging, accessible and important to ALL students.

—National Science Teaching Association, "Sensemaking" (2025)

As you review these unit plans, please keep an eye out for patterns in how the Elicit–Investigate–Interrogate–Act framework is used:

1. How does the framework engage students in sensemaking of science content?
2. How does the framework scaffold students in sensemaking of social justice topics?
3. What are the different methods of debates that are used, and how can you use them in your classroom?
4. Where else can you use the Claim–Evidence–Reasoning framework in your teaching?

Each unit we'll discuss begins with a teacher background section, standards, and a timeline followed by instructions for the teacher and student pages. While there is some preparation in materials and for instruction, these units were created with the goal of keeping the materials limited to what you might have on hand or those that are easily accessible.

While the units' lessons were designed to require minimal prep, we know with all teaching that you may have to make minor adjustments to best fit the needs of your students, school, and community. Engaging in social justice is hard work! We hope these units and lesson plans empower you to take the leap to instill and nurture empathy within your classroom.

UNITS IN THIS CHAPTER

TITLE	TOTAL LESSONS IN THE UNIT	DISCIPLINARY CORE IDEAS	SOCIAL JUSTICE STANDARDS
4.1 Water Negotiators	5	Earth's Systems	Action 16
4.2 Diaper Deserts	4	Matter and Its Interactions	Justice 14 Action 20
4.3 Honorable Harvest	4	From Molecules to Organisms: Structures and Processes	Diversity 6 Action 18

UNIT PLAN 4.1
Water Negotiators

Teacher Background

In the southwestern United States, the right to water is a critical issue deeply connected to the region's history and culture. In this unit students conduct and carry out an investigation on population growth and evaporation before applying the information to water scarcity occurring in the United States. Students will engage in a role-playing activity to simulate negotiations of water rights between farmers, ranchers, industry representatives, and Indigenous communities. By engaging with diverse viewpoints, students will gain a holistic understanding of water rights issues and the need for inclusive and creative solutions.

Standards

TABLE 4.1

EARTH'S SYSTEMS		
Students who demonstrate understanding can:		
Develop a model using an example to describe ways the geosphere, biosphere, hydrosphere, and/or atmosphere interact.		
Science and Engineering Practices	**Disciplinary Core Ideas**	**Crosscutting Concepts**
Planning and Carrying Out Investigations	Earth's Systems and Earth and Human Activity	Cause and Effect
Social Justice Connection		
Anchor Standard, Action 16: Students will express empathy when people are excluded or mistreated because of their identities and concern when they themselves experience bias.		
In this unit, students will investigate how water influences both personal and professional aspects of life while exploring diverse perspectives on water usage and scarcity. They will examine the various ways water is utilized and consider how individual viewpoints on water-related concerns may differ. By learning about global and local water conservation efforts, students will recognize how individuals and communities address inequities and take responsibility for improving lives. As part of this exploration, students may engage in activities, such as writing a thank-you note to acknowledge efforts in water preservation and sustainability.		

Objectives

Students will:

- Analyze past and present implications of factors leading to water scarcity.

- Plan and carry out an investigation to explore evaporation of water.
- Evaluate and defend water allocations based on stakeholder perspective and need.

Timeline

TIMELINE	INSTRUCTIONAL PHASE	DESCRIPTION	MATERIALS
Day 1	Elicit	Observing water levels in Lake Mead	Per student: • Elicit student page
Days 2 and 3	Investigate	Designing and conducting an investigation to explore evaporation of water	Per student: • Investigate student page Per small group (3 or 4 students): • Water • Various containers (e.g., plastic bags, plastic cups, bins) • Measurement tools (e.g., rulers, graduated cylinders, measuring cups)
Day 4	Interrogate	Debating to decide water allocation among stakeholders	Per small group (4 students): • Water Negotiators' Roles page (cut) Per student: • Interrogate student page
Day 5	Act	Writing a thank-you letter for conservation efforts	Per student: • Act student page

ELICIT PHASE

Changing Water Levels in Lake Mead

1. ASK: What water sources do we depend on here in our town?
2. Press students for information related to how they use water in their everyday lives both out of necessity and for recreation. Consider the strengths of your community (e.g., farming, ranching, industry) to open dialogue. Tell students that they will look at a picture of the Hoover Dam on Lake Mead on the Arizona–Nevada border. Lake Mead is the largest reservoir in the United States and is used by the states of Arizona, California, and Nevada. The lake is a main source of water for residents as well as agricultural, commercial, and industrial businesses.

3. As you share the picture of Lake Mead and the Hoover Dam, prompt students to draw pictures or add comments to the Notice and Wonder chart on their Elicit student page.

   a. "Notice" prompts might include:
      i. What colors or textures do you notice in the picture?
      ii. What do you notice about the water level in the picture?
      iii. Are there any signs of water movement or erosion in the picture?
      iv. Are there any patterns you notice? Does anything break that pattern?

   b. "Wonder" prompts might include:
      i. Where the water is going and who is using it.
      ii. Whether they have seen dams elsewhere.

4. Here is an example of what a completed Notice and Wonder chart might look like:

NOTICE	WONDER
• There is a white line on the rocks above the water line. • The water level below the dam is lower. • There is a bridge with cars on it.	• Is the water rising or falling over time? • Has it been hotter or drier than years before? • Who needs this water? • Will the water get replaced?

As students complete the chart, follow up with prompts that ask them to use evidence in the pictures to support their ideas. You might also prompt them to connect what they have learned about water cycles, weather, human activity, and climate change.

SMALL STEPS FOR BIG IMPACT: Focus on the Facts

▶ Many students, and adults, automatically begin to inference the causes of their observations. However, it is imperative that you keep students focused on the evidence of what they see and what they wonder. Remind students that scientists depend on evidence as answers so they must slow down to collect all the evidence before jumping to an explanation. To guide students in observing like a scientist, you could use the following prompts:

(Continued)

(Continued)

Setting the Stage

- Scientists don't jump to conclusions—they carefully observe, gather evidence, and ask questions before making explanations. Today, we will practice thinking like scientists by slowing down and focusing only on what we see and wonder before we explain.

Observing Without Explaining

- For now, we are only collecting evidence. Describe exactly what you see, hear, or feel using these sentence stems:
  - I see . . .
  - I hear . . .
  - I feel . . .

Wondering Before Explaining

- What do you wonder about this object or phenomenon? Generate questions using these sentence stems:
  - Why does it . . . ?
  - How did it . . . ?
  - What might it . . . ?

Connecting to Evidence-Based Thinking

- What evidence supports your idea? Do we need more data? Let's propose explanations that link back to our evidence.

Using these prompts can support students as they reflect on why scientists have to slow down and collect all the evidence first.

INVESTIGATE PHASE

Investigating Changes and Conditions

1. ASK: We know that the population in this area is increasing. We're also going to investigate other factors that may be contributing to the water change. What do we already know about desert communities in regions like Arizona and Nevada?

    a. Potential Probing Questions

       i. Do you think temperatures and the climate are getting warmer or cooler around the world? What makes you think that? What evidence have you heard or seen?

          A. Does anybody agree or disagree with the evidence shared by [insert student's name]? Why?

       ii. If water is evaporating, where do you think it goes?

2. SAY: Next, we are going to investigate what conditions cause water to evaporate the fastest. Hopefully, it will give us some insight into what is happening at Lake Mead and the Hoover Dam.

3. Divide students into small groups of 3 or 4.

4. Distribute one Elicit student page to each student.

5. If this is the first time using this four-question strategy, work through questions 1, 3, and 4 together.
    a. For question 1, a scaffolding question may include:
        i. What materials do we have in the classroom right now?
    b. For question 2, students may use words or a drawing to communicate their thinking. For instance, some students may hold the misconception that water simply disappears when it evaporates. Remind students matter cannot disappear, and continually press students to explain where they believe water goes and what the cause is.
    c. Question 3 builds off of question 1 to develop some independent variables. Remind students you are looking for ideas of what they can change to see if it makes a difference.
    d. Question 4 focuses on the dependent variable and informs data collection and experimental design. Encourage students to revisit question 1 and potentially add to the list with new ideas.

6. In their small groups, students select an option from questions 3 and 4 to create their own testable question.

SMALL STEPS FOR BIG IMPACT: Create an Anchor Chart

▶ The four-question strategy found in Part One of the Investigate student page can be used to scaffold open inquiry with any grade level (Cothron et al., 2006). You can choose to differentiate for readiness by creating an anchor chart together as a class or by having students independently brainstorm potential opportunities. We suggest modeling an anchor chart as a whole group so students know how they might proceed through the activity and what questions to ask. You will see an example of the four-question strategy on the Investigate teacher page.

7. In their small groups, students create their investigative procedures. Some helpful hints include:
    a. Start each step with a verb so the procedures read like a recipe.
    b. Ensure students are controlling variables.
    c. Reinforce the idea of multiple trials.
    d. Instruct small groups to have you check their procedures before moving on to gathering supplies. Once you have decided procedures are adequate, students should set up their investigation.

SMALL STEPS FOR BIG IMPACT: Consider Whole-Class Demonstrations

▶ When time, resources, and energy limit the ability to conduct multiple small-group investigations, consider using whole-class demonstrations as an effective alternative. To maintain a student-centered approach, have students vote on which variable they would like to test or manipulate as a class. Whole-class demonstrations can be used to conserve resources and lead rich conversations that empower students to ask and answer questions as authentic scientists.

SMALL STEPS FOR BIG IMPACT: Mark It

▶ After verifying students' procedures, mark your initials on their papers to indicate they are ready to move on. This not only holds students accountable for creating high-quality procedures but also gives you a quick reference for grading later.

8. It may take about a week to see the results. Students recording their results should take no more than 5–10 minutes a day.

9. Once all small groups have answered their research question, it is time for a whole-group consensus discussion.
    a. Begin with the initial question: What conditions cause water to evaporate the fastest?
    b. Have each small group share their claim, and *always* prompt for evidence to support their claims.

10. Once the whole group agrees that a claim has enough evidence to be supported, add it to an anchor chart. Possible answers may include:
    a. When the temperature is higher.
    b. When the air is drier (low humidity).
    c. If it is windy.
    d. When there is a larger surface area exposed.

11. SAY: When water evaporates, it changes from a liquid to a gas. It does not simply disappear! Tiny water molecules start to move faster and break free from the surface of the water, floating up into the air as water vapor.
    a. ASK: Where do the water molecules gain the extra energy?
        i. Higher temperatures, windy days, and so on.

12. Redirect students to the picture from the Elicit phase.
13. ASK: Which of these conditions is prevalent in the southwestern part of the United States where Lake Mead is located?

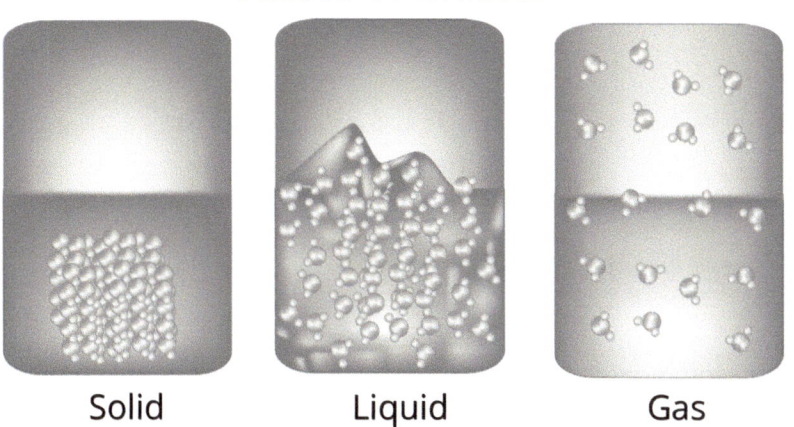

States of Matter

Solid   Liquid   Gas

SOURCE: iStock.com/KKT Madhusanka

INTERROGATE PHASE

Debate: Who Deserves the Most Water?

1. Divide your class into four home expert groups for a debate. Assign each home expert group a role (i.e., Chief Tsosie, Sarah Tompson, Carlos Martinez, and Aliyah Johnson) and distribute enough role cards from the Interrogate student page so each student understands their perspective in the debate.

2. Within the home expert groups, have students collaborate to develop arguments for why the stakeholder they are representing deserves to have the most water. Provide at least 10 minutes to allow each student to understand and discuss their role's perspective and what they need to be successful.

3. At the conclusion of the allotted time, have each home expert group member number off. For example, Chief Tsosie's group will have #1, #2, #3, and so on.

4. Moving in sequential order, have each group member with the #1 give a brief statement in defense of their perspective's water rights. Once each of the four perspectives' #1s have shared, move on to the #2s, and so forth.

5. While students share their arguments, instruct the rest of the group to listen carefully so they can build on others' ideas and log potential counterarguments to different perspectives on the student Interrogate page.

6. Once the debate has concluded, regroup students based on their assigned numbers. For example, Chief Tsosie #1 will work in a small group with Sarah Tompson #1, Carlos Martinez #1, and Aliyah Johnson #1. These are their negotiation groups.

Expert Groups					**Negotiation Groups**			
1	2	1	2		1	1	2	2
3	4	3	4	→	1	1	2	2
1	2	1	2		3	3	4	4
3	4	3	4		3	3	4	4

7. Each negotiation group must now reach a consensus, and complete the Interrogate student page, as to which percentage each stakeholder should receive in water allocation.

SMALL STEPS FOR BIG IMPACT: Try the Jigsaw Method

▶ The jigsaw method is a collaborative learning strategy that helps students engage deeply with content while developing critical thinking skills and dispositions, teamwork, and communication skills. While we often see this method for students to practice peer teaching, in this lesson we are reenvisioning this structure to create an environment for small-group negotiations. Here are some tips for facilitating a successful jigsaw activity:

- Be clear with your behavior expectations during the transitions. Remind students to walk and push in their chairs before regrouping. You may find it beneficial to include a visual timer or verbally count down to keep students on track.
- Encourage active listening. Remind students that being an active listener is just as important as being an expert.
- Hold students accountable. Require students to take notes, draw pictures, or summarize key points to ensure engagement and understanding.

SMALL STEPS FOR BIG IMPACT: Limit Decision Time

▶ To differentiate the process, consider limiting the students' decision time to mimic real-life negotiation constraints. To differentiate for readiness, one small group may choose to represent a new perspective and form their argument on their own. Alternative stakeholders include environmental protection workers, city mayors, or even citizens of Mexico.

> **SMALL STEPS FOR BIG IMPACT: Leverage AI**
>
> ▶ Use artificial intelligence (AI) to make activities such as the water rights debate more contextual for your community! The example perspectives presented in this unit were purposefully created with AI to suggest how resources exist to support (and enhance) your activities. When using AI, just like any resource, we encourage you to make intentional modifications to make the activity more meaningful for your students. We also find it helpful in diversifying information, such as including names and experiences from diverse perspectives. Nevertheless, when using AI, be sure to fact-check! For example, when we tried using AI for this activity, the initial AI-generated output mentioned using the Lakota people. However, the Lakota live in the northern plains and not the Colorado River basin.

8. Once each group has reached a consensus, invite students to share out as a whole group using a Claim–Evidence–Reasoning format. Potential sentence stems you may wish to provide for students are:

    a. We believe _____ should be allocated the most water because _____.

    b. Other groups such as _____ should not have a higher water allocation because _____.

ACT PHASE

Create a Thank-You Letter for Conservation Efforts

1. Reflecting on the debate and the perspectives of the people and businesses discussed, write a thank-you letter to an organization or group working to conserve and protect the Colorado River. You may wish to research local farming groups, Indigenous communities, foundations, or nonprofit organizations. Examples include the Colorado Water Trust, the Nature Conservancy, the Walton Family Foundation, and Protect Our Rivers. For more information on Indigenous peoples in the Colorado River basin, see www.waterandtribes.org. If students wish to learn more about their local contexts, they can also research organizations and groups supporting a local body of water or your community's watershed.

2. Have students brainstorm organizations and groups related to the Colorado River or a geographical location of interest. Discuss:

    a. The organization or group's name.

    b. Involvement/use of the water.

3. ASK:
   a. What is being done to address water conservation? (Examples include creating water-saving technologies, adjusting practices, and supporting healthy ecosystems.)
   b. Who is impacted by the initiatives, and how?
   c. What evidence will you include to support how initiatives are supporting water conservation?
4. Have students collaboratively complete the Act student page. In the body of the letter, expect students to make connections to the science of evaporation, such as including an illustrated model depicting the evaporation process.
5. To support students in writing their thank-you letters, provide them with sentence starters such as the following noted in Chapter 3. As always, we encourage you to differentiate and use technology if that is what your students need to be successful.

Thank you for your work in protecting the Colorado River.

   a. **Recognition of Effort:** We learned about your efforts to use water sustainably, which include . . .
   b. **Connection to Science Content:** We learned that evaporation is important to the water cycle. Your method helps keep water in the river by . . .
   c. **Examples of Sustainable Practices and Solutions:** We admire how you use traditional knowledge to conserve water, such as . . .
   d. **Connection to Local Impact:** Your work helps ensure enough water for everyone who uses the river to do . . .
   e. **Actions Inspiring Work:** We're starting a project at our school about saving water and how evaporation works. We plan to . . .
   f. **Ongoing Support:** We hope to share your story about your efforts with our community to learn from your example. We want our community to know . . .

Closure

Have students share their thank-you letters with the class. If possible, see if the class can send the letters to the organization or group. By sharing their letters, students are raising public awareness of what organizations and groups are doing to conserve water and considering ways they might be able to support similar water conservation initiatives.

Name: _____

ELICIT: Water Negotiators

Guiding Question: What do you notice and wonder about Lake Mead and the Hoover Dam?

Lake Mead and the Hoover Dam

iStock.com/LPETTET

NOTICE	WONDER

Name: _____

INVESTIGATE: Water Negotiators

PART ONE

Guiding Question: What conditions cause water to evaporate the fastest?

1. What materials are readily available for conducting experiments on evaporation?

   _____
   _____
   _____
   _____
   _____

2. What does it mean for something to evaporate?

   _____
   _____
   _____
   _____
   _____

3. How can I change the set of evaporation materials to affect the action?

   _____
   _____
   _____
   _____
   _____

4. How can I measure or describe potential changes due to evaporation?

   _____
   _____
   _____
   _____
   _____

PART TWO

Research Question: How does _____ affect _____?

Procedures:

DATA COLLECTION	VARIABLE YOU ARE MEASURING (QUESTION 4) _____				
VARIABLE YOU ARE CHANGING (QUESTION 3) _____	DAY 1	DAY 2	DAY 3	DAY 4	DAY 5

Conclusion:

1. What is the answer to your research question?

   _____
   _____
   _____
   _____

2. In your data table, circle evidence that supports your answer.

3. How can your data help explain what is happening in the Colorado River?

   _____
   _____
   _____
   _____
   _____
   _____
   _____

Name: _____

INTERROGATE: Water Negotiators

PART ONE

My Role: _____

Why I Deserve [More/Less/the Same Amount of] Water:

Other Perspectives:

PERSPECTIVE	COUNTERARGUMENTS
Farmers	
Indigenous peoples	
Industry representatives	
Ranchers	

PART TWO

With your group, sketch a pie chart showing what you think the best plan of action would be to conserve the Colorado River. Label each pie piece with the percentage agreed upon. Keep in mind the amount of water evaporating will continue to increase.

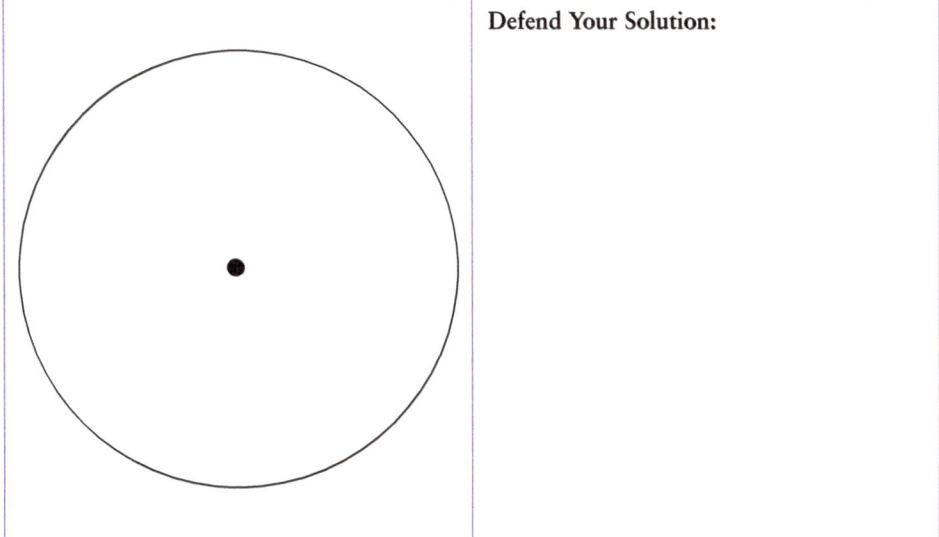

Defend Your Solution:

CHAPTER 4 • UNIT PLANS FOR CRITICAL THINKING AND ACTION

Name: _____

ACT: Water Negotiators

Dear _____ [Individual, Group, or Organization's Name],

Thank you for your work in protecting the _____

_____

_____

_____

_____

_____

_____

Sincerely,

[Visual]

INVESTIGATE (TEACHER PAGE)
Water Negotiators

Sample Four-Question Strategy

Guiding Question: What conditions cause water to evaporate the fastest?

1. What materials are readily available for conducting experiments on evaporation?
   a. Water.
   b. Containers (plastic cups, Ziploc bags, bins).
   c. Locations (by the window, in a cabinet, under a light, outside).
   d. Measurement (calendar, rulers, graduated cylinder).

2. What does it mean for something to evaporate?
   a. Use students' answers as a pre-assessment to guide future instruction.

3. How can I change the set of evaporation materials to affect the action?
   a. We can change the amount of water.
   b. We can change the container (open or closed container, surface area exposed).
   c. We can change the location of the water.

4. How can I measure or describe the response of evaporation to the change?
   a. Count the number of days until everything has evaporated.
   b. Measure the volume of water each day for a week.
   c. Measure the height of water each day for a week.

INTERROGATE
Water Negotiators' Roles

Chief Tsosie of the Navajo Nation	Sarah Tompson, Rancher
My name is Chief Tsosie of the Navajo Nation. We have taken care of this land and its water for many generations. Water is very important to us for our culture and daily life. In the past, communities like ours have often been treated unfairly and not been given enough water, even though treaties and laws say we should have it. We need water to grow food, protect nature, and keep our traditions alive. It's important that we get a fair share of water so our communities can be healthy and strong.	My name is Sarah Tompson, and I run a cattle ranch in Utah. Water is essential for my livestock and crops, and without enough of it, my ranch can't survive. In recent years, we've faced water shortages that have made it hard to keep our animals healthy and our business running. I believe that as a rancher who contributes to the local economy and provides food for our community, I deserve a fair share of water. It's important that we find a balance so that everyone, including farmers and ranchers, can thrive.
Carlos Martinez, Farmer	**Aliyah Johnson, Industry Representative**
My name is Carlos Martinez, and I grow alfalfa on my farm. Alfalfa needs a lot of water, but it's crucial because it feeds cattle and supports the livestock industry. Recently, water shortages have made it tough to keep my crops healthy and productive. As a farmer who plays a key role in the food supply chain, I believe I deserve a fair share of water. It's important that we ensure enough water for farming so we can continue to provide for our community and support local agriculture.	My name is Aliyah Johnson, and I advocate for the semiconductor manufacturing industry in the southwestern United States. This industry is vital for states like Arizona and Utah, providing jobs and driving technological advancements. Semiconductors are essential components in many devices, including smartphones, computers, and medical equipment. However, manufacturing requires a significant amount of water, and recent shortages have threatened our operations. As someone who supports this crucial industry, I believe we deserve a fair share of water to ensure we can continue to innovate and contribute to the economy. It's important that we secure enough water to keep our factories running and support the livelihoods of thousands of workers.

UNIT PLAN 4.2
Diaper Deserts

Teacher Background

While we often hear of food deserts, diaper deserts also plague low-income communities around the United States. Lack of access to diapers jeopardizes infants' health and even hinders caregivers' ability to maintain steady employment due to day care requirements. In this unit, students will be introduced to the concept of diaper deserts, investigate the physical properties of diapers, and explore the communities most likely to be at risk of becoming a diaper desert.

Standards

TABLE 4.2

MATTER AND ITS INTERACTIONS		
Students who demonstrate understanding can:		
Conduct an investigation to determine whether the mixing of two or more substances results in new substances.*		
Note: In this unit, new substances will not be created. Students will be expected to defend why diapers absorbing water is a physical change because new substances are not created.		
Science and Engineering Practices Engaging in Argument From Evidence	**Disciplinary Core Ideas** Chemical Reactions	**Crosscutting Concepts** Cause and Effect
Social Justice Connection *Anchor Standard, Justice 14:* I know that life is easier for some people and harder for others based on who they are and where they were born. *Anchor Standard, Action 20:* I will work with my friends and family to make our school and community fair for everyone, and we will work hard and cooperate in order to achieve our goals. In this unit, students will explore how the location of communities affects families' ability to obtain cost-efficient diapers. They will examine which communities are the most impacted by diaper deserts and collaboratively organize a diaper drive that can be used to collect diapers for their own community.		

Objectives

Students will:

- Analyze an infographic to determine which communities are predominantly impacted by diaper deserts.

- Plan and carry out an investigation to determine if the changes that occur when a diaper absorbs water are physical or chemical.

- Outline a plan of action to help families in their own community obtain diapers.

Timeline

TIMELINE	INSTRUCTIONAL PHASE	DESCRIPTION	MATERIALS
Days 1 and 2	Elicit	Making observations about diaper deserts in the local area	Per student: • Elicit student page
	Investigate	Considering chemical and physical changes in diapers	Per student: • Investigate student page Per small group (3 or 4 students) • Half of a diaper • Water
Day 3	Interrogate	Finding diaper deserts in the local area	Per student: • Interrogate student page • Computer/tablet with internet access
Day 4	Act	Organizing a diaper drive	Per student: • Act student page

ELICIT PHASE

Unpacking Diaper Information

1. ASK: How many of you have younger siblings, cousins, or friends who use diapers? About how many diapers would you estimate they use in a day?

    a. Prompt students to share experiences when diapers did not get changed immediately or if there are scenarios where clean diapers might not be readily available.

2. SAY: Today, we are going to be talking about diapers, some of the chemistry involved, and the importance of having access to diapers.

3. Pass out one Elicit student sheet per student.

4. Have students independently complete the Notice and Wonder chart based on the information on the infographic.
5. Have students share their Notice and Wonder charts with a peer while listening for similar ideas.
6. ASK:
   a. What is a diaper desert?
      i. Why do we use the term *desert* to describe this issue?
   b. Who is most at risk of living in a diaper desert? What patterns do you notice?
      i. To guide observations related to patterns, consider asking students to reflect on discussing specific socioeconomic, geographic, or demographic factors and what impact these factors might have.
   c. Who is impacted by living in a diaper desert?
      i. Children who might develop sores and get sick from not having clean diapers.
      ii. Parents and caregivers who may not be able to go to work because many day cares require caregivers to provide a certain number of diapers for their children to attend day care.
   d. Can we reuse diapers?
      i. Leave this question unanswered as it transitions into the Investigate phase.
         A. If students bring up the idea of disposable diapers, it is a valid idea but often not advantageous as it requires multiple loads of laundry, which may be difficult if there is not a washer or dryer or a vehicle to drive to a Laundromat.

INVESTIGATE PHASE

Investigating Physical Versus Chemical Changes

1. ASK: What do we know about diapers?
   a. What is the primary purpose of a diaper?
   b. What are common signs that a diaper needs to be changed?
      i. Do you think that indicates a physical or chemical change? Why?

SMALL STEPS FOR BIG IMPACT: Argue With Evidence

▶ Take your time on this question and allow students the space and support they need to engage in the Science and Engineering Practice of engaging in argument from evidence. Encourage each student to explain their thinking by asking "why," and guide them to draw on personal experience or prior knowledge as part of their reasoning. To support diverse

(Continued)

(Continued)

learners, consider scaffolding the process with sentence starters such as "I agree/disagree with _____ because _____" or "I'd like to add _____." These prompts can help students articulate their ideas more confidently. Encourage students when responding to refer to their classmates by name to give ownership of the ideas back to the contributor—this not only builds a sense of community and shared ownership over ideas but also allows you to track engagement and create space for every voice to be heard.

2. Pass out an Investigate student page to each student and have them complete questions 1 and 2 in groups of 3 or 4.
3. Discuss question 2:
   a. If they believe it is a chemical change, students should be looking for a new substance, an odor, a temperature change, precipitate, or gas bubbles.
   b. If students believe it is a physical change, they should look for a change in the appearance or form of a substance, including its shape, size, or state of matter, but not in the substance itself.
4. As a whole group, determine procedures to pour water onto the diaper and where the diaper will be kept for 2–5 days. Pass out materials for small groups. *Be sure to have students wash their hands after manipulating the diapers.*

SMALL STEPS FOR BIG IMPACT: Save Resources

▶ You may choose to do this investigation with one diaper as a whole class to conserve supplies. When completing the investigation, place the diaper under a document camera connected to an overhead projector or large screen. You can use technology to zoom in on specific layers, materials, or reactions during water absorption. Where resources are limited, demonstrating with intention is a powerful way to engage students while modeling sustainability.

5. After waiting 2–5 days, have students complete their final documentation and begin the Claim–Evidence–Reasoning process.
6. ASK:
   a. What evidence is there that this is a chemical change? (Remind students to consider what constitutes a chemical change in comparison to a physical change.)
      i. There is no evidence of a chemical reaction, where bonds between atoms are broken and new bonds are formed.

b. What evidence is there that this is a physical change?
   i. No new substance is formed: While the shape of the diaper does change, no new chemical substance is created.
   ii. Reversibility: The process can be reversed by drying the diaper, which will release the absorbed water, returning the diaper to its original state.
   iii. Observable physical properties: The diaper's physical properties, such as size, weight, and texture, change as it absorbs water.
7. After the discussion, have students complete the Claim–Evidence–Reasoning chart.

INTERROGATE PHASE

Researching Diaper Data

1. We now know that adding water to diapers creates a physical change. Even though this physical change is reversible, we don't want to reuse diapers.
   a. ASK: Why do we not reuse diapers?
      i. Even though the water evaporates, bacteria and other microorganisms from urine and feces pose a risk of infections and skin irritations for babies.
2. Have students work in partners to complete the Interrogate student page. They will need access to a computer/tablet and the internet.
3. Discuss the patterns and accessibility issues your students find when they have concluded their research.
4. When discussing the challenge question, remind students of the added resources and financial considerations needed to use online retailers (e.g., subscription and shipping fees) and reusable diapers (e.g., the cost of laundry and/or ability to get to a Laundromat).
5. ASK: What actions can we take in our classroom to address diaper deserts?

ACT PHASE

Organizing a Diaper Drive

1. Have the class complete the Act student page. You may choose to do this individually, in small groups, as a jigsaw activity, or as a whole group. Think about other groups you have at your school that may want to help such as the student council, student advisory committees, or even the parent–teacher association.

SMALL STEPS FOR BIG IMPACT: Share Results

▶ Completing the Act student page is a great "fast finisher" activity—perfect for students who complete their work ahead of time and are ready for an additional challenge! If only a small group of students complete this outline, consider having them present their plan to the rest of the class. This not only validates and celebrates their effort but also empowers all students by sharing ideas that can spark further curiosity, critical thinking, and discussion.

Closure

Consider tapping into the energy and leadership within your school community to bring the diaper drive to life. Collaborate with student groups—such as your student council, service clubs, or peer leaders—or partner with teacher leaders at your school who have connections to community service opportunities. Work with a local organization or social service agency that can help distribute the collected diapers to families in need. This collaboration not only ensures your donations reach the right hands but also builds meaningful community partnerships. To amplify the impact and celebrate students' efforts, promote the initiative through local social media pages, school newsletters, or community bulletins. Consider having students create flyers, videos, or social media posts to raise awareness, turning the drive into a real-world learning opportunity that builds skills in communication, organization, and civic engagement.

Name: _____

ELICIT: Diaper Deserts

Guiding Question: What do you notice and wonder about the following infographic?

DIAPER DESERTS: NEIGHBORHOOD CHARACTERISTICS

"Priority" areas are identified by the need for diaper access based on average median income and low access to stores that sold most common diaper sizes.

72% THE NUMBER OF PRIORITY NEIGHBORHOODS MADE UP OF RENTER-OCCUPIED HOUSING.

67%

DEMOGRAPHICS OF PRIORITY NEIGHBORHOODS

Of the priority areas, 67% of the neighborhoods' inhabitants identify as Black, African American, Hispanic, or Latino.

Massengale, K. E., Jones, M. A., Liao, J., Park, C., & Old, M. (2022). Priority areas for child diaper access: Low-income neighborhoods with limited retail access to the basic need of diapers. *Health Equity*, *6*(1), 767–776. https://doi.org/10.1089/heq.2021.0192

Notice

Wonder

Name: _____

INVESTIGATE: Diaper Deserts

PART ONE

Research Question: Does adding water to a diaper create a physical or chemical change?

1. Predict: Do you think adding water to a diaper is a physical or chemical change? Why?

2. What type of evidence should you be observing to either support or falsify your prediction?

Data Collection: Draw and label your observations.

Before Adding Water	
While Adding Water	
Immediately After Adding Water	
_____ Days Later	

PART TWO

Research Question: Does adding water to a diaper create a physical or chemical change?

Claim *Compose one sentence that answers the research question.*	
Evidence *Describe at least three pieces of evidence from your observations to support your claim.*	
Reasoning *Explain how your evidence supports your claim.* THINK: How does what you know about physical and chemical changes help link your observed evidence to your claim?	

Name: _____

INTERROGATE: Diaper Deserts

1. Complete the chart identifying which retailers have the most cost-efficient diapers.

Retailers	Brand of Diapers: _____ Size of Diapers: _____		
	Largest Package Available *(Example: 78 Diapers)*	Cost of the Package	Cost per Diaper *Size of Package/Cost of Package*
Sam's Club			
Walmart			
Dollar General			
Walgreens			

2. What patterns are you noticing about the size of the retailer and cost of diapers?

   _____

   _____

   _____

3. Identify communities near you. Using the internet and maps, find the distance from the community center to the retailers you found earlier with the most cost-efficient diapers.

COMMUNITIES NEAR YOU	DISTANCE FROM RETAILER TO COMMUNITY CENTER		
	(EXAMPLE: SAM'S CLUB)	_____	_____

COMMUNITIES NEAR YOU	DISTANCE FROM RETAILER TO COMMUNITY CENTER		
	(EXAMPLE: SAM'S CLUB)	_____	_____

4. What patterns in distance and accessibility do you notice?

_____
_____
_____
_____
_____

5. **Challenge Question:** There are positives and negatives to alternatives such as using online retailers and reusable diapers. Choose one alternative to disposable diapers and list at least one positive and one negative implication.

_____
_____
_____
_____
_____

Name: _____

ACT: Diaper Deserts

Understanding the Need

1. What is a diaper desert?

2. Why is it important to help families in diaper deserts?

Planning the Drive

1. Who will be involved in organizing the diaper drive?

2. When will the diaper drive happen?

3. How long will the diaper drive last?

Collecting Diapers

1. What types of diapers will you collect (e.g., sizes, brands)?

2. How will you encourage people to donate diapers?

3. How will you physically collect the diapers, and where will you store them?

Promoting the Diaper Drive

1. How will you let people know about the diaper drive?

2. Who can help you spread the word?

Distributing the Diapers

1. Who will receive the donated diapers?

2. How will you deliver the diapers to those in need?

UNIT PLAN 4.3
Honorable Harvest

Teacher Background

Society often devalues and silences Indigenous practices when compared to traditional Western science. Indigenous wisdom holds valuable space in science, particularly through the concept of respectful harvesting of natural resources, which emphasizes taking only what is needed, ensuring the sustainability of resources, and maintaining a reciprocal relationship with nature. This approach aligns closely with Western science's principles of sustainable harvesting, which focuses on managing resources to prevent depletion and ensure long-term ecological benefits. Unlike Western science, many Indigenous cultures view plants, animals, and decomposers as being family with an interconnectedness among all living things, seeing them as relatives with their own spirits and roles. This perspective is particularly impactful for the youngest scientists who can pull from their own life experiences with human family members. In this unit on life cycles, we focus on mushrooms to help extend students' thinking beyond the more commonly used caterpillar or frog life cycle.

Standards

TABLE 4.3

FROM MOLECULES TO ORGANISMS: STRUCTURES AND PROCESSES		
Students who demonstrate understanding can:		
Develop models to describe that organisms have unique and diverse life cycles but all have in common birth, growth, reproduction, and death.		
Science and Engineering Practices Engaging in Argument From Evidence	**Disciplinary Core Ideas** Growth and Development of Organisms	**Crosscutting Concepts** Patterns
Social Justice Connection *Anchor Standard, Diversity 6:* Students will express comfort with people who are both similar to and different from them and engage respectfully with all people. *Anchor Standard, Action 18:* Students will speak up with courage and respect when they or someone else has been hurt or wronged by bias. In this unit, students will explore ways to learn about people, including their traditions and culture, concerning agricultural practices. Students will make comparisons with their culture's ways of interacting with nature, mainly looking for similarities and differences. These comparisons will allow students to respect cultural differences and strategize treating others respectfully. Students will apply their newly acquired knowledge to create a petition that outlines ways to advocate for their beliefs, with a particular emphasis on supporting and amplifying the voices of those whose practices have been restricted or marginalized.		

Objectives

Students will:

- Explore how patterns can be used to make predictions.
- Use models to communicate their predictions.
- Advocate for or against Indigenous harvesting practices in national parks.

Timeline

TIME	INSTRUCTIONAL PHASE	DESCRIPTION	MATERIALS
Day 1	Elicit	Reading an "Honorable Harvest" poem and exploring reciprocal relationships	Per student: • Elicit student page
Day 2	Investigate	Part I: Dissecting a mushroom through an Indigenous harvesting practice	• Store-bought mushroom(s) Per student: • Investigate student page
		Part II: Mushroom Life Cycle Card Sort activity	Per small group (3 or 4 students): • Set of mushroom cards Per student: • Investigate student page
Day 3	Interrogate	Participating in a debate as to whether Indigenous peoples should be able to harvest in national parks without a permit	Per student: • Interrogate student page
Day 4	Act	Writing a petition in support of students' positions on Indigenous peoples harvesting in national parks	Per student: • Act student page

ELICIT PHASE

Reciprocal Relationships

1. ASK: Think silently. Is there a time you have helped a friend? What did you do to help them? How did they respond? Did they help you back?

    a. Students may share times when they have or have not received anything in return. Focus on the examples where both individuals benefited through shared advice, mutual comfort, or cooperation to accomplish a task. Emphasize how respectful and mutual relationships benefit both people.

2. SAY: Indigenous culture is about sharing and being fair to humans, plants, animals, and all Earth's resources. Some of you just described a *reciprocal relationship*. A reciprocal relationship with nature means giving and getting in a way that is good for everyone, including the Earth. We're about to read a poem from a member of the Citizen Potawatomi Nation about the "Honorable Harvest" (Kimmerer, 2013, pp. 177–178), an oral tradition passed down for people to remember how to take care of plants, fruits, and vegetables in a way that is good for everyone, including the plant!

############ **SMALL STEPS FOR BIG IMPACT: Know Your Place** ############

▶ Be prepared by familiarizing yourself with both the historical and current presence of Indigenous communities in your region. Understanding their histories, traditions, and contributions helps lay a respectful and accurate foundation for classroom discussions. Go beyond textbooks by researching Indigenous nations' websites, visiting local cultural centers, or connecting with community members or elders who can provide firsthand perspectives.

Importantly, enlist the knowledge and voices of your students, especially those who may have personal or cultural connections to Indigenous communities. This not only honors student identity and lived experience but also reinforces the message that Indigenous cultures are not relics of the past—they are vibrant, evolving, and very much alive today. Creating space for students to share, ask questions, and reflect helps build a more inclusive and accurate understanding of Indigenous life.

3. ASK: As we read the "Honorable Harvest" poem, circle a statement that reminds you of helping a friend.
    a. With a partner, share what you circled and your reasoning for circling it. What was similar in your responses? What was different? What is this poem talking about? How is a reciprocal relationship represented in this poem?
    b. How does the way Indigenous cultures view their relationship with plants and animals differ from the perspective we often take in science class?
        i. Students should understand that, unlike the perspective that views plants and animals solely as resources for human, Indigenous cultures often regard them as relatives or family members. These beings deserve respect and care, much like one would show to a sibling, parent, or cousin.

INVESTIGATE PHASE

Part I: Mushroom Dissection

1. Tell students they will use their observation skills to determine if a mushroom has been harvested *respectfully*—in a way that ensures sustainability of the decomposer. You may choose to manipulate one mushroom under a document camera or in front of a small group. You may also provide one store-bought mushroom per small group of students. *Teaching students that wild mushrooms can be dangerous is important. Let them know the mushrooms they are using are from the store—the only truly safe place to harvest them from unless you are an adult mushroom expert.*

2. ASK: What signs can we look for to determine if this mushroom was harvested respectfully in a way that allows it to keep growing and reproducing?

   a. Students may offer ideas such as it being stepped on or ripped. Probe for students' understanding of a life cycle, such as "Do you think this is a baby mushroom or an adult mushroom?"

   b. Probe for student misconceptions about mushrooms being plants reproducing through seeds or that there are no longer roots.

SMALL STEPS FOR BIG IMPACT: Look Beyond the Butterfly

▶ We deliberately chose to focus on mushrooms to investigate life cycles in this lesson. Traditionally, students encounter familiar organisms like butterflies, plants, or frogs when studying this concept. While these examples are valuable, they can unintentionally reinforce a narrow view of life cycles and ecological roles. By introducing mushrooms, we challenge common misconceptions—particularly the idea that decomposers are not living or that they do not have life cycles on their own. This choice not only broadens students' understanding of biodiversity but also introduces them to often-overlooked organisms that play essential roles in ecosystems. Additionally, it provides an opportunity for students to engage with fresh, unfamiliar content that can spark curiosity and deepen inquiry.

3. As you manipulate the mushroom, prompt students to draw pictures or add comments to the Notice and Wonder chart on their Investigate student page. Here is an example of what a completed Notice and Wonder chart might look like:

NOTICE	WONDER
• It is white.	• Where do mushrooms grow?
• It looks a bit shriveled.	• Are mushrooms plants?
• It looks like an umbrella.	• What happens if I pick a mushroom?
• There are no roots.	• How long does a mushroom live?

SMALL STEPS FOR BIG IMPACT: Observe Without Inference

▶ As students complete a Notice and Wonder chart, they may naturally begin to make inferences—drawing conclusions or assumptions based on what they see. While this instinct is an important part of scientific thinking, it's crucial to emphasize the difference between observation and inference. Observations involve carefully noticing and describing what is directly seen, heard, or measured, without interpretation. Remind students that the goal right now is to focus solely on accurate, objective observations and to generate thoughtful questions based on what they notice. This helps build the foundational skill of evidence-based inquiry, where conclusions are supported by data rather than assumptions. Encourage students to slow down, look closely, and describe details precisely.

4. Should students need suggestions to prompt their noticings and wonderings, here are some helpful prompts:
   a. Where do you see mushrooms on the playground? At your house?
   b. What are some patterns you notice about these areas?
   c. What does the mushroom's texture look like? Does it look smooth, rough, or something else?
   d. Does the mushroom look wet or dry?
   e. What parts of the mushroom do you see?
   f. How long does it take for a mushroom to grow?
5. As students complete the chart, have them share their noticings and wonderings in small groups and/or in a whole-group discussion. As students compare their responses, there may be some disagreements. For example, if students disagree with each other about whether the mushroom is young or old, say, "This sounds like something we can

add in the Wonder section." Listen in for common misconceptions your students may hold about mushrooms, including:

a. Mushrooms are plants.

b. Mushrooms photosynthesize to eat.

c. All mushrooms are poisonous.

d. Mushrooms only grow in the dark.

e. Mushrooms are vegetables.

f. Mushrooms grow from seed.

SMALL STEPS FOR BIG IMPACT: Monitor Shifts in Understanding

▶ Making a physical note of student misconceptions during a lesson can be used to guide responsive teaching. When students share ideas that reveal misunderstandings, whether during discussion, written responses, or hands-on activities, jotting these down allows you to track their thinking. These notes can prompt you to revisit those specific misconceptions later in the lesson or during future instruction, rather than letting them go unaddressed.

By documenting these moments, you create a reference point for targeted check-ins with individual students or small groups. This ongoing monitoring allows you to notice shifts in understanding, clarify confusion, and provide timely support or enrichment. It also helps you adjust your instructional approach on the spot, reinforcing concepts where needed and celebrating growth when students revise their thinking. Over time, these notes can serve as valuable data for identifying patterns, informing your teaching strategies, and supporting student learning more effectively.

6. ASK: Based on your observations, do you think this mushroom was harvested respectfully?

   a. Provide time for partners or small groups to discuss their thoughts. Be sure to ask students to explain their thinking based on their observations.

   b. Remind students what you mean by "harvested respectfully." By using the term *respectful*, you mean establishing a reciprocal relationship with nature ensuring you only take what you need so you get to eat the mushroom but the mushroom is also able to regenerate.

Part II: Mushroom Life Cycle Card Sort

1. Create small groups of 3 or 4 students and pass out one set of the Mushroom Life Cycle Card Sort per group.

2. Tell students their first task is to look for patterns within the cards and group cards with similarities. For this first round, students may sort the cards into as many groups as they would like, but they must have a reason for placing each card in a particular group.

    a. As you circle the room, prompt students to use evidence from the pictures to justify their groups. Questions may include "Tell me about this group?" or "Why did you put this picture here?" Be sure to listen in for previously discussed misconceptions!

3. When complete, conduct a gallery walk and ask students to focus on similarities and differences in how different groups of students sorted the cards. ASK:

    a. Did any sorted groups look similar?
    b. What were some differences you noticed?
    c. Did what you see make you change your mind about how you sorted your own groups?

Provide time for students to discuss and re-sort if necessary.

4. Tell students mushrooms have life cycles just like humans.

    a. Instruct the small groups to do their best to demonstrate the life cycle of a mushroom using as many cards as they would like.
    b. Continue to ask small groups what evidence they have from the demonstration and the pictures to justify their answers.

5. Conduct a second gallery walk and allow small groups to re-sort their pictures if necessary.

SMALL STEPS FOR BIG IMPACT: Use a Gallery Walk

▶ A gallery walk can be used as an instructional strategy that allows students to purposefully move around the classroom and engage with their peers' work in meaningful ways. You can use a purposeful gallery walk to encourage students to view a variety of solutions or responses displayed around the room—these might be written explanations, diagrams, models, or data sets. In the mushroom life cycle case, students can observe how other groups sorted their pictures to ask questions, gather new evidence and new perspectives, and use critical thinking to assess and potentially reevaluate the way they sorted their cards.

(Continued)

(Continued)

Be sure to give students one explicit question or task to complete while engaging in the gallery walk. Students could note different ways other groups classified the pictures and/or leave a sticky note asking a specific question. Having one group member stay at their station to present while the others rotate through the stations offers a valuable opportunity for students to practice asking thoughtful questions and exploring alternative ideas or misconceptions. Be sure to build in time for all group members to reconvene and potentially adjust their thinking after seeing how others solved the problem. By seeing multiple perspectives, students gain a deeper understanding of content and the many valid ways to approach a problem, while also developing their ability to articulate and defend their own reasoning. And, as always, be sure to lead with your behavior expectations, reminding students to keep their hands to themselves, remain on task, and walk (not run) to each station.

SMALL STEPS FOR BIG IMPACT: Brush Up on Background Content

▶ Take time to build or refresh your understanding of mushrooms. Spores and seeds differ in a variety of ways. Spores are much simpler than seeds. For example, spores are unicellular, and seeds are multicellular. Mushrooms typically reproduce asexually with spores, while seeds result from sexual reproduction. Seeds store food to help germinate, while a spore does not. Also, spores are often microscopic, while many seeds are visible to the human eye. Understanding these differences can help you guide students in making accurate observations and drawing meaningful comparisons.

6. Share a picture of a mushroom's life cycle with the whole class. Be sure your picture includes the mushroom's *spores*, *hyphae*, *mycelium*, and *fruiting body*. Discuss each step before having students rearrange their pictures according to a mushroom's life cycle, beginning with a spore. Expect students to use key vocabulary words while they are rearranging their mushroom's life cycles:

   a. First, a mature mushroom releases *spores*, sometimes through its *gills* under the cap of the mushroom or sometimes through a hole in the top of the mushroom. Spores are not seeds! They are tiny and typically dispersed by wind, water, or animals.

   b. Next, spores germinate with the right conditions. When there is enough moisture, the right temperature, and nutrients, they germinate and produce *hyphae*, which look like string.

c. Hyphae from different spores meet and form *mycelium*. Mycelium forms a network of threads that grows through soil and wood to absorb nutrients and help mushrooms grow.

d. Eventually, the mycelium forms dense clusters, which lead to the development of the mushroom we see above ground—also called the *fruiting body*.

e. Finally, when mushrooms are mature, they release spores, and the cycle begins again.

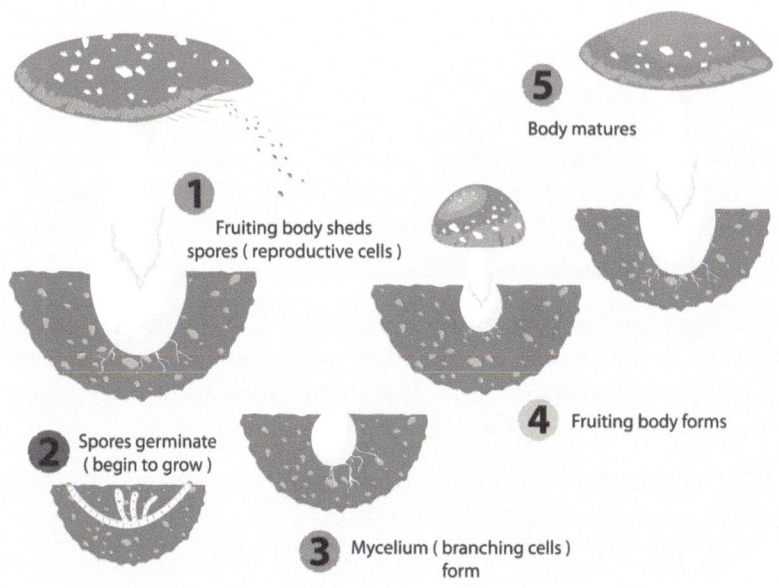

SOURCE: iStock.com/mapichai

7. ASK: What plants and animals depend on the mushroom's life cycle? (Interesting talking points may include the following.)

   a. Insects, birds, and mammals (including humans) all eat mushrooms for essential nutrition. Some of these animals also play an important role in spreading spores.

   b. Mushrooms decompose once-living things, recycling nutrients back into the soil to benefit both plants and animals.

   c. Trees and plants depend on the mushroom's mycelium to help transport and absorb water and nutrients. Plants can even "talk" to one another through the mycelium, alerting each other to potential pests.

8. Tell students that many plants and animals depend on mushrooms, so we must harvest them respectfully.

9. ASK: Based on this new information, was this mushroom harvested respectfully? (If students have changed their minds, ask them to elaborate on what evidence they used to justify their answer.)

    a. Potential Answer: Yes, it was harvested respectfully because the mycelium was not attached, meaning it is still in the ground and can create additional fruiting bodies. In addition, minimal (or no) spores were visible, meaning they had already been released to germinate elsewhere.

INTERROGATE PHASE

Change-Your-Mind Debate

1. Provide one Interrogate student page per student. Read the paragraph to the whole class and provide time for students to share their experiences at national parks or their interactions with Indigenous cultures, and field questions about the text.

2. Provide time for students to think and complete questions 1 and 2 independently. Circle the room and be sure students are listing pieces of evidence to support their claim. If students need additional prompts, you may consider the following:

    a. What impact does preventing traditional hunting and gathering practices have on Indigenous cultures?

        i. What is one of your family traditions? What would happen if you now had to get a permit to do it?

    b. Which plants and animals are benefiting from either perspective?

    c. How would this decision affect your life?

    d. Who do you think says yes or no to a permit application?

3. In your classroom, designate opposite sides as "Yes" or "No" with an "Undecided" middle ground.

4. Facilitate a debate by having students take turns presenting their claims and justifications, alternating between opposing sides. Encourage students to actively listen to differing perspectives and thoughtfully respond with counterarguments or points of agreement. Throughout the debate, students should be given the freedom (and even encouraged) to revise their positions as they encounter new information. This approach promotes critical thinking and reinforces the idea that changing one's mind in light of new evidence is a strength, not a weakness, in scientific and civic reasoning.

SMALL STEPS FOR BIG IMPACT: Act Out Your Change of Mind

▶ To support students in developing their decision-making skills and confidence in taking a stance, consider incorporating physical movement into classroom discussions. One effective strategy is to use a "move if you agree" approach, where students position themselves in the room based on their opinion or choice. As the discussion unfolds and students hear different perspectives, encourage them to move to the other side if their thinking changes. This simple act of physically changing position not only reinforces that it's OK to revise one's thinking based on new evidence or reasoning but also makes learning visible and engaging. Be sure to pause at key moments to ask students to explain why they moved or stayed, helping them articulate their reasoning and listen to differing viewpoints.

SMALL STEPS FOR BIG IMPACT: Differentiate on the Go

▶ To differentiate for readiness, adjust the number of vocabulary words or pieces of evidence students must use. It is quick and easy to adjust the expectations on individual students' pages as they work! You can also provide sentence starters, visual supports, or guiding questions for students who need extra scaffolding, while substituting extension prompts for those ready to go deeper. This flexible approach keeps all learners engaged and challenged at their own level without interrupting the flow of the lesson.

5. When discussions have slowed, bring students back to a whole-group discussion. ASK:
   a. For those in the neutral zone, what were the key points from each position?
   b. For those who changed your minds, what piece of evidence made you rethink your original stance?
6. Have students independently complete the Claim-Evidence-Reasoning chart.

ACT PHASE

Create a Petition

1. Reflecting on the debate, students will now create a petition that supports their stance.
2. Have students find a partner with a similar claim and pass out one Act student page per pair.

3. Briefly contextualize the content with your geographical location. Discuss:
   a. Local Indigenous nations.
   b. National parks within proximity to your school.
4. ASK:
   a. Who are the stakeholders? Who would this choice affect?
   b. To whom should we write a petition? Who oversees this decision?
      i. Tip: It is the park's superintendent.
   c. How will you determine what the most important evidence is to support your stance?
5. Have students collaboratively complete the Act student page.
6. Have students share their petition with another class to seek signatures. By having students share their petition, they need to support their claim with evidence and make a compelling case.

Closure

7. ASK:
   a. How do respectful harvesting rules help protect mushrooms and nature more broadly?
   b. Who do you think is most affected when resources are overused or polluted? Is it fair?
   c. Can you think of any examples in the news or community where people work for environmental justice? What are they doing, and who benefits?
   d. Who usually has the power to decide how resources are used? Why might it be important for communities to have a say?
   e. How can a petition be used to advocate for change?
8. **Suggested Option for Extension**: Have your students conduct research on the National Park Service website (NPS.gov) looking for Indigenous communities affiliated with harvesting at the national park nearest you.

Name: _____

ELICIT: Honorable Harvest

Guiding Question: How do we know if this store-bought mushroom was harvested sustainably?

> Know the ways of the ones who take care of you, so that you may take care of them.
>
> Introduce yourself. Be accountable as the one who comes asking for life. Ask permission before taking. Abide by the answer.
>
> Never take the first. Never take the last. Take only what you need.
>
> Take only that which is given.
>
> Never take more than half. Leave some for others.
>
> Harvest in a way that minimizes harm.
>
> Use it respectfully. Never waste what you have taken. Share.
>
> Give thanks for what you have been given.
>
> Give a gift, in reciprocity for what you have taken.
>
> Sustain the ones who sustain you and the earth will last forever.

SOURCE: From Robin Wall Kimmerer's *Braiding Sweetgrass* (2013, pp. 177–178)

SOURCE: iStock.com/ruxi_coroiu

Name: _____

INVESTIGATE: Honorable Harvest

Mushroom Dissection Notice and Wonder Chart

NOTICE 	WONDER 
Color: Texture (circle or add your own): • Smooth • Bumpy • Soft • Rough • • Shape:	How does _____? Where does _____? What if _____?

- Was this mushroom harvested respectfully? (Circle your answer.)

  YES   NO

- In your observation above, circle at least two pieces of evidence to support your claim.

Name: _____

INTERROGATE: Honorable Harvest

Guiding Question: Should Indigenous peoples be able to harvest in national parks without a permit?

_____

For thousands of years, Indigenous peoples lived on the land that is now called U.S. national parks. For example, 27 nations, like the Tukudika, have ties to Yellowstone National Park. They built their homes, celebrated, hunted, and gathered food there. But then, they were forced to leave when the National Park Service took over. After that, the Indigenous peoples couldn't hunt, gather, or visit sacred sites.

In 2016, new rules allowed Indigenous peoples to hunt and gather food again, but they have to follow special steps to get a permit:

1. Provide a written request that shows their nation has a history with the park, explain why they need the plants, and list the plants and methods for harvesting.

2. Make an agreement with the national park supervisor through additional discussions and paperwork.

3. Complete an environmental assessment.

4. Follow the agreement and renew the permit every five years.

_____

1. Given what you know about life cycles and traditional harvesting practices of Indigenous peoples, do you believe this is fair? (Circle your answer.)

    YES   NOT SURE   NO

2. List at least three pieces of evidence to support your claim:

    a. _____

    b. _____

    c. _____

Postdebate Reflection

Complete the following Claim–Evidence–Reasoning organizer using at least three of the following vocabulary words:

- Mushroom
- Spore
- Mycelium
- Decompose
- Fruiting body
- Respect
- Reciprocal relationship

Should Indigenous peoples be able to harvest in national parks without a permit?

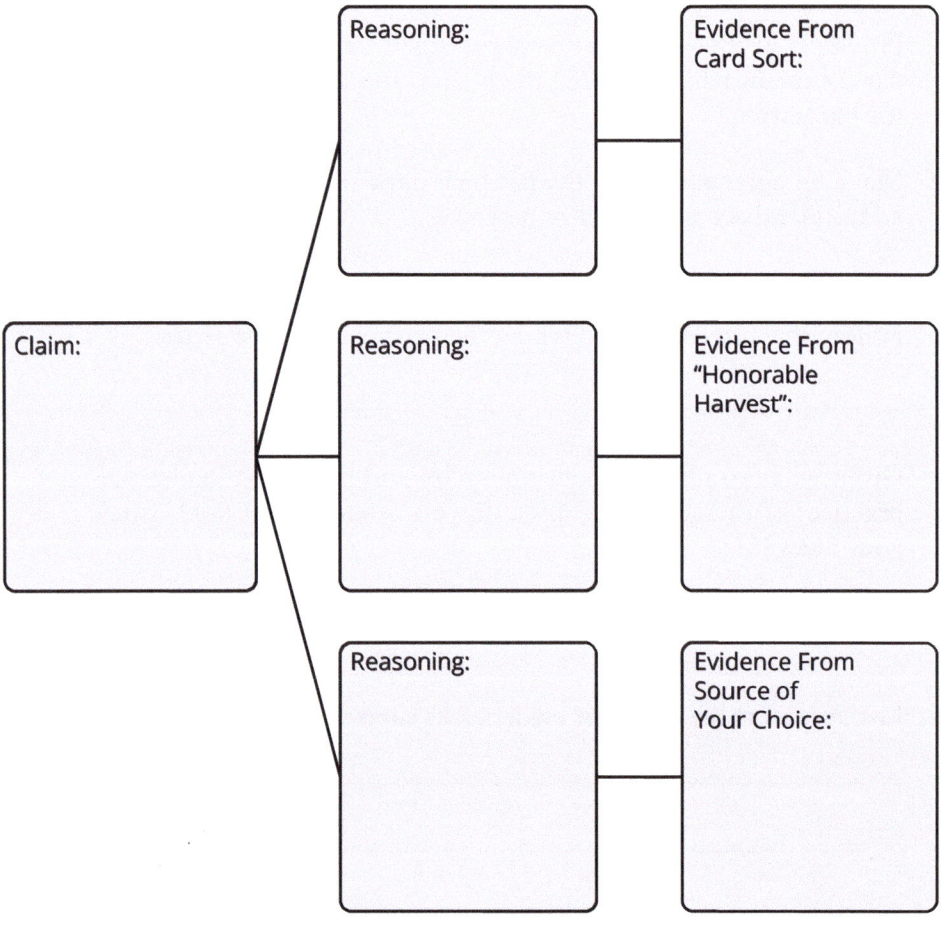

Name: _____

ACT: Honorable Harvest

A Petition

Title:
To: _____ *List who has the power to make this change.*
List two stakeholders whom your petition will impact: 1. _____   2. _____   3. _____
We are writing to urge citizens to (circle one) **MAINTAIN THE PROCESS / MAKE IT EASIER / MAKE IT MORE DIFFICULT** for Indigenous peoples in our region to harvest at national parks for these two reasons: 1.   2.
It is important for everybody because _____

	If you agree to the petition, please sign below:	
NAME	**DATE**	

MUSHROOM LIFE CYCLE CARD SORT

Print and cut one set of cards per small group.

(Continued)

(Continued)

From right to left: puffball mushroom image by iStock.com/ApisitWilaijit; mycelium network image by iStock.com/ChristinaPrinn; mycelium image by iStock.com/Kichigin; western pine mushroom image by iStock.com/Teresa Otto; parasol mushroom image by iStock.com/wayra; mushroom grown image by iStock.com/MOHAMMAD TANVEERUL HOQUE; mycelium image by iStock.com/Kichigin; brown champignons image by iStock.com/yul38885 yul38885; slime mold image by iStock.com/Iuliia Morozova; mushroom image by iStock.com/Jiyi; willow bracket image by iStock.com/Kristyna Sindelkova

GENERAL UNIT TEMPLATE

Title

Teacher Background

Standards

Title		
Students who demonstrate understanding can:		
Science and Engineering Practices	Disciplinary Core Ideas	Crosscutting Concepts
Social Justice Connection		

Objectives

Sociocultural-Informed Phenomenon

Timeline

DAYS	INSTRUCTIONAL PHASE	OBJECTIVES	MATERIALS
	Elicit		
	Investigate		
	Interrogate		
	Act		

Elicit:

Investigate:

Interrogate:

- Debate—use suggested formats from Chapter 3
- Use the Claim–Evidence–Reasoning (CER) framework from Chapter 3

Act:

- Use an option from the Act Menu in Chapter 3

CHAPTER SUMMARY

- Allowing students to *Explore before Explain* provides teachers the opportunity to tailor instruction to the needs of their students. Using the Notice and Wonder chart should be a tool to gather students' ideas and observations to revisit throughout the unit.

- Providing opportunities to view issues from multiple perspectives is one strategy to engage students in sensemaking.

- Using debates requires students to listen to one another and argue with evidence, bringing authenticity and student buy-in to proposed social justice issues.

REFLECTION QUESTIONS

1. What are some ways that you can use the Elicit–Investigate–Interrogate–Act framework to design units and lessons to support making sense of both scientific concepts and social justice issues in your context?

2. How does digging deeper into content, rather than wider, increase critical thinking expectations for students?

3. Consider how the Claim–Evidence–Reasoning framework was woven through the units. How can this strategy provide powerful ways for students to communicate their thinking, develop scientific reasoning, and engage in arguing with evidence across content areas and grade levels?

CHAPTER 5

Grab-and-Go Lessons

Don't wait for tomorrow; do today what you can, and do it well.
—Henry Ford

This chapter provides a collection of grab-and-go lessons designed for quick implementation with minimal prep. Unlike the more in-depth units found in Chapter 4, these shorter lessons require only the printing of student worksheets. Each lesson follows the four phases of the Elicit–Investigate–Interrogate–Act framework and includes prompts to help students begin thinking about how social justice themes connect to their own lives and communities.

Our goal in offering these grab-and-go lessons is twofold: to make instructional planning a little easier and to provide concrete examples of how to embed critical thinking and action into science instruction, even when time is limited. These lessons are especially helpful for teachers who have only 20 to 30 minutes available for science at a time and wish to offer a stand-alone lesson. Or, you can easily modify the lesson to focus on one phase per day if you wish to guide students through deeper meaningful discussions, data analysis, and collaborative problem-solving with minimal prep required on your end.

That said, we invite you to treat these lessons as starting points. We encourage you to extend, modify, and reimagine them to better fit the needs of your students and their communities. Additionally, we hope you use them as inspiration to spark new ideas, or as templates to help formulate your own lessons. After all, the goal of this work is to empower you as a designer of meaningful, relevant science learning experiences, and to help you feel confident in bringing your students into conversations that matter.

As you browse the grab-and-go lessons, you'll notice that they follow a similar pattern to the units presented in the previous chapter. While the units in Chapter 4 consisted of multiple lessons scaffolding opportunities to engage in the phases of the Elicit–Investigate–Interrogate–Act framework, these lessons are condensed in nature, presenting options for following the framework but with limited time in mind. Let's do a deeper dive into how these grab-and-go lessons are structured.

1. The Elicit phase still asks students to engage in a Notice and Wonder activity. In both the expanded units and these grab-and-go lessons, students engage in the Science and Engineering Practice of asking questions and defining problems, typically using data and data visualizations to elicit students' observations and questions.
2. The Investigate phase asks students to dig into text and graphs to investigate, infer implications, and strengthen their data literacy skills.
3. The Interrogate phase calls on students to engage the Claim–Evidence–Reasoning framework with evidence presented in the previous two phases.
4. The Act phase offers differentiation by allowing students to choose the method they prefer for taking action to address the social justice issue. To guide this phase, we reference the Learning for Justice (2022) Social Justice Standard AC.3-5.20.

SMALL STEPS FOR BIG IMPACT: Meet Students at Their Level

▶ You can respond to individual readiness needs by adjusting the number of questions students should ask about the data. If a student shows a particular interest in one of their questions, allow them to conduct additional research if they finish work quickly or need an incentive! Encourage students to share their findings with peers, which can spark new questions and deepen classroom discussion.

SMALL STEPS FOR BIG IMPACT: Change the Sequence of Student Interactions

▶ You can differentiate the *process* of interacting with the data by changing the sequence of student interactions. For example, students can work independently and share with a partner before offering ideas in a whole-group setting. This gradual buildup allows students to process their thoughts, gain confidence, and refine their understanding through peer feedback. It also encourages broader participation and deeper engagement during whole-group discussions.

In addition, each grab-and-go lesson has a concluding section titled "Local Insights" (see Table 5.1). In this phase, students will carry the main social justice theme explored in the lesson into their own context. Students will work to investigate if some of the same issues occurring at a larger level apply to their context. These are complex tasks! Your students have the opportunity to dive into open inquiry, look to the real world to decide on data collection procedures, organize messy data, and generate solutions to local issues important to them. We've purposely built in a lot of flexibility in how you choose to use these templates so that you can make the lessons appropriate for your students' interests and readiness.

SMALL STEPS FOR BIG IMPACT: Get Creative

▶ Karli Gilbertson used the prompts provided to create a graphic organizer when teaching Lesson 5.3: Invasive Carp to her fourth graders. At the end of the lesson, her students generated a formal persuasive argument for allowing gum in the classroom on Fridays during the final weeks of the school year. Ms. Gilbertson carried the theme of collective agency from the beginning to the end of the lesson, giving her students an authentic reason to interrogate and act in their local context. This seemingly small topic became a meaningful exercise in civic voice, critical thinking, and persuasive communication, all tailored to the students' interests. Feel free to get creative using these lessons as inspiration to spark conversations about fairness, responsibility, and collective problem-solving in ways that feel personal and achievable for your students.

Local Insights Brainstorm

Unfair School Rules:

Rule: _____

Who made the rule or decision?

Why did they make the rule or decision? What was the problem they were trying to solve?

How does the rule or decision affect the students? Consider both good and bad implications.

(Continued)

(Continued)

Claim: An unfair rule at school is
Evidence 1:
Evidence 2:
Reasoning:
Alternatives:

SOURCE: Karli Gilbertson

TABLE 5.1 The Sequence of a Grab-and-Go Lesson

PHASE	ACTIVITY
Elicit	Completing a Notice and Wonder chart using a graph as a stimulus
Investigate	Annotating graphs and text to work with science content
Interrogate	Engaging the Claim–Evidence–Reasoning framework
Act	Taking action (options are provided for students to choose from)
Local Insights	Investigating the main social justice theme found in the lesson and challenging students to consider the issue within their own context (open-ended)

We've also included Table 5.2, which will help you align the lessons to your grade level, the Next Generation Science Standards Disciplinary Core Ideas (DCIs; NGSS Lead States, 2013, p. 1), and the corresponding Social Justice Standards (Learning for Justice, 2022). We look forward to learning about how your students take on these challenges!

TABLE 5.2 Grab-and-Go Lessons Aligned With Grade Levels, DCIs, and Social Justice Standards

GRADE	TITLE	DISCIPLINARY CORE IDEA	SOCIAL JUSTICE STANDARD
Lower Elementary	5.1 Accessibility: Inclined Planes	Engineering Design	AC.3-5.20
Lower Elementary	5.2 Politics and Plastics	Earth and Human Activity	AC.3-5.20
Upper Elementary	5.3 Invasive Carp	Ecosystems: Interactions, Energy, and Dynamics	AC.3-5.20
Lower Elementary	5.4 Fossil Fuels and Nonrenewable Energy	Earth and Human Activity	AC.3-5.20

Name: _____

LESSON 5.1 ACCESSIBILITY
Inclined Planes

Elicit

Look at the infographic that follows and complete a Notice and Wonder chart. Here are some questions to guide your thinking:

- What buildings do you visit?
- What types of tasks do you or your family have to complete in the building?

SOURCE: Data from Perea Burns, S., Mendonca, R. J., & Smith, R. O. (2024). Accessibility of public buildings in the United States: A cross-sectional survey. *Disability & Society*, *39*(11), 2988–3003. https://doi.org/10.1080/09687599.2023.2239996

NOTICE	WONDER
1.	1.
2.	2.
3.	
4.	

Name: _____

INVESTIGATE

A ramp is a simple machine called an inclined plane. Inclined planes make it easier to move people or objects between different heights instead of lifting something straight up. For example, in the following picture the student must exert a lot of effort to lift herself and the stack of books she is carrying in her next step! A ramp would allow her to use less effort because it would spread her climb over a longer distance.

When building a ramp, we need to think about a few things. The height tells us how long the ramp should be. The surface needs to have friction so no one slips. The ramp should not be too steep, or people may go down too fast. It is also very important the ramp ends in a safe and flat space to avoid wheelchair users or strollers moving quickly into dangerous traffic.

SOURCE: iStock.com/CreativaImages

1. The Americans with Disabilities Act (ADA) requires businesses and public buildings to be physically accessible to individuals with disabilities, including ramps where necessary. When designing ramps, what should engineers take into consideration to ensure wheelchair users can enter and exit buildings safely and easily?

   _____

   _____

   _____

   _____

   _____

2. Here is a picture of a new hamburger restaurant. Help them be accessible to all new customers! Sketch a new ramp, a parking lot, a sidewalk, and any other features you feel would allow all customers to access the restaurant. Please label all new additions.

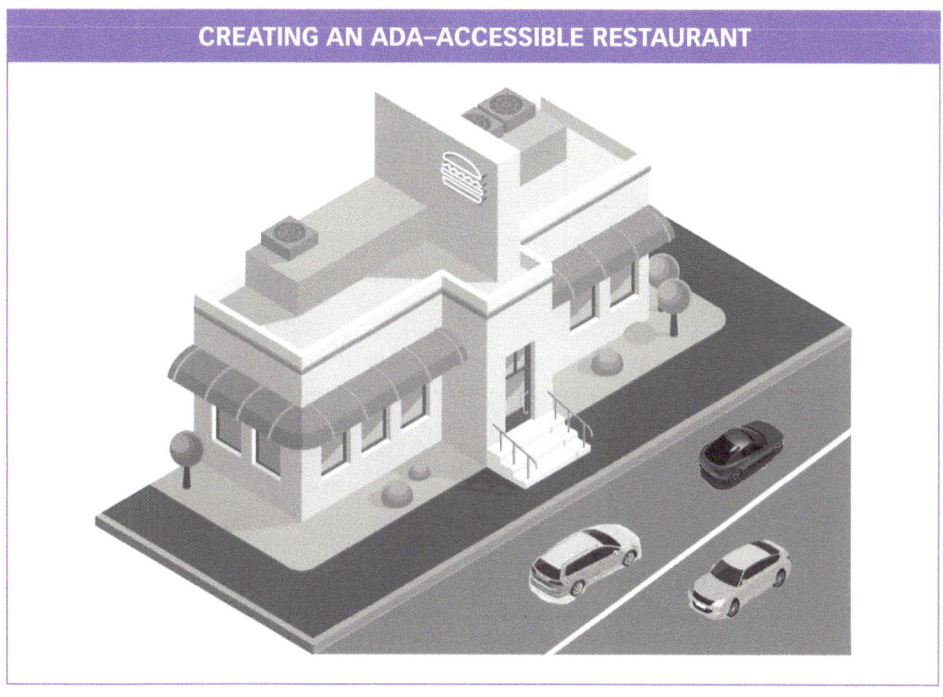

CREATING AN ADA–ACCESSIBLE RESTAURANT

SOURCE: iStock.com/Medesulda

Name: _____

INTERROGATE

The pie charts that follow show how frequently the inaccessibility of public transportation impacts 805 surveyed people with disabilities.

Of the four tasks, which one do you think is the most important to fix first?

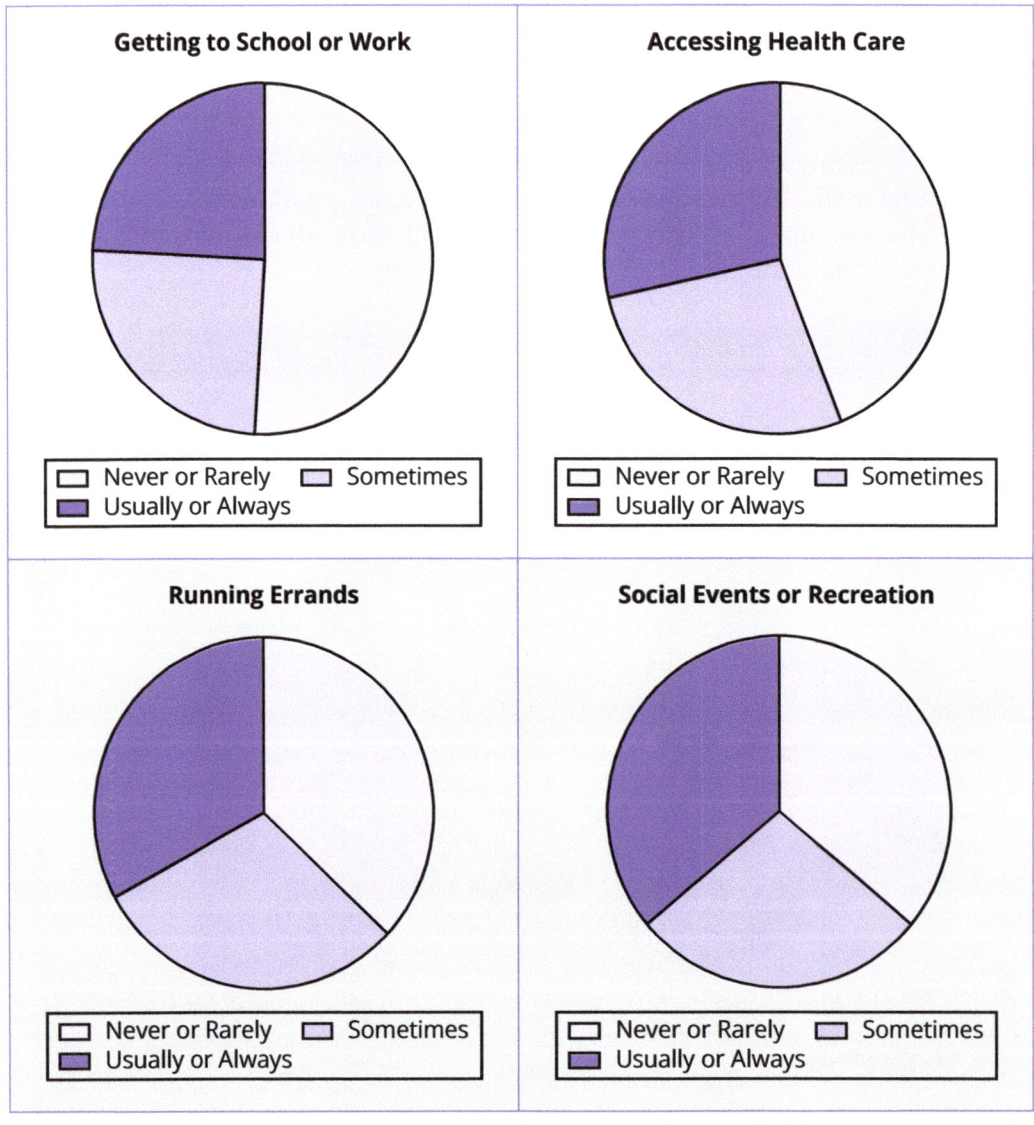

SOURCE: Data from Bezyak, J. L., Sabella, S., Hammel, J., McDonald, K., Jones, R. J., & Barton, D. (2019). Community participation and public transportation barriers experienced by people with disabilities. *Disability and Rehabilitation, 42*(23), 3275–3283. https://doi.org/10.1080/09638288.2019.1590469

1. **Claim:** Circle the activity you believe should be the most accessible to every person.

2. **Evidence:** List at least three pieces of evidence from the charts and your own experience.

   _____

   _____

   _____

   _____

   _____

3. **Reasoning:** How does your evidence support your claim?

   _____

   _____

   _____

   _____

   _____

Name: _____

ACT

Conduct an accessibility check of your school or a building of your choosing.

ADA CHECKLIST	
Are inside and outside walkways at least 36 inches wide?	❏ Yes ❏ No
Is there a ramp to get into and out of the building?	❏ Yes ❏ No
Is the ramp easy to find?	❏ Yes ❏ No
Do all inaccessible entrances have signs indicating the location of the nearest accessible entrance?	❏ Yes ❏ No
Are there ramps in the curbs? If so, is the curb ramp at least 36 inches wide? (Yes/No)	❏ Yes ❏ No
On ramps, is the handrail's gripping surface circular and between 34 and 38 inches above the ramp surface?	❏ Yes ❏ No
Are you able to open the door with one hand and without tight grasping, pinching, or twisting of the wrist?	❏ Yes ❏ No
Are edges of carpets or mats securely attached to minimize tripping hazards?	❏ Yes ❏ No

SOURCE: New England ADA Center. (2017). *ADA checklist for existing facilities*. A project of the Institute for Human Centered Design. https://www.adachecklist.org/checklist.html

1. If you checked "no" to any indicators, describe at least two solutions for each.

   _____
   _____
   _____
   _____
   _____

2. Who can you share your observations and solutions with to help all people?

_____

_____

_____

_____

_____

Name: _____

LOCAL INSIGHTS

This lesson invited you to think about how physical barriers can limit some individuals' ability to access places and carry out everyday tasks, such as attending school or visiting the doctor. In this section, you'll apply that understanding by exploring ways to help people with disabilities navigate your school more easily.

> OBJECTIVE: I will work with my friends and family to make our school and community fair for everyone, and we will work hard and cooperate in order to achieve our goals. (AC.3-5.20)

1. Brainstorm a list of questions somebody with a disability might ask to ensure that their visit to your school is accessible.

   _____

   _____

   _____

   _____

   _____

2. List two people you could ask for feedback on your questions. Who would know best?

   _____

   _____

   _____

   _____

   _____

3. Create a map or presentation that can be used to communicate accessibility routes both outside and inside of your school. You may choose to include:

   a. A key

   b. Labels

   c. Helpful hints

4. Share your map with others!

Brainstorming

Name: _____

LESSON 5.2
Politics and Plastics

Elicit

Look at the two facts that follow. Then, think about how you can show them using pictures, symbols, or drawings. Your goal is to help others *see* what the numbers are saying. THINK: What symbols or visuals could you use? How might you show the difference between a large number and a small number?

Facts:

- In the world, the amount of plastic produced from 2008 to 2023 is more than all the plastics made in history before then.
- In the world, recycling rates for plastics have averaged below 10% since 1950 (Dauvergne, 2023).

Use pictures to show how much plastic was made and how little of it gets recycled:

Using your model, what do you notice and wonder considering the timeline and number of plastics produced and recycled?

NOTICE	WONDER
1. 2. 3. 4.	1. 2.

Name: _____

INVESTIGATE

SOURCE: iStock.com/varniccha kajai

Think about all the ways you use plastic in your everyday life. How did you use plastic today? We have come to rely on plastic products in our everyday lives! However, many plastics are harmful to our planet because, unlike natural materials, plastics do not decompose and often find their way into water sources such as oceans and rivers.

While many people believe recycling can fix the problem, only 9% of global plastic waste is recycled while 79% accumulates in landfills and in oceans. Recycling plastic is a time-consuming, expensive, and sometimes hazardous job. There are many different types of plastic, which requires all recycled materials to be manually cleaned and sorted at recycling plants. The cleaned plastics are then shredded into small pieces, melted down, and formed into pellets that can be used to make new plastic products. The plastic that cannot be recycled in the United States is sometimes sent to countries such as Malaysia, Thailand, and Indonesia where waste pickers work in hazardous conditions for low pay to sort out items that are potentially of value (Calil et al., 2021).

In addition, the recycling process can make the plastic weaker, so it's not as good for making new products. Contamination from food, chemicals, and other substances can also make recycling harder, leading to lower-quality recycled plastic. Because of these challenges, not all plastics can be recycled.

Complete the following:

1. Why is it important to clean plastics before recycling them?

   _____
   _____
   _____
   _____
   _____

2. Why is it difficult to recycle some types of plastic?

   _____
   _____
   _____
   _____
   _____

3. How does recycling plastic help protect the environment?

   _____
   _____
   _____
   _____
   _____

4. List at least one question you are still curious about.

   _____
   _____
   _____
   _____
   _____

Name: _____

INTERROGATE

Look at the bar chart that shows how the amount of pollution affects the number of visitors to beach communities and days they stay at the beach. The number of days is counted by adding up the total number of days spent at the beach by each visitor. For example, if you had a family of 3 people and you stayed 2 days, the total number of days visitors stayed at the beach would be 6. Now consider that each of your family members spends approximately $30 each day of the vacation.

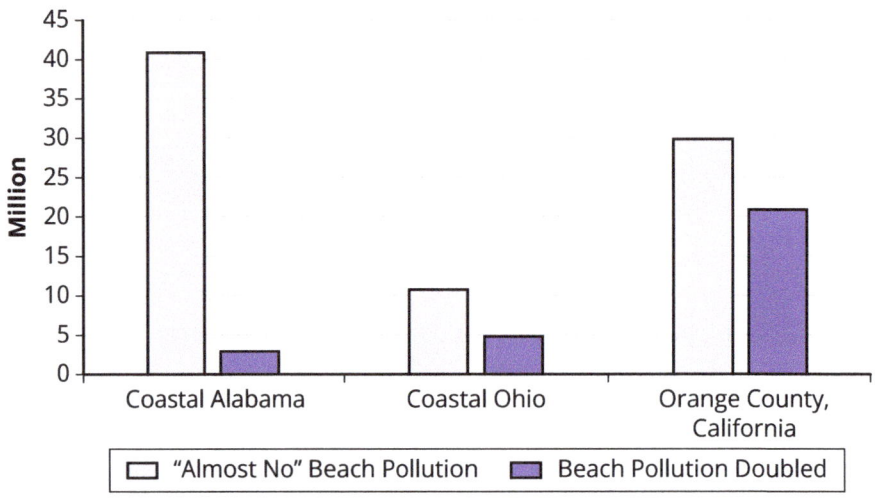

SOURCE: English, E., Wagner, C., & Holmes, J. (2019, July). *The effects of marine debris on beach recreation and regional economies in four coastal communities: A regional pilot study.* Final report submitted by Bear Peak Economics, CW Research and Consulting, and Abt Associates to National Oceanic and Atmospheric Administration Marine Debris Division. https://www.abtglobal.com/sites/default/files/2024-09/2019.07.Econ_.Impacts.Marine.Debris.complete.wFN_30Aug2019_508.pdf

1. **Claim:** Who is impacted by the loss of tourists to beach communities?

   _____
   _____
   _____
   _____
   _____

2. **Evidence:** Create a bubble map using information from the bar chart and your own experiences to brainstorm those who are affected by plastic pollution on the beach. Think about who benefits from tourism and a clean beach.

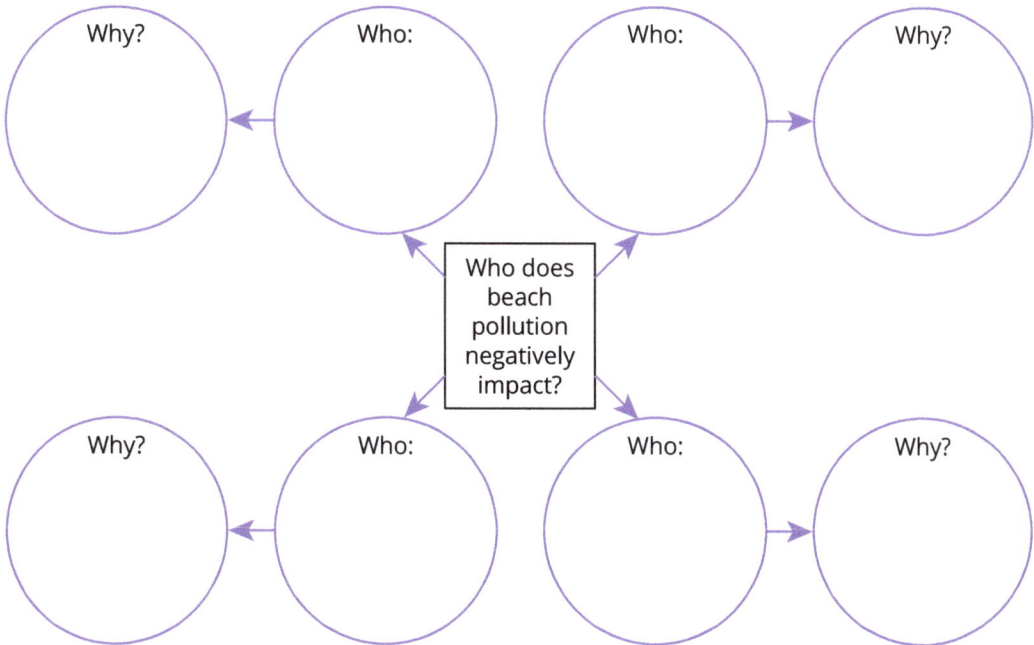

3. **Reasoning:** How does your evidence support your claim?

_____
_____
_____
_____
_____

Name: _____

ACT

You choose!

- ❏ Educate Others:
    - ❏ Design an advertisement campaign to teach others about how to properly recycle plastics or use less plastic in their day-to-day lives.
- ❏ Advocate for Change:
    - ❏ Write a persuasive letter to your school to use less plastics.

Name: _____

LOCAL INSIGHTS

This lesson prompted you to consider how the use of disposable plastics can negatively impact communities. In this section, you'll apply that understanding by exploring how you and your classmates use plastics in your everyday life.

> OBJECTIVE: I will work with my friends and family to make our school and community fair for everyone, and we will work hard and cooperate in order to achieve our goals. (AC.3-5.20)

1. Create a list of plastic items used by your classmates at lunch or snack times.

   _____
   _____
   _____
   _____
   _____

2. Create a plan to track the number of plastic products you or your class use(s) throughout the day. Is it possible for you and your class to use less plastic?

   _____
   _____
   _____
   _____
   _____

3. In science, all decisions are based on evidence. Come up with a plan to collect evidence showing if you or your class can reduce your plastic usage across one week.

   _____
   _____
   _____
   _____
   _____

4. Engage the Claim–Evidence–Reasoning framework to prove you either are or are not able to reduce your plastic usage across a week. Use your data collection as evidence and celebrate any successes with your community!

Name: _____

LESSON 5.3
Invasive Carp

Elicit

Look at the line graph that follows and complete a Notice and Wonder chart. Questions to guide your thinking may include:

- Line graphs are used to communicate data over time. What range of years is this graph representing?
- The graph shows you the population of what type of fish?
- Where were the fish counted?

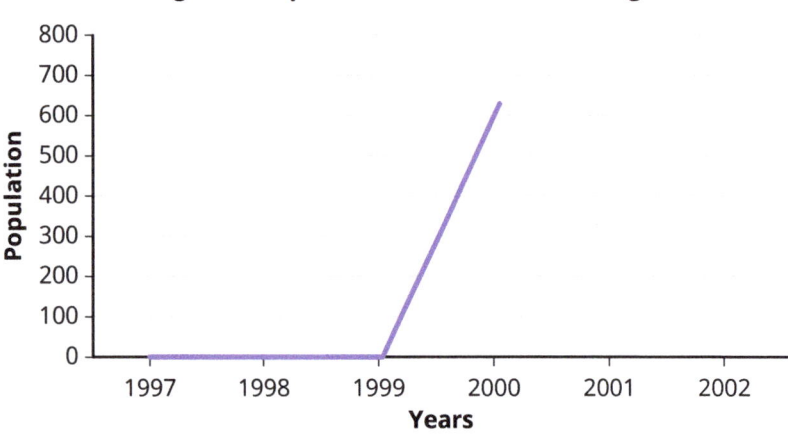

SOURCE: Irons et al., 2011

Complete the Notice and Wonder chart using the information in the graph:

NOTICE	WONDER
1.	1.
2.	2.
3.	3.

Name: _____

INVESTIGATE

SOURCE: iStock.com/ivanmateev

In 1963, bighead carp and other types of invasive carp were introduced to the United States to help clean ponds and support commercial fish farms. These fish act like natural vacuum cleaners, eating up to 40% of their body weight in plankton each day! They also eat mollusks, helping to keep ponds clean. The carp were useful for fish farms because they grew quickly and could be sold as food, making them a profitable choice.

Three years later, these carp were accidentally released in Arkansas and spread to 16 states, moving up the Mississippi River. They have no natural predators in these waters and take up resources that native fish need to survive. This has led to the decline of native fish species and has caused economic problems in the United States and Canada. The spread of these types of carp has hurt local ecosystems and cost a lot of money.

1. Extend the line on the following graph to show what you predict happened to the bighead carp population in 2001 and 2002.

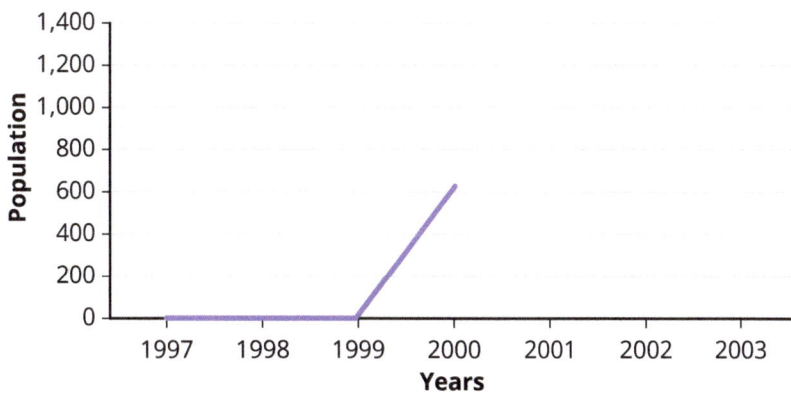

SOURCE: Irons et al., 2011

2. What do you believe happened to the population of plankton as a response to the growing bighead carp population?

   _____
   _____

3. Fish that naturally live in these areas also depend on plankton to survive. Using your graph as evidence, discuss what happened to the native fish population in 2000 and beyond. You may wish to use the sentence stem that follows:

   a. Since native fish eat plankton, the native fish population [increased/decreased] in 2000 and beyond because _____.

   _____
   _____
   _____
   _____
   _____

Name: _____

INTERROGATE

Use the following bar graph to examine how communities are impacted by the accidental release of invasive carp.

Was the introduction of invasive carp into U.S. waterways the best option for all stakeholders?

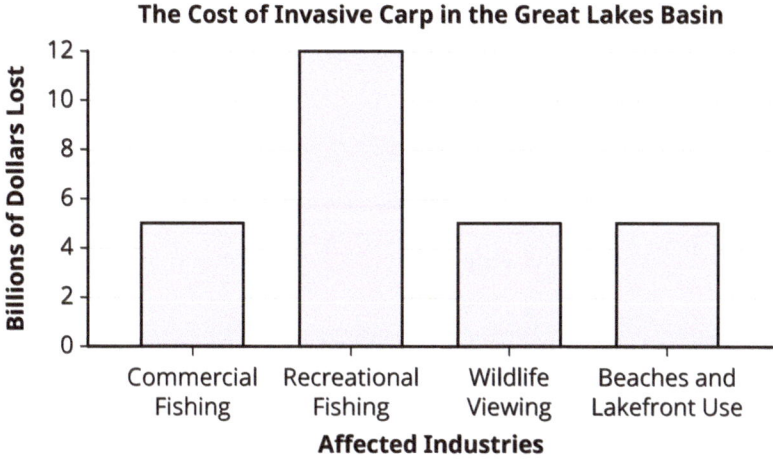

SOURCE: Asian Carp Canada, 2015

1. **Claim (select one):**

   ❑ The introduction of invasive carp *was* the right solution for all stakeholders.

   ❑ The introduction of invasive carp *was not* the right solution for all stakeholders.

2. **Evidence:**

STAKEHOLDERS	HELP/HURT	EVIDENCE
Fish Farms in 1963	❑ Help ❑ Hurt	

(Continued)

(Continued)

STAKEHOLDERS	HELP/HURT	EVIDENCE	
Commercial Fishers Today	❑ Help ❑ Hurt		
	❑ Help ❑ Hurt		
	❑ Help ❑ Hurt		

3. **Reasoning:** How does your evidence support your claim?

_____

_____

_____

_____

_____

Name: _____

ACT

You choose!

- ☐ Research invasive carp food webs. Create a flyer or infographic to draw awareness to people and ecosystems affected by invasive carp. Note the cause-and-effect issues and how the invasive carp benefit some people and negatively impact others.
- ☐ Identify groups working to intervene in the invasive carp crisis and see what action steps they are taking. How are the groups carrying out collective action? What strategies do you see as more effective for achieving their goal?

Name: _____

LOCAL INSIGHTS

This lesson prompted you to consider how the decisions and actions of one group of people negatively impacted the lives of others. In this section, you'll be asked to do the same!

> OBJECTIVE: I will work with my friends and family to make our school and community fair for everyone, and we will work hard and cooperate to achieve our goals. (AC.3-5.20)

1. Brainstorm a list of recent decisions or rules that have been made at your school without students having any input. You may want to think about areas and times in your school such as recess, hallways, lunchtime, or dismissal time. For each rule you brainstorm, discuss:

    a. Who made the rule or decision?

    b. Why did they make the rule or decision?

    c. What was the problem they were trying to solve?

    d. How does the rule or decision affect the students? Consider both good and bad implications.

    -

    -

    -

    -

2. Circle which rule or decision you think is the most unfair to students. A rule or decision that is made for student safety cannot be selected.

3. In science, all decisions are based on evidence. Outline a plan to collect evidence that proves the rule or decision is unfair to students. You may want to consider the following questions:

   a. What data can you collect to prove the rule does not need to be in place?

   b. What data can you collect to prove there is a better solution?

   _____
   _____
   _____
   _____
   _____

4. Engage the Claim–Evidence–Reasoning framework to support your argument for overturning the rule or decision. You must provide at least one alternative solution to solve the initial problem.

   _____
   _____
   _____
   _____
   _____
   _____

Name: _____

LESSON 5.4
Fossil Fuels and Nonrenewable Energy

Elicit

Look at the pie chart that follows and complete a Notice and Wonder chart. Questions to guide your thinking may include:

- What is this pie chart telling you?

- Do you think it resembles how you use energy in your home? Why or why not?

- What do you think is in the "other" section?

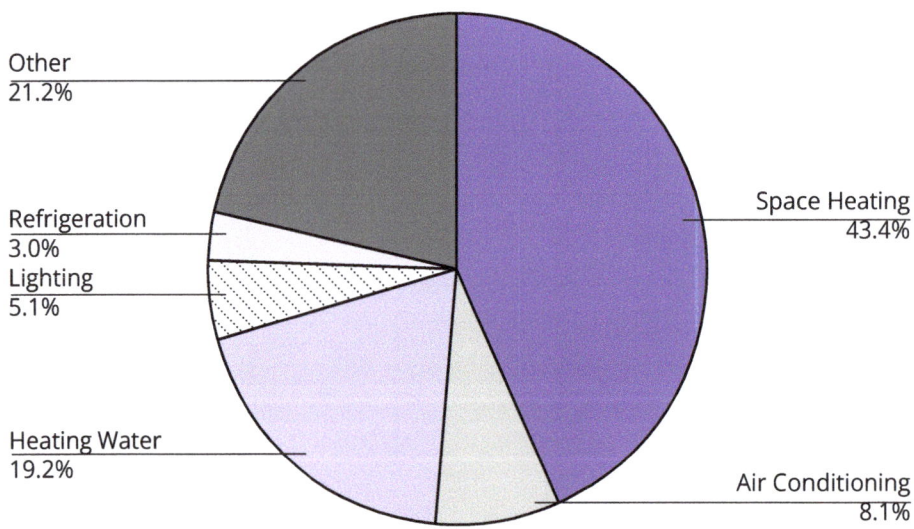

SOURCE: Data interpreted from U.S. Energy Information Administration, 2015 Residential Energy Consumption Survey

NOTICE	WONDER
1.	1.
2.	2.
3.	3.
4.	
5.	

Name: _____

INVESTIGATE

Read and annotate the passage that follows:

1. Circle the benefits of renewable and nonrenewable energy.
2. Draw a box around the negative implications of renewable and nonrenewable energy.

Energy and fossil fuels come from natural resources like coal, oil, natural gas, sunlight, wind, and water. Nonrenewable resources, such as coal and oil, produce electricity and power vehicles. These resources cause air pollution when burned, which affects the health of people, animals, and plants. For example, burning coal releases harmful gases into the air that can make the air dirty and hard to breathe. However, nonrenewable resources are often more reliable and can quickly produce large amounts of energy.

Renewable resources, like sunlight and wind, cause less pollution. Solar panels or wind turbines do not release as many harmful gases into the environment. However, renewable resources can sometimes be less reliable and can negatively impact the large areas of land needed for technology, such as solar panels and wind turbines. A significant advantage of renewable resources is that they are sustainable and can be replenished naturally.

SOURCE: iStock.com/VectorMine

1. What are some examples of renewable and nonrenewable energy resources mentioned in the passage?

   _____
   _____
   _____
   _____
   _____

2. List at least four ways you use energy in your home or community.

   _____
   _____
   _____
   _____
   _____
   _____
   _____
   _____
   _____

3. Which energy sources do you use that come from nature? Name some that can run out and some that cannot.

   _____
   _____
   _____
   _____
   _____

4. Why do you think using wind and sunlight for energy is better for the environment?

_____

_____

_____

_____

_____

5. Why do people still use nonrenewable energy even though it can pollute the air?

_____

_____

_____

_____

_____

6. Would you rather the energy used in your home come from renewable or nonrenewable sources? Why?

_____

_____

_____

_____

_____

Name: _____

INTERROGATE

The bar graph that follows shows the types of communities that live within 3 miles of a power plant that uses nonrenewable energy.

1. What do you notice about where most power plants are located?

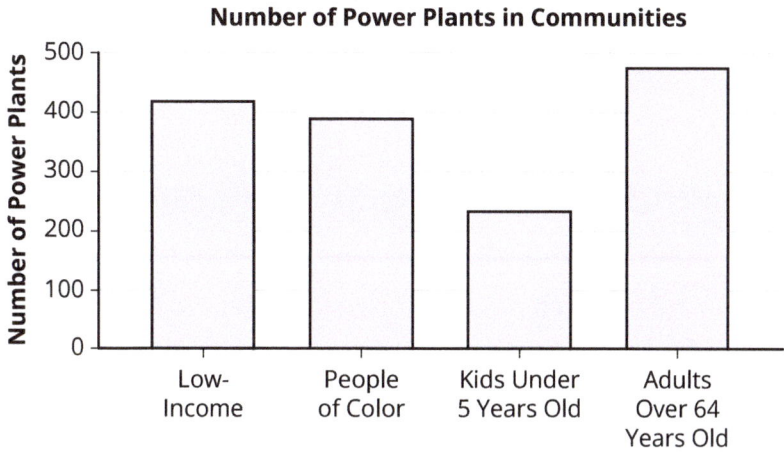

SOURCE: Data captured on January 10, 2025, from EPA's "Power Plants and Environmental Justice." Available now on the Wayback Machine (https://archive.org).

2. **Claim:** Do you think the location of power plants in the United States is fair for everyone?

_____
_____
_____
_____
_____

3. **Evidence:** Complete the following table:

Groups of People Affected by Power Plants	Do fossil fuel power plants help or hurt these people?	How? *Use evidence from the bar graph and your previous investigation.*
	☐ Help ☐ Hurt	
	☐ Help ☐ Hurt	

4. **Reasoning:** Explain in at least three sentences why your evidence supports your claim.

_____

_____

_____

_____

_____

5. If you lived in a neighborhood with lots of power plants, how would you feel? What might you want to change?

_____

_____

_____

_____

_____

6. What actions can students, leaders, or community members take if they think a neighborhood is being treated unfairly when it comes to pollution or energy use?

_____

_____

_____

_____

_____

7. What other questions or sources of data might you wish to future investigate?

_____

_____

_____

_____

_____

Name: _____

ACT

You choose!

- ❑ Create a flyer communicating a *pattern* of data you noticed in this lesson to alert others about equity issues in air pollution and a call for environmental justice.

- ❑ Create a short skit, commercial, or social media video (3–5 minutes) that explores how air pollution affects certain groups of people more than others based on who they are and where they were born.

- ❑ Write a proposal to a school leader identifying a cause of pollution at your school and at least one potential solution.

Name: _____

LOCAL INSIGHTS

This lesson prompted you to consider how life is easier for some people and harder for others based on who they are and where they were born.

> OBJECTIVE: I will work with my friends and family to make our school and community fair for everyone, and we will work hard and cooperate to achieve our goals. (AC.3-5.20)

1. Brainstorm common resources or areas students frequently use in your school—for example, a water fountain, the playground, the library, or the restrooms. Now, think about your school's layout. Are there any classrooms, grade levels, or areas of the building that do not have easy access to any of the resources you listed? List the specific classroom(s) or area(s). Describe what resources are not easily available in those locations.

   _____
   _____
   _____
   _____
   _____

2. In the list you created, circle an issue you feel can be solved with a creative solution.

3. In science, all decisions are based on evidence. Outline a plan for collecting evidence to show your identified issue is unfair to the students. You may want to consider some questions:

   a. How much time do you have to collect data?
   b. What type of data are you collecting? Consider the number of students, lack of students, or number of resources in a location.
   c. Make a prediction. What are you anticipating the data to show?

   _____
   _____
   _____
   _____
   _____

4. Use the Claim–Evidence–Reasoning framework to explain your argument about which classroom or area of your school is most affected by limited access to resources.

   a. Make a clear claim about the location.

   b. Support your claim with evidence from your observations or experiences.

   c. Explain your reasoning to show why this issue matters.

Then, propose at least one solution to improve access to the resource(s). Be creative! Your solution could involve changing schedules, improving processes, or inventing a new idea that helps solve the problem.

_____

_____

_____

_____

_____

CHAPTER SUMMARY

- Consistently using the Elicit–Investigate–Interrogate–Act framework will streamline planning for you and give your students a familiar lesson structure.

- Throughout these grab-and-go lessons, students are analyzing real-world data and, therefore, practicing authentic data literacy.

- In the Local Insights section of each lesson, students are pushed to engage in deeper thinking by identifying a real-world problem, deciding what data they need to collect, and analyzing those data to draw a conclusion. While this process is challenging, it reflects the authentic practice of scientific inquiry.

REFLECTION QUESTIONS

1. What phases of the Elicit–Investigate–Interrogate–Act framework do you believe are most impactful for students engaging with science content?

2. What phases of the framework do you find are most impactful for supporting students in social justice work?

3. What ideas do you have for further integrating science and social justice across all four phases of the framework?

PART III

Looking Ahead and Taking Action

CHAPTER 6

Navigating Today's Classrooms With Purpose

It always seems impossible until it's done.

—Nelson Mandela

Advocating for science instruction at the elementary level isn't for the faint of heart. We all know the struggle—there are only so many hours in the school day, and science often takes a back seat to subjects that get more attention on state and district tests. How many times have we had to squeeze in extra mathematics or English language arts, even if it meant cutting into science time? It's frustrating, but let's be real—when something isn't prioritized in standardized testing, it's easy for it to get pushed aside. That's why making the case for dedicated science instruction can sometimes feel like an uphill battle. And, what if we start talking about weaving in social justice? Well, we might as well be mission control calling in, "Houston, we have a problem!"

SMALL STEPS FOR BIG IMPACT: Make Time for Science

▶ Consider squeezing in science time in those weeks before holidays, during the last weeks of school, or when your electives get canceled. Thankfully, many elementary students have a genuine interest in science. Leverage that interest and make your life easier during those chaotic times of the year.

Teaching science through a social justice lens is not easy work, but it's meaningful work. To do it well, you need to be crystal clear on three things:

- Your purpose
- Your people
- Your growth opportunities

Think back to the teaching manifesto you created in the introduction. That wasn't just an exercise—it was a way to ground yourself in why you do what you do. Keeping your *why* front and center will help you stay committed, even when things get tough.

And here's the thing—this isn't work you have to take on alone. When you're open about your goals, you invite support from colleagues, administrators, students, and families. That kind of backing can be the fuel that keeps you going. So, let's take a moment to reflect on how we can approach this work in ways that are both effective and sustainable, ensuring that we take "pulse checks" to keep us tuned into healthy ways of approaching this work—because when we get it right, we're not just teaching science; we're preparing students to understand the world and change it for the better.

> *When we get it right, we're not just teaching science; we're preparing students to understand the world and change it for the better.*

KNOWING YOUR PURPOSE, PRIORITIES, AND PROFESSIONAL RESPONSIBILITIES

Teaching science through a social justice lens is a bit like juggling—you're juggling your professional responsibilities with your passion for empowering students. On one hand, you have the non-negotiables: meeting curriculum standards, assessing student progress, communicating with families, and maintaining a safe and efficient classroom. These non-negotiables establish your foundation, your steady rhythm. Without them, everything else risks falling apart. But here's the exciting part—once you've got that foundation solid, you can start adding in the real magic: lessons that challenge students to think critically about the world around them, encourage empathy, and see science as a tool for change.

SOURCE: iStock.com/CraigRJD

This is where you get to think outside the box. Imagine your lesson plans as a road map—yes, there are required stops along the way, but you get to decide the most engaging and meaningful route. Maybe that means incorporating real-world problems like climate justice, environmental racism, or the ethics of scientific advancements. Maybe it means bringing in community voices, using hands-on inquiry, or designing projects that give students a sense of agency. The key is making science relevant and personal so students don't just memorize facts but feel inspired to use what they learn to make a difference.

> *The key is making science relevant and personal so students don't just memorize facts but feel inspired to use what they learn to make a difference.*

Of course, none of this work happens in isolation. Communication is everything, and how you go about it should feel right for you. Like building a bridge—you need strong connections between you, your students, their families, and administrators. If your goal is to incorporate social justice into science instruction, be transparent about why it matters. Make sure your intentions are clear, not as a directive but as an invitation for learning and reflection. Now, we aren't saying you have to make a grand announcement or broadcast your intentions through the intercom! Instead, you can create space for conversations that encourage curiosity, critical thinking, and meaningful dialogue.

An important reminder is that this work isn't about pushing an agenda—it's about opening doors for deeper understanding. That may mean doing more listening than talking at times! Some conversations will happen naturally in the flow of a lesson, while others may emerge in one-on-one discussions with students, colleagues, or families. Not everyone will see things the same way, and that's OK. A democratic approach means respecting different perspectives while staying true to your values as an educator. Model that behavior for your students! When people are given the space to explore and engage with complex ideas on their own terms, they're more likely to form authentic connections rather than feeling like they're being told what to think.

> *This work isn't about pushing an agenda—it's about opening doors for deeper understanding.*

And when it comes to students, the goal is to cultivate an environment where they feel safe asking questions, pushing back, and making connections to their own lives. Your role isn't to hand them all the answers—it's to guide them in thinking critically about the world around them. When we approach science education this way, we're not just teaching content; we're empowering students to be thoughtful, informed, and engaged members of their communities.

SOURCE: iStock.com/BrianAJackson

Most importantly, make room for growth, both for your students and for yourself. Teaching this way means embracing a mindset of continuous reflection, adjusting as you learn what works and what doesn't. Some days, it might feel like a messy experiment, but isn't that what science is all about? Just like in a lab, trial and error are part of the process. When we create space for curiosity, challenge assumptions, and encourage deeper thinking, we're not just teaching science—we're shaping future problem-solvers. And that's what makes this work worth doing.

FINDING YOUR PEOPLE AND SPHERE OF INFLUENCE

Teaching science through a social justice lens isn't something you should take on alone. Finding your people—those who listen, support, and challenge you—can make all the difference in sustaining this work. Your sphere of influence isn't just within the four walls of your classroom; it extends to colleagues, administrators, families, and the broader community. When you connect with others who share your vision or are open to learning, you build a network that strengthens your teaching and ensures that the impact of your work extends beyond just one class or one school year. Having a strong support system means you have people to celebrate wins with, troubleshoot challenges, and remind you why this work matters when obstacles arise.

Partnerships, both in and out of school, are essential in making this work sustainable. Look for advocacy groups, digital networks, and local organizations that align with your goals. Whether they are national organizations focused on equity in education, local environmental justice groups, or online teacher communities, these networks can provide resources, ideas, and moral support. Consider bringing in guest speakers, partnering with community-based organizations on student projects, or collaborating with local museums, science centers, or institutions of higher education. These partnerships don't just benefit your teaching—they also give students opportunities to see science and social justice in action beyond the textbooks and worksheets.

And, when building partnerships, it's important to remember the essence of **reciprocity,** ensuring that both school members and community members benefit from the collaboration. While community organizations can provide great resources for the classroom, mutual exchanges of knowledge, expertise, and support must be at the forefront of the partnership. For instance, when working with local environmental groups, consider how students can contribute through science projects, advocacy efforts, or service-learning initiatives that align with the organization's goals. In turn, these groups can provide real-world context for students, offering hands-on learning

> **Reciprocity** is the practice of exchanging ideas, support, and resources for mutual benefit. For instance, one person might respond to another's action with a similar action, where benefits are returned in kind.

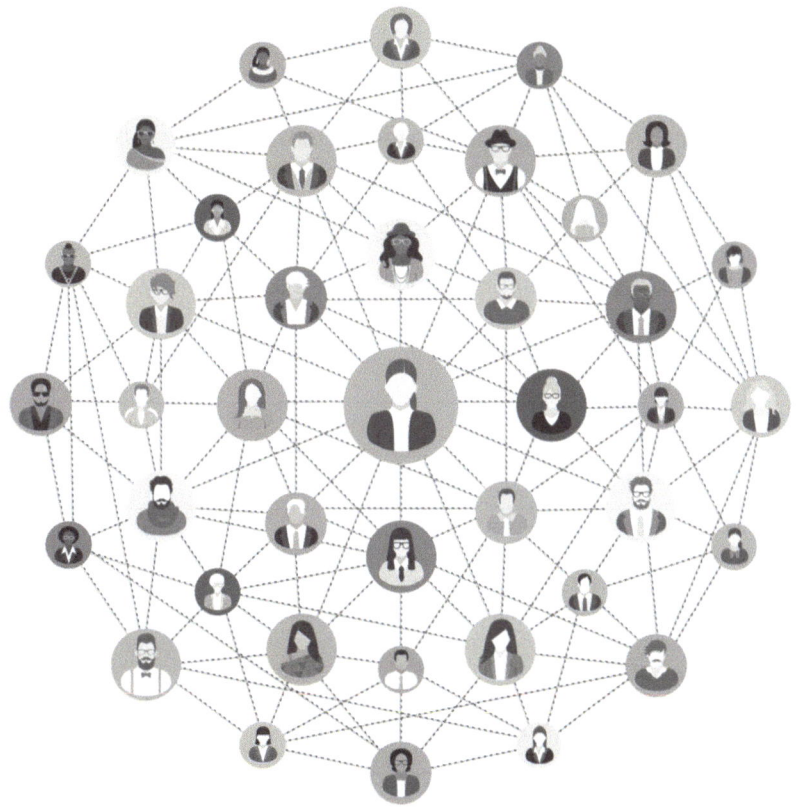

SOURCE: iStock.com/aelitta

experiences that make science and social justice tangible. By fostering reciprocal relationships, teachers can help students develop a sense of agency while also supporting the community's ongoing work. Thus, developed partnerships can create meaningful and lasting connections.

When building partnerships, it's important to remember the essence of reciprocity, ensuring that both school members and community members benefit from the collaboration.

Your sphere of influence also includes your students. Your students are capable of deep thinking, engaging in meaningful discussions, and taking action. When given the chance, they will take what they learn and build on it in ways you may not have imagined. A lesson on environmental justice might inspire students to start a recycling initiative, while a discussion on health disparities could lead to a student-driven research project. By fostering a culture of inquiry, agency, and critical thinking, you aren't just teaching content—you're equipping students with the tools to create change in their own communities.

Your students are capable of deep thinking, engaging in meaningful discussions, and taking action. When given the chance, they will take what they learn and build on it in ways you may not have imagined.

SMALL STEPS FOR BIG IMPACT: Map Your Sphere of Influence

▶ Think about the people who have supported you in your teaching journey. These might be colleagues, mentors, family members, friends, or even students. Create a list of 5–10 individuals who are part of your sphere of influence. For each person, briefly describe or map:

- How they support you emotionally, professionally, logistically, or otherwise
- A specific moment or example when their support made a difference
- Whether their support is ongoing or situational

_____
_____
_____
_____
_____

After your list is complete, consider these reflection questions:

- Are there types of support you feel you're lacking?
- What steps might you take to strengthen or expand your network?
- How can you be a support to others in your teaching community?

_____
_____
_____
_____
_____

> *Give students the trust and space to lead.*

Your influence is more powerful when it's shared. Surround yourself with people who believe in this work, seek out allies in your community, and give students the trust and space to lead. The more voices involved, the stronger and more lasting the impact. Social justice in science education isn't just about the lessons we teach—it's about the connections we build and the change we help inspire.

CURATING PATIENCE FOR GROWTH OPPORTUNITIES

Engaging in social justice work within the science classroom requires patience—not just for your students but for yourself. Even the most well-planned lessons don't always unfold the way we hope. Maybe only a handful of students grasp the deeper connections you're trying to make, or you run out of time before a discussion truly takes off. Perhaps an activity that felt powerful in theory falls flat in practice. These moments can be frustrating, but they are also part of the process.

Social justice education, like science itself, is about inquiry, iteration, and refinement. Each student, classroom, and community is different. Give yourself grace as you iron out the wrinkles and capitalize on the cultural assets your students bring to the classroom. Just as we encourage students to embrace the trial-and-error nature of scientific exploration, we must also allow ourselves to learn and grow through each attempt.

SMALL STEPS FOR BIG IMPACT:
Recall and Reframe a Growth Opportunity

▶ Think back to a lesson or classroom experience that didn't go as planned. Whether the activity was a miss, your students were disengaged, or your goals weren't met, these moments, while uncomfortable, can be powerful learning opportunities. To help reframe the misstep as a growth opportunity, consider the following:

1. What was your goal for the lesson? What did you hope students would understand and be able to do?

2. What actually happened? Describe the moments when the lesson started to diverge from your original goals.

3. What might have contributed to the outcome?

4. What did this experience teach you about your teaching practice?

5. What supports or adjustments could help you improve this lesson in the future?

6. Now, reframe the narrative. What did you learn that you wouldn't have considered if the experience had gone perfectly?

_____
_____
_____
_____
_____

It's important to recognize that missteps are not failures! Missteps are like detours on a hiking trail. Remember, detours are part of the process, not the end! Sometimes, you take a wrong turn or trip over an unexpected obstacle. That doesn't mean you've lost your way or can't keep trudging

> *Use a misstep to offer insight into the landscape of your teaching. . . . They also open doors for creative solutions, deeper engagement, and opportunities to recalibrate and grow stronger as an educator and as a community member.*

forward—it simply means you've encountered a challenge that teaches you something new about the path. Use a misstep to offer insight into the landscape of your teaching. While these moments can reveal where the terrain is rougher than expected, they also open doors for creative solutions, deeper engagement, and opportunities to recalibrate and grow stronger as an educator and as a community member. After taking a moment to regroup, you get back on track, often with a clearer understanding of the terrain and a stronger resolve to continue your journey.

SOURCE: iStock.com/ldelfoto

And, for the times when the connection between a science concept and a social justice initiative feels like an uphill climb, it's important to pause and reflect, much like a hiker takes a moment to catch their breath. Sometimes, the terrain you're navigating is more challenging than anticipated—perhaps because students are unfamiliar with the concepts, or the material stirs uncomfortable emotions. Resistance, whether internal or external, is a sign that you're pushing boundaries, and that's where the learning happens. It's in those moments of discomfort and uncertainty that transformation begins. Embrace these challenges as part of the natural flow of change. Just like hikers adjust to weather changes or unexpected routes, you too can adapt. Reflect on how you can approach things differently next time—perhaps by breaking the lesson into smaller, more digestible steps or by providing students with more opportunities to voice their concerns and ideas. Remember, social justice work isn't about perfection; it's about persistence.

SOURCE: iStock.com/esolla

As you push forward, think of each misstep or challenge as a stepping stone toward growth rather than a setback. Each step, no matter how small, contributes to the journey toward creating a more just and equitable classroom. You might not see immediate results, just as a hiker might not reach the summit after one detour, but with persistence, patience, and a willingness to adjust, you will continue moving forward. Each step along the way is a lesson in itself—an essential part of the journey that, when reflected upon, enriches your understanding of both the content and the students you are guiding.

KEEP A JOURNAL TO CHRONICLE PROGRESS

To help you navigate the journey, you may wish to keep a journal. Keeping a journal can offer a space to reflect, process, and celebrate those small wins that might otherwise go unnoticed. Sometimes, it's the quiet moments—the student who finally "gets" a concept after struggling with it, or the quiet nod of understanding when a difficult idea clicks—that can be the most telling. These small victories are the breadcrumbs that guide you, and by documenting them, you begin to see the incremental progress you're making. It's easy to get busy overlooking how far you've come. But when you take a moment to pause and write down your thoughts, you allow yourself to reflect on both the triumphs and the challenges, giving you a clearer sense of direction and purpose.

> **SMALL STEPS FOR BIG IMPACT:**
> **Reserve Time for Reflection and Growth**
>
> ▶ Set aside 5–10 minutes each day or week to thoughtfully reflect on both the highlights and the challenges of your practice. Reflection, whether written in a journal or saved in your phone as a recording, not only supports emotional processing but also deepens awareness of recurring patterns in teaching—revealing strengths and pinpointing areas for development.
>
> Over time, reviewing written or spoken entries allows you to track your growth, identify consistent student needs, and experiment with small, strategic adjustments. Including a "Next Steps" thought bubble encourages a growth mindset by transforming challenges into actionable goals. Whether you're reflecting on how a student reached an aha moment or considering new ways to handle a difficult situation, reserving the time to engage in reflection can empower you to take ownership of your teaching journey and continuously refine your craft.

Encouraging Growth Mindset

As you track these moments, you may also notice patterns—areas where certain approaches are working well, or where you might need to adjust. This helps you stay connected to your goals, especially when the path feels uncertain or when progress feels slow. Celebrate the small wins, because in social justice work, those are often the most meaningful. Maybe a student who was shy at the beginning of the semester starts to engage more openly in discussions about equity or environmental justice. Maybe a group of students will lead a class discussion

SOURCE: iStock.com/ Deepak Sethi

on the real-world application of a science concept in their community. These moments of growth are your milestones, and they deserve recognition. Don't forget to celebrate—you are elevating new voices and perspectives while *doing* social justice work along with your students.

Even on days when progress feels slow, remember that change doesn't happen all at once. Seeds take time to grow, and just like in the garden, some might sprout faster than others. But rest assured, every seed you plant is important. Those thoughtful questions, moments of insight, and sparks of curiosity are the foundation for deeper understanding and action in the future. When the results aren't immediate, it's crucial to remember that your work today is laying the groundwork for tomorrow's breakthroughs. Trust that by planting these seeds and nurturing them with care, you're contributing to a larger movement—one that will eventually bear fruit in ways you can't yet predict.

Most importantly, give yourself permission to pace yourself. When you first dive into integrating social justice into your science teaching, there's so much to consider, and it can feel like you need to make a huge change right away. But here's the thing: You don't have to do it all at once. Give yourself permission to start small and take things at a pace that feels manageable. Maybe you introduce a social justice theme within one lesson or unit and see how it goes. It could be as simple as having a discussion about equity in a scientific context or exploring an issue like environmental justice in your local community. You don't need to completely overhaul your curriculum overnight. Start with one small, meaningful step and build from there, using your students' interests and successes to determine next steps.

> *You don't have to do it all at once. Give yourself permission to start small and take things at a pace that feels manageable.*

As you gain confidence in blending social justice with science, you'll naturally find new ways to weave it into your teaching. Maybe you'll invite a guest speaker who has firsthand experience with social justice issues related to science, or you might find an exciting community project that you can connect to your curriculum. The key is to let these efforts evolve organically and allow the process to unfold over time.

SMALL STEPS FOR BIG IMPACT: Connect Science to the Community

▶ Consider how you can connect real-world social justice issues to meaningful community engagement within your teaching context. Is there a guest speaker you could invite who has firsthand experience with topics like environmental justice, health disparities, or access to clean water—areas that relate to your curriculum? How can you collaborate with a field trip partner to connect their content with your classroom's social justice work? You might tap into the rich knowledge and experiences of families within your classroom or school community. You can ask for help identifying local projects or community initiatives that align with your learning goals and could bring authentic, real-world relevance to your lessons by connecting with families and community stakeholders.

The journey isn't just about what you're teaching—it's about how you're learning along the way too. You'll learn from your students, from your own reflections, and from the feedback you get from the broader community. All of these elements contribute to a richer, more robust understanding of how to integrate social justice into science education.

SOURCE: iStock.com/FatCamera

Lastly, trust in your students and trust in yourself. Your students are more capable of meaningful engagement than you might think, and by creating space for them to explore these topics, you're empowering them to take ownership of their learning. Trust that they will rise to the occasion. And trust yourself—your experience, your creativity, and your commitment to this work are all

> *Every step you take, no matter how small, is a step toward creating a more just, equitable, and thoughtful classroom.*

invaluable. Every step you take, no matter how small, is a step toward creating a more just, equitable, and thoughtful classroom. You're not just teaching science; you're shaping future leaders who will carry these lessons with them into their communities.

HOLDING ON TO HOPE

Engaging in social justice work, especially within the classroom, is not only about making change—it's about healing. When we tackle issues of equity and justice, we're addressing long-standing inequities that have harmed communities and individuals for generations. This work can feel overwhelming at times, but it's also profoundly healing because it opens doors to new possibilities, new ways of thinking, and new ways of being. Each small act of justice, whether it's amplifying a student's voice or addressing a systemic issue in the curriculum, helps heal the broader community by fostering understanding, empathy, and a deeper sense of connection. The work may be hard, but it is deeply rewarding and brings joy because it offers hope for a more just and equitable future.

Hope is a powerful force when doing social justice work. It is the fuel that keeps you going even when the road feels long or the challenges seem insurmountable. This hope is contagious—it spreads to students, their families, and the wider community, creating a collective sense of possibility. Even on days when the results aren't immediately visible, remember that each step you take contributes to a larger vision.

SOURCE: iStock.com/Wavebreakmedia

As much as hope and joy are key drivers, we must also recognize the need for self-care and sustainability. Teachers doing social justice work are often deeply invested, which can lead to burnout if we're not careful. To maintain faith in your work, it's essential to take time to rest and recharge. This means not just physical rest but also emotional and mental rest. Take moments to reflect, celebrate your small victories, and reconnect with why you started this work in the first place. Surround yourself with a supportive community of fellow educators, mentors, or advocacy groups who share your vision. They can help remind you of the bigger picture when the day-to-day challenges feel draining.

Hold onto the hope that the work you're doing now is part of a larger, ongoing process of transformation—not just for your students but also for the future of the communities you serve. By nurturing yourself and celebrating progress, you can continue engaging in this vital work, energized and inspired for the long journey ahead.

> *Hold onto the hope that the work you're doing now is part of a larger, ongoing process of transformation—not just for your students but also for the future of the communities you serve.*

CHAPTER SUMMARY

- Your lesson plans are like a road map where you chart your journey, including what community voices, hands-on inquiry, and projects you wish to share in your classroom.

- Strong relationships are essential—connect with students, families, and administrators to communicate your goals and gain support for your work.

- Cultivate a learning environment for your students where they feel safe questioning ideas, and they can see the connections between science and their own lives.

- You don't have to do this alone—partner with advocacy groups, digital networks, and local organizations to help sustain and grow your impact.

- Be mindful of your sphere of influence. Surround yourself with people who share your vision and believe in the importance of this work.

- Challenges will happen, but use missteps as growth opportunities to develop creative solutions that strengthen your persistence and build resilience.

- Capture your small victories through written or spoken journaling. Reflecting on your progress will give you a clearer sense of where you've been and where you're headed.
- Start small, trust the process, and stay hopeful—change takes time, but every step matters.

REFLECTION QUESTIONS

1. Who in your school or community supports your vision for integrating social justice into science teaching, and how can you strengthen those relationships?

2. What are the existing structures or policies in your school that either help or hinder your ability to make change? How might you work within or around them?

3. Who's in your sphere of influence? How can you use partnerships with families, local organizations, or advocacy groups to support your social justice work and help your students see themselves as scientists and changemakers?

4. How do you sustain your sense of hope and purpose when facing resistance or challenges in integrating social justice into your science teaching, and what strategies help you stay committed to your goals?

5. How do you celebrate moments of progress in your journey toward teaching science through a social justice lens, and why is it important to recognize these milestones? How have these small wins influenced your next steps?

CHAPTER 7

Your Call to Action

Change will not come if we wait for some other person, or if we wait for some other time. We are the ones we've been waiting for. We are the change that we seek.

—Barack Obama, 44th president of the United States

Up to this point, we have discussed what a teacher needs to know to effectively design and integrate social justice science lessons. In this chapter, we'll talk about how to take action in the context of your classroom, your school, and your community.

SOURCE: iStock.com/Oleh Kuzminskyi

TAKING ACTION IN YOUR CONTEXT

Teachers have the education, experience, and skills to initiate change. As a teacher, you make an impact on the people you serve, including your students and the families and communities they interact with. This impact contributes to the deeply rewarding and demanding journey of engaging in social justice science teaching.

As you embark on your next steps, don't forget to take time to reflect, as such reflection will keep you questioning, looking for innovative ways to make a difference, and fueling (or renewing) your purpose. While there are multiple questions that can be asked to spark reflection, we highlight three questions essential to this work.

1. *Whose knowledge and ways of knowing are being valued in your classroom, and how are you actively challenging dominant narratives to make science more inclusive and just?*

    Throughout this book, we acknowledge the elephant in the room. Science education has traditionally prioritized Western perspectives, often overlooking Indigenous knowledge systems, cultural innovations, and the contributions of scientists from diverse backgrounds. Teachers can disrupt this pattern by integrating multiple perspectives into their lessons, such as exploring how Indigenous communities use ecological knowledge for sustainable harvesting and debating community use of water informed by water scarcity. By making science instruction more inclusive, students can see themselves as part of the scientific community and recognize the value of diverse ways of knowing to advocate for unjust practices. Thus, it is important to check in often with your science instruction and resources to see whose voices and experiences you are prioritizing in your curriculum and practice.

SOURCE: iStock.com/masterzphotois

SMALL STEPS FOR BIG IMPACT: Reflect on Diverse Perspectives in Your Physical Classroom

▶ Take a moment to observe your classroom. Ask yourself, "Are diverse perspectives not only present but truly valued and regularly shared?" Think about the stories, identities, experiences, and biases that surface in your materials and throughout your activities. Putting diverse faces on your classroom texts and walls is an easy first step. Ensuring the culture, values, traditions, and values of those diverse faces are embedded into your instruction is next, but hopefully those pictures will serve as your daily reminder to ask yourself how your students are engaging with these perspectives. Are they developing the confidence to question dominant narratives? Are they learning to recognize bias and seek out counternarratives? Most importantly, are they mirroring your leadership in embracing complexity, nuance, and equity in the content they engage with?

If you find that certain voices are missing or consistently underrepresented, it may be time to examine the choices behind your materials and your classroom culture. Could any of these unintentionally reinforce stereotypes or sideline the contributions and realities of historically marginalized communities?

2. *How do your instructional choices help students see themselves and others as capable scientists and advocates for change?*

Teachers should reflect on how their instructional choices actively support students in seeing themselves and others as capable scientists and advocates for change. This reflection is critical because the way science is taught influences students' sense of empathy and their belief in their ability to make a difference. Without intentional efforts, traditional science instruction can unintentionally exclude diverse perspectives and disconnect students from the relevance of science in their lives. By designing learning experiences that not only allow students to engage in scientific practices and thinking but also encourage students to recognize and address real-world issues, teachers create opportunities for meaningful engagement in science.

So, what are you doing in your context to make this happen? Are you using hands-on, inquiry-based investigations, such as testing local water quality, analyzing environmental injustice data, or developing sustainable solutions for school waste? If so, are these instructional choices allowing students to apply scientific knowledge while considering broader social implications? By moving beyond awareness to action, you can help students develop a sense of agency, empowering them to use science as a tool for advocacy and meaningful change.

> *Without intentional efforts, traditional science instruction can unintentionally exclude diverse perspectives and disconnect students from the relevance of science in their lives.*

SMALL STEPS FOR BIG IMPACT: Reflect on an Instructional Change You Can Make

▶ Think about your current science instruction. What is one instructional change you can make that will help students see themselves and their peers as capable scientists and change agents? Record your instructional change idea: One change I can make is . . .

_____

_____

_____

Now that you've identified a goal, consider the support, resources, or collaboration needed to implement your change effectively. For instance, do you need to seek curricular materials, local partnerships, professional development, or co-teaching opportunities? Record your needs and possible next steps: To make this change happen, I will need . . . (Tip: If you're not sure who to contact for support, your first action step can be reaching out to a colleague, coach, or administrator for guidance.)

_____

_____

_____

Next, set a vision for what success might look like to help you stay focused and track progress over time. Consider what success looks like for both you and your students: I will know this change is successful when . . .

_____

_____

_____

3. *How are you expanding your knowledge, building resilience, and refining your teaching practices to inspire action toward a more just society?*

   Engaging in equity-focused teaching requires continuous learning, resilience, and intentional practice to inspire action toward a more just society. Expanding knowledge can involve exploring diverse perspectives in science, highlighting contributions of historically marginalized scientists. Building resilience means acknowledging the challenges of social justice work, seeking support from professional communities, and embracing reflection as a tool for growth. Refining teaching practices involves designing lessons that encourage students to think critically about real-world issues, such as climate justice or environmental racism, and empowering them to propose and implement solutions. For example, students might investigate air quality in their neighborhoods, research sustainable energy alternatives, or advocate for greener school policies. By staying informed, adapting to challenges, and fostering student agency, teachers can create classrooms that not only deepen scientific understanding but also inspire meaningful action for a more just society. What are you doing to encourage action, and how are your students growing their knowledge alongside you?

   > *Building resilience means acknowledging the challenges of social justice work, seeking support from professional communities, and embracing reflection as a tool for growth.*

SOURCE: iStock.com/Liudmila Chernetska

SMALL STEPS FOR BIG IMPACT: Create Your Resilience Anchor Statement

▶ In two sentences, describe what keeps you committed to teaching science for social justice, how you will care for yourself in the process, and whom or what you will lean on for support. This statement serves as your personal anchor, a reminder of your purpose and your plan to sustain yourself through challenges. You can use the following sentence starters to guide your statement:

- The reason I choose to center justice in my science teaching is . . . , and I will nurture it by . . .
- To sustain myself in this work, I will . . . , and I draw strength from . . .

_____

_____

_____

REVISITING YOUR TEACHING MANIFESTO

When you first opened this book and dove into the introduction, we asked you to write your teaching manifesto, reflecting on your *why* for doing social justice science education work. You might have had some ideas, but curiosity primarily led you here. It could have also been that you wished to participate in a professional development or professional learning community and this book was selected as a conversation starter. Whatever the case, we are glad you joined us on this journey considering ways to effectively design and implement social justice science lessons in your context.

Although we are at the end of this book, we know the journey is far from over. The same is true for examining your beliefs about teaching and justice. There will be growth and shifts in your thinking. Maybe these shifts happened while you read this book. Maybe some will occur as you and your students get busy using science as a tool to initiate change. Thus, we encourage you to update your teaching manifesto based on new experiences and insights. View your manifesto as a snapshot in time that is prone to change as you change and refine your commitment. And, if you

> *View your manifesto as a snapshot in time that is prone to change as you change and refine your commitment.*

benefit from intentional goal setting like we do, it might be helpful to set check-in points to assess your progress and inform your next phase of work.

Leaving a legacy in education involves inspiring both students and colleagues to continue the work of equity and justice long after we are no longer in the classroom. By cultivating a passion for social justice and demonstrating its relevance in our teaching, we empower the next generation of educators and learners to advocate for change and approach the world with a critical, compassionate lens. Documenting our impact, through student successes, collaborative initiatives, and contributions to the field, serves as a testament to the enduring effects of our work and provides a foundation for others to build upon. Ensuring that a justice-centered approach remains embedded in our practice requires intentional reflection, a commitment to continuous learning, and the creation of systems that prioritize equity at every level of instruction. By leaving behind a framework of values and practices that champion inclusivity and activism, we ensure that the work continues, evolving and expanding with each new generation.

> *Leaving a legacy in education involves inspiring both students and colleagues to continue the work of equity and justice long after we are no longer in the classroom.*

CHAPTER SUMMARY

- Recognizing the intellectual and emotional labor of teaching science for social justice is crucial, and prioritizing self-care, mindfulness, boundaries, and support is essential for sustaining this work.

- Each lesson that sparks curiosity, each student who sees themselves as a scientist, and each conversation challenging injustice add to the broader movement.

- Committing to ongoing learning, flexibility, and viewing science as a tool for empowerment helps teachers stay dedicated to making a lasting impact.

- By making science more inclusive, students see themselves as part of the scientific community and value diverse ways of knowing. Regularly assess whose voices and experiences are prioritized in your curriculum and practice.

- Reflect on how your teaching choices empower students to see themselves and others as capable scientists and advocates for change.

Inspire students and colleagues to carry forward the work of equity and justice. Cultivate a passion for social justice and show its relevance to empower future teachers and learners to advocate for change with a critical, compassionate lens.

REFLECTION QUESTIONS

1. In what ways can reflection inform and support the sustainability of social justice work?
2. Upon reviewing your teaching manifesto, what aspects would you consider revising, expanding upon, or adding?
3. How do you envision leaving a legacy in your work?

References

Advisory Committee on Water Information Open Water Data Initiative. (n.d.). *Drought in the Colorado River basin*. Developed by the Department of Interior, U.S. Geological Survey, and U.S. Bureau of Reclamation, with contributions from the U.S. Environmental Protection Agency, Oregon State University, and the Western States Water Council. https://labs.waterdata.usgs.gov/visualizations/OWDI-drought/en/index.html

Aragaki, W., & Milks, K. (2026). *Place-based science teaching: Connecting students to curriculum, community, and caring for our planet*. Corwin.

Asian Carp Canada. (2025). *Current research*. https://www.asiancarp.ca/surveillance-prevention-and-response/current-research/

Atwater, M. M., Russell, M., & Butler, M. B. (Eds.). (2013). *Multicultural science education: Preparing teachers for equity and social justice*. Springer Science & Business Media.

Bartell, T. G., Yeh, C., Felton-Koestler, M. D., & Berry, R. Q., III. (2023). *Upper elementary mathematics lessons to explore, understand, and respond to social injustice*. Corwin.

Barton, A. C. (2003). *Teaching science for social justice*. Teachers College Press.

Berry, R. Q., III, Conway, B. M., IV, Lawler, B. R., & Staley, J. W. (2020). *High school mathematics lessons to explore, understand, and respond to social injustice*. Corwin.

Bezyak, J. L., Sabella, S., Hammel, J., McDonald, K., Jones, R. J., & Barton, D. (2019). Community participation and public transportation barriers experienced by people with disabilities. *Disability and Rehabilitation*, 42(23), 3275–3283. https://doi.org/10.1080/09638288.2019.1590469

Bishop, R. S. (1990). Mirrors, windows, and sliding glass doors. *Perspectives: Choosing and Using Books for the Classroom*, 6(3), ix–xi.

Bowler, P. J., & Morus, I. R. (2005). *Making modern science: A historical survey*. University of Chicago Press.

Brookfield, S. D. (2012). *Teaching for critical thinking: Tools and techniques to help students question their assumptions*. Jossey-Bass.

Bybee, R. W. (2015). *The BSCS 5E instructional model: Creating teachable moments*. National Science Teaching Association Press.

Calabrese Barton, A., & Tan, E. (2019). Designing for rightful presence in STEM: The role of making present practices. *Journal of the Learning Sciences*, 28(4–5), 616–658. https://doi.org/10.1080/10508406.2019.1591411

Calabrese Barton, A., & Tan, E. (2020). Beyond equity as inclusion: A framework of "rightful presence" for guiding justice-oriented studies in teaching and learning. *Educational Researcher*, 49(6), 433–440. https://doi.org/10.3102/0013189X20927363

Calil, J., Gutiérrez-Graudiņš, M., Munguía, S., & Chin, C. (2021). *Neglected: Environmental justice impacts of marine litter and plastic pollution*. United Nations Environment Programme. https://wedocs.unep.org/bitstream/handle/20.500.11822/35417/EJIPP.pdf

Committee on Chemical Safety. (2011). *Safety in the elementary science classroom* (3rd ed.). American Chemical Society. https://www.acs.org/content/dam/acsorg/about/governance/committees/chemicalsafety/safetypractices/safety-in-the-elementary-school-science-classroom.pdf

Cothron, J. H., Giese, R. N., & Rezba, R. J. (2006). *Students and research: Practical strategies for science classrooms and competitions*. Kendall/Hunt.

Dauvergne, P. (2023). The necessity of justice for a fair, legitimate, and effective treaty on plastic pollution. *Marine Policy, 155*, Article 105785. https://doi.org/10.1016/j.marpol.2023.105785

Dewey, J. (1910). *How we think*. Heath.

English, E., Wagner, C., & Holmes, J. (2019, July). *The effects of marine debris on beach recreation and regional economies in four coastal communities: A regional pilot study*. Final report submitted by Bear Peak Economics, CW Research and Consulting, and Abt Associates to National Oceanic and Atmospheric Administration Marine Debris Division. https://www.abtglobal.com/sites/default/files/2024-09/2019.07.Econ_.Impacts.Marine.Debris.complete.wFN_30Aug2019_508.pdf

Facione, P. A. (2023). *Critical thinking: What it is and why it counts*. Insight Assessment. https://insightassessment.com/wp-content/uploads/2023/12/Critical-Thinking-What-It-Is-and-Why-It-Counts.pdf

Gay, G. (2000). *Culturally responsive teaching: Theory, research, and practice*. Teachers College Press.

Gutstein, E. (2006). *Reading and writing the world with mathematics: Toward a pedagogy for social justice*. Routledge.

Halpern, D. F. (2014). *Thought and knowledge: An introduction to critical thinking* (5th ed.). Psychology Press. https://ia801301.us.archive.org/9/items/Thought_and_Knowledge_An_Introduction_to_Critical_Thinking_by_Diane_F._Halpern/Thought_and_Knowledge_An_Introduction_to_Critical_Thinking_by_Diane_F._Halpern.pdf

Hansson, L., & Yacoubian, H. A. (2020). *Nature of science for social justice*. Springer International.

Irons, K. S., Sass, G. G., McClelland, M. A., & O'Hara, T. M. (2011). Bigheaded carp invasion of the La Grange Reach of the Illinois River: Insights from the long-term resource monitoring program. *American Fisheries Society Symposium, 72*, 31–50.

Jain, P., Forbes, H., & Esposito, L. A. (2022). Two new alkali-sink specialist species of *Paruroctonus* Werner 1934 (Scorpiones, Vaejovidae) from central California. *ZooKeys, 1117*, 139–188.

Johns Hopkins Medicine. (n.d.). *The importance of HeLa cells*. The Legacy of Henrietta Lacks. https://www.hopkinsmedicine.org/henrietta-lacks/importance-of-hela-cells

Johnson, D. W., Johnson, R. T., & Smith, K. A. (1991). *Active learning: Cooperation in the college classroom*. Interaction Books.

Kang, J., Hense, J., Scheersoi, A., & Keinonen, T. (2019). Gender study on the relationships between science interest and future career perspectives. *International Journal of Science Education, 41*(1), 80–101. https://doi.org/10.1080/09500693.2018.1534021

Kimmerer, R. W. (2013). *Braiding sweetgrass: Indigenous wisdom, scientific knowledge and the teachings of plants*. Milkweed Editions.

Kimmerer, R. W. (2020). *Robin Wall Kimmerer*. https://www.robinwallkimmerer.com/

King, M. L., Jr. (1963, April 16). *Letter from a Birmingham jail*. University of Pennsylvania African Studies Center. https://www.africa.upenn.edu/Articles_Gen/Letter_Birmingham.html

Koestler, C., Ward, J., del Rosario Zavala, M., & Bartell, T. (2023). *Early elementary mathematics lessons to explore, understand, and respond to social injustice*. Corwin.

Kuhn, T. S. (1962). The structure of scientific revolutions. In O. Neurath, R. Carnap, & C. Morris (Eds.), *International encyclopedia of unified science* (Vol. 2, no. 2). University of Chicago Press.

Ladson-Billings, G. (1995). Toward a theory of culturally relevant pedagogy. *American Educational Research Journal, 32*(3), 465–491.

Leap, S. R., Soled, D. R., Sampath, V., & Nadeau, K. (2024). Effects of extreme weather on health in underserved communities. *Annals of Allergy, Asthma, & Immunology, 133*(1), 20–27. https://doi.org/10.1016/j.anai.2024.04.018

Learning for Justice. (2022). *Social justice standards: The Learning for Justice antibias framework*. Southern Poverty Law Center. https://www.learningforjustice.org/frameworks/social-justice-standards

Levy, B. S., & Patz, J. A. (2015). Climate change, human rights, and social justice. *Annals of Global Health, 81*(3), 310–322. https://doi.org/10.1016/j.aogh.2015.08.008

Lopez-Carmen, V. A., Redvers, N., Calac, A. J., Landry, A., Nolen, L., & Khazanchi, R. (2023). Equitable representation of American Indians and Alaska Natives in the physician workforce will take over 100 years without system change. *The Lancet Regional Health-Americans, 26,* Article 100588.

MacKenzie, A. H., Lindeman, P., Roberts, K., Thomas, W., Lorrain, C., Parker, J., Baker, M. F., Horak, J., & Sheldrake, J. (2020). Editor's corner: Social justice in the science classroom. *The Science Teacher, 87*(7), 6–7. https://doi.org/10.1080/00368555.2020.12293510

Maillard, K. N. (2019). *Fry bread: A Native American family story.* Roaring Brook Press.

Massengale, K. E. C., Jones, M. A., Liao, J., Park, C., & Old, M. (2022). Priority areas for child diaper access: Low-income neighborhoods with limited retail access to the basic need of diapers. *Health Equity, 6*(1), 767–776. https://doi.org/10.1089/heq.2021.0192

Masten, S. J., Davies, S. H., & Mcelmurry, S. P. (2016). Flint water crisis: What happened and why? *American Water Works Association, 108*(12), 22–34. https://doi.org/10.5942/jawwa.2016.108.0195

Matthews, M. R. (2024). Thomas Kuhn and science education: Learning from the past and the importance of history and philosophy of science. *Science & Education, 33,* 609–678. https://doi.org/10.1007/s11191-022-00408-1

McNeill, K. L., & Krajcik, J. (2011). *Supporting grade 5–8 students in constructing explanations in science: The claim, evidence and reasoning framework for talk and writing.* Pearson Education.

Moldavan, A. M., & Gupta, D. (2024). Culturally relevant science learning: Helping students culturally connect with science through picture books. *Science & Children, 61*(1), 70–76. https://doi.org/10.1080/00368148.2023.2292390

Moll, L., Amanti, C., Neff, D., & González, N. (1992). Funds of knowledge for teaching: Using a qualitative approach to connect homes and classrooms. *Theory Into Practice, 31,* 132–141.

Montessori, M. (1917). *The advanced Montessori method* (Vol. 1). Frederick A. Stokes.

Moulding, B., & Bybee, R. (2017). *Teaching science is phenomenal.* ELM Tree.

NASA. (2023). *NASA astronaut Dr. Ellen Ochoa.* https://www.nasa.gov/people/nasa-astronaut-dr-ellen-ochoa/

National Diaper Bank Network. (2024). *What is diaper need?* https://nationaldiaperbanknetwork.org/the-need/

National Research Council. (2012). *A framework for K–12 science education: Practices, crosscutting concepts, and core ideas.* Committee on a Conceptual Framework for New K–12 Science Education Standards. Board on Science Education, Division of Behavioral and Social Sciences and Education. National Academies Press.

National Science Teaching Association. (2000). *Multicultural science education* [Position statement]. https://www.nsta.org/nstas-official-positions/multicultural-science-education

National Science Teaching Association. (2020). *National Science Teaching Association releases official statement on social justice and science education* [Press release]. https://www.nsta.org/press-release/national-science-teaching-association-releases-official-statement-social-justice-and

National Science Teaching Association. (2025). *Sensemaking.* https://www.nsta.org/sensemaking

New England ADA Center. (2017). *ADA checklist for existing facilities.* A project of the Institute for Human Centered Design. https://www.adachecklist.org/checklist.html

NGSS Lead States. (2013). *Next Generation Science Standards: For states, by states.* National Academies Press. https://nap.nationalacademies.org/read/18290/chapter/1

Nilson, L. B. (2021). *Infusing critical thinking into your course: A concrete, practical approach.* Stylus.

OpenAI. (2025). *Microsoft CoPilot* (January 3 version) [Large language model]. https://copilot.microsoft.com/

Paris, D. (2012). Culturally sustaining pedagogy: A needed change in stance, terminology, and practice. *Educational Researcher*, 41(3), 93–97.

Parsons, E. S., Jowell, A., Veidis, E., Barry, M., & Thadaney Israni, S. (2024). Climate change and inequity. *Pediatric Research*, 1–8. https://www.nature.com/articles/s41390-024-03153-z

Paul, R., & Elder, L. (2010). *The miniature guide to critical thinking concepts and tools*. Foundation for Critical Thinking Press.

Perea Burns, S., Mendonca, R. J., & Smith, R. O. (2024). Accessibility of public buildings in the United States: A cross-sectional survey. *Disability & Society*, 39(11), 2988–3003. https://doi.org/10.1080/09687599.2023.2239996

Perry, W. G. (1968). *Forms of intellectual and ethical development in the college years: A scheme*. Holt, Rinehart, & Winston.

PhET Simulations. (2018, July 17). *What is PhET?* [Video]. YouTube. https://www.youtube.com/watch?v=OjZ6qvi21Qo&t=1s&ab_channel=PhETSimulations

Piaget, J. (1970). *Genetic epistemology*. Columbia University Press.

Piaget, J. (1972). *Psychology and epistemology: Toward a theory of knowledge*. Penguin.

Rodriguez, A. J., & Morrison, D. (2019). Expanding and enacting transformative meanings of equity, diversity and social justice in science education. *Cultural Studies of Science Education*, 14, 265–281. https://doi.org/10.1007/s11422-019-09938-7

Shin, D. D., Lee, M., Ha, J. E., Park, J. H., Ahn, H. S., Son, E., Chun, Y., & Bong, M. (2019). Science for all: Boosting the science motivation of elementary school students with utility value intervention. *Learning and Instruction*, 60, 104–116. https://doi.org/10.1016/j.learninstruc.2018.12.003

Silberman, M. (1996). *Active learning: 101 strategies to teach any subject*. Pearson.

Singh, R. (2020). *111 trees: How one village celebrates the birth of every girl*. Kids Can Press.

Tan, E., & Calabrese Barton, A. (2023). *Teaching toward rightful presence in middle school STEM*. Harvard Education Press.

University of California Museum of Paleontology. (2022). *Understanding science 101: How science works*. University of California, Berkeley. https://undsci.berkeley.edu/understanding-science-101/how-science-works/the-real-process-of-science/

U.S. Energy Information Administration. (2015). *Residential Energy Consumption Survey*. https://www.eia.gov/consumption/residential/data/2015/

Valencia, M., Bocken, N., Loaiza, C., & De Jaeger, S. (2023). The social contribution of the circular economy. *Journal of Cleaner Production*, 408, Article 137082.

Vieira, R. M., & Tenreiro-Vieira, C. (2016). Fostering scientific literacy and critical thinking in elementary science education. *International Journal of Science and Math Education*, 14, 659–680. https://doi.org/10.1007/s10763-014-9605-2

Vogel, M. (2019, April 29). Social justice in science class. *Learning for Justice*. https://www.learningforjustice.org/magazine/social-justice-in-science-class

Vygotsky, L. S. (1962). *Thought and language*. MIT Press.

Vygotsky, L. S. (1978). *Mind in society: The development of higher psychological processes*. Harvard University Press.

Windschitl, M., Thompson, J., & Braaten, M. (2008). Beyond the scientific method: Model-based inquiry as a new paradigm in preference for school science investigations. *Science Education*, 92(5), 941–967. https://doi.org/10.1002/sce.20259

Windschitl, M., Thompson, J., & Braaten, M. (2020). *Ambitious science teaching*. Harvard Education Press.

Wolcott, S. K. (1999). Developing and assessing critical thinking and life-long learning skills through student self-evaluations. *Assessment Update*, 11(4), 16.

Index

Absorption, 86
Academic skills, 1
Action domain, 43
Active participants, 28, 39, 77, 79
Act Menu, 105–106 (table), 105–107
Act phase
   Act Menu, 105–106 (table), 105–107
   change agent, 101
   elementary students, 101
   sociocultural-informed phenomenon, 101
   student's action, 102–103
   teacher support, 103–105
Agency, 1, 2, 5, 28, 29, 32, 39–44, 107, 134, 165, 211, 213, 225, 227
Agrobiodiversity, 62–63
Air and water pollution, 28
Ambitious Science Teaching, 80
Americans with Disabilities Act (ADA), 171
Artificial intelligence (AI), 93, 119
Asset-based approach, 76–77

Biological Sciences Curriculum Study (Bybee), 80
Bishop, R. S., 31, 33, 66
Brainstorming, 29, 68, 70, 105
Brookfield, S. D., 19 (table)
BSCS 5E Instructional Model, 80
Bybee, R., 80

California Academy of Sciences, 24
Change agent, 7, 101, 107
Chronic illness, 6
Claim–evidence–reasoning (CER), 100–101
Classroom Care Council, 29
Classroom community, 10, 11, 75, 80
Classroom norms, 11, 79–80
Classrooms with purpose
   growth opportunities, 214–217
   holding on to hope, 220–221

   journal to chronicle progress, 217–220
   people and sphere of influence, 212–214
   priorities and professional responsibilities, 210–212
   science instruction, 209
   science time, 209
   teaching science, 210
Collaborative learning, 99
Colorado River, 106–107
Community-driven approach, 70
Community organizations, 103, 212
Critical thinking
   building scientific knowledge, 21
   classrooms, 18
   cognitive skills and dispositions, 21, 22 (figure)
   definitions, 19, 19–20 (table)
   developmental models, 19, 19–20 (table)
   intentional instructional design and classroom practices, 18
   interrogate phase, 99–100
   kindergarten, 19
   metacognition, 21
   self-regulation, 21
Crosscutting Concepts (CCCs), 93, 94, 94 (table), 108
Crystallography, 65
Culturally important phenomena, 86
Culture, 86
   classroom, 43, 79, 80
   diverse, 65
   Indigenous, 66, 140
   science knowledge, 48
   students, 25
Cystic fibrosis (CF), 6

Decision-making process, 79, 105, 152
Dewey, J., 47
Diverse preservice, 8–9

Diverse scientists, 33, 64, 67
Diversity domain, 43
Dynamic community, 66

Ecological knowledge, 32, 64, 89, 224
Elder, L., 20 (table), 21
Electrical energy, 84
Elementary school, 4, 28
Elementary science methods
    student inventory assessment, 8
Elicit–Investigate–Interrogate–Act framework, 11, 81, 81 (figure), 109, 163
Empowering students, 2, 4, 28, 43, 68, 107, 210, 211
Environmental hazards, exposure to, 11
Environmental justice, 11, 88, 152, 202, 212, 213, 217, 218
Environmental pollution, 28
Equity-based practices, 39, 68
Evaporation, 84, 86, 99, 106, 107, 111, 112, 120, 122, 127
Evidence-backed solutions, 60

Facione, P. A, 20 (table)
Ford, H., 163
A Framework for K–12 Science Education (National Research Council, 2012), 92
Funds of knowledge, 75, 77, 108

Gorman, A., 75
Grab-and-go lessons
    accessibility, 168–177
    Elicit–Investigate–Interrogate–Act framework, 163–165
    fossil fuels, 194–204
    grade levels, DCIs and social justice standards, 166, 167 (table)
    instructional planning, 163
    invasive carp, 186–193
    nonrenewable energy, 194–203
    politics and plastics, 178–185
    sequence, 165, 166 (table)
    students and communities, 163
GRC (Gather, Reason, Communicate) framework, 80

Halpern, D. F., 20 (table)
Hardy–Weinberg principle, 58
High-interest phenomena, 85, 88–89, 96, 97
High-quality education, 5–6
    learning experiences, 68
    science instruction, 11
How We Think (Dewey), 47
Human endeavor, 22, 62

Identity domain, 43
Indigenous cultures, 64, 66, 141, 143, 150
Indigenous ecological knowledge, 32
Inquiry-based learning, 1
Inquiry-driven process, 52
In-service teachers, 8–10
Instructional change, 226–227
Intellectual empathy, 21, 22
Interrogate phase
    claim–evidence–reasoning, 100–101
    critical thinking, 99–100
    evaporation, 99
    high-interest phenomenon, 96–97
    sociocultural-informed phenomenon, 97–98, 99
    states of matter, 98, 98–99 (table)
Investigate phase
    collaborative student groups, 95–96
    instructional considerations, 94
    Next Generation Science Standards (NGSS), 92
    planning, 93
    safety, 94–95
    science education, 92
    three-dimensional science teaching, 93–94, 94 (table)
Invisible disability, 6

Justice-centered approach, 229

K–12 classrooms and education, 5, 6
Kimmerer, R. W., 32
King, M. L., Jr., 2

Ladson-Billings, G., 25
Laws of nature, 51
Learning environments, 1, 4, 33, 37, 40, 44, 75, 78–81, 221
Learning for Justice (2022) Social Justice Standards, 5, 10, 11, 39, 40 (figure), 41 (figure), 43, 44, 164, 166
Learning process, 78
Letter From a Birmingham Jail (King), 2
Local community, 28, 64, 68, 72, 88, 218

Maillard, K. N., 64
Mandela, N, 209

Meaningful connections, 9, 78
Meitner, L., 17
Metacognition, 21
Montessori, M., 81

National Science Teaching Association (NSTA), 37, 38, 109
Nature of Science (NOS), 48–49, 48 (figure)
Newton's law, 7, 57, 71
Next Generation Science Standards (NGSS), 5, 10, 11, 37–39, 44, 48, 48 (figure), 49, 92, 94

Obama, B., 223

Paul, R., 20 (table), 21
Penicillin, 23
Perry, W. G., 19 (table)
Phenomena, 1
  constructivist education theories, 81
  content knowledge, 84
  definition, 81
  elementary science classroom, 83
  evaporation, 84
  paradigm shifts, 82
  physical location, 85
  sociocultural-informed phenomena. *See* Sociocultural-informed phenomena
  student perspectives, 87, 88 (table)
  three-dimensional science teaching, 83
  types, 85–89, 88 (table)
  Western civilization, 82
Physical classroom, 225
Physical location phenomena, 85
Piaget, J., 81
Problem-solving methods, 1, 103–104
Purpose and action, science
  agrobiodiversity, 62–63
  critical thinking and skepticism, culture of, 50
  cultural contexts, 64
  cumulative effort, 62
  empirical evidence, 49–50
  epistemologies, 65–68
  evidence-based reasoning, 49–50
  Indigenous cultures, 64
  Indigenous ecological practices, 62
  knowledge acquisition, 64
  knowledge, perspectives and systems of, 62
  laws, 57
  model, 54–56
  Nature of Science (NOS), 48–49, 48 (figure)
  Ndebele Village in South Africa, 62, 63 (figure)
  plant knowledge, 63
  process, 50, 51 (figure)
  scientific community influence, 62
  scientific knowledge, 50–54
  scientific literacy, 49
  tried-and-true scientific method, 47
  value of community, 69–71

Racial group, 66
Real-world context, 212–213
Reciprocity, 212, 213
Resilience, 67, 227–228

Safety in the Elementary Science Classroom (Committee on Chemical Safety), 95
Science
  Classroom Care Council, 29
  classroom culture, 43
  classroom environment, 26, 35
  community deserves investment, 35
  critical thinking, 34
  emotional empathy, 24
  empathy, 21, 22
  equity, 38–39
  evidence-based solutions, 34
  fairness, 39–44, 40 (figure), 41 (figure)
  mirrors, windows and sliding glass doors, 31–33
  penicillin, 23
  polio and COVID-19 vaccines, 24–25
  scientific community, 30
  scientific inquiry, 34
  scientific knowledge, development of, 24
  scorpion, 23
  sense of fairness, 26–29
  social endeavor, 23
  social justice, 36
  socioeconomic status, issues of, 35
  students' assets and communities, 25–26, 25 (figure)
  students' perceptions, 30
Science and Engineering Practices (SEPs), 93, 94 (table)
Science education
  diverse backgrounds, 224
  high-quality, 37
  learning environments, 37
  social justice, 37

Science instruction
  elementary contexts, 9
  high-quality, 11, 39
  social justice, 211
  sociocultural-informed phenomena, 88
  three-dimensional, 5
  traditional, 225
Science, technology, engineering, and mathematics (STEM), 2–3, 5, 7, 38, 39, 65–66
Scientific community, 30–32, 39, 59, 62, 65, 78, 224, 229
Scientific exploration, 48, 215
Scientific facts, 24, 59, 71
Scientific inquiry, 33, 34, 36, 43, 45, 49, 53–54, 81, 103, 206
Scientific laws, 56–58, 58–59 (figure), 71
Scientific literacy, 49, 50, 67
Scientific theories, 57–59, 71
Scorpion, 23
Self-efficacy, 9, 67
Self-preservation, 1
Self-reflection, 9, 21, 100
Sexual reproduction, 147
Singh, R., 64
Social change, 43, 44, 70
Social criticism, 1
Social issue, 8, 43, 103
Social justice
  activity questionnaire, 223–229
  benefits, 2, 4
  challenges, 227
  community, 70, 71
  develop agency in science, 39
  education, 5
  elementary schools, 9, 10
  elementary science classrooms, 75
  framing, 5
  grab-and-go science, 11
  inclusive classroom community, 80
  injustice, issues of, 3
  integration, 36, 42, 218
  issues, 11, 64, 103
  phenomena. *See* Phenomena *vs.* pollution, 11
  principles, 42
  science classroom, 214
  science frameworks, 80
  science lesson, 81, 81 (figure)
  student engagement, 40
  teachers, 1–2, 3
  teaching science, 3
  value of community, 69
"Social Justice in Science Class" (Vogel), 1
Social Justice Standards. *See* Learning for Justice (2022) Social Justice Standards
Sociocultural-informed phenomena
  cultural and linguistic backgrounds, 88
  diaper deserts, 89, 91
  diverse people and perspectives, 88
  local community issues/environmental justice, 88–89
  observation, 89, 90–91 (table)
  polluted local stream, 89
  student perspectives, 87, 88 (table)
  students' assets and community, 89
  students' cultural beliefs and practices, 89
Southern Poverty Law Center, 39–40
Spratt, G. A., 47
Student-centered learning, 9, 80, 105
Student-drawn models, 107
Student learning
  academic year, 75–76
  classroom norms, 79–80
  diversity as an asset, 76–77
  first day of school, 75
  inclusive environment, 78–79
  teacher's role, 76

Teacher education, 5, 8
Teaching Tolerance Social Justice Standards. *See* Learning for Justice (2022) Social Justice Standards
Thermodynamics, 65
Three-dimensional science learning, 11

Uncertainty, 6, 216
Unit plans
  diaper deserts, 129–140
  Elicit–Investigate–Interrogate–Act framework, 109
  honorable harvest, 141–160
  template, 161
  water negotiators, 111–128
U.S. Public Health Service, 24

Value of community, 10, 69–71
Vogel, M., 1
Vygotsky, L. S., 81

Wolcott, S. K., 20 (table)
Wright, O., 47

Preparing students for a future we can't imagine

Jo Boaler, Cathy Williams

Introduce data science to your students across disciplines with real world stories and teacher testimonials to transform your classroom experience.
Grades K-8

Bertha Vazquez, Kimi Waite, Lauren Madden

Use this inspiring road map to integrate climate change lessons into your existing curriculum and foster student agency across disciplines.
Grades K–12

Irina Lyublinskaya, Xiaoxue Du

Integrate AI literacy into K–12 classrooms, blending theory, practical lesson plans, and ethical considerations to empower students as critical thinkers.
Grades K–12

Whitney Aragaki, Kirstin Milks

Learn more about centering place (and the people who inhabit it) in science instruction across locations, from places rich in Native culture like Hawai i and Alaska to urban areas that have multiple histories and myriad cultural influences.
Grades K–12

To order your copies, visit corwin.com

CORWIN

Whether you're training students for an increasingly technological job market, striving for equitable access in STEM, or encouraging innovation and joy through scientific exploration, our books are here to support you every step of the way.

Aneesha Badrinarayan

Learn more about exploring science like scientists do and embracing an asset-based approach to formative and summative assessment.
Grades K–12

Richard Cox, Jr., Brandy Howard

This resource offers accessible guidance for teachers, instructional coaches, and administrators, detailing specific moves to facilitate imaginative learning.
Grades K–8

Christa Jackson, Kristin L. Cook, Sarah B. Bush, Margaret Mohr-Schroeder, Cathrine Maiorca, Thomas Roberts

Help educators create integrated STEM learning experiences that are inclusive for all students and allow them to experience STEM as scientists, innovators, mathematicians, creators, engineers, and technology experts!
Grades PreK–5 and Grades 6–12

Sarah B. Bush, Kristin L. Cook

Going far beyond a collection of STEAM activities, this book shows educators—as well as school and district leaders—how to build a STEAM ecosystem that can measurably improve every learner's mathematics and science achievement.
Grades PreK–5

To order your copies, visit corwin.com

CORWIN

Free professional learning from leading education experts

 Live and on-demand webinars

Get a certificate for PD hours!

 Videos

 Podcasts

 Study guides

 New teacher toolkit

 Lessons and strategies

 Checklists and assessments

 Plain language summaries of education research

 Book excerpts

 Other downloadables

 Blogs

Leave a review! If you enjoyed this book, let us know by leaving a review on **GoodReads.com** or **Amazon.com**.

corwin.com/resources

CORWIN

CORWIN

To help every educator help every student

We believe that every single student deserves a great education

We believe that knowing our impact is both a privilege and a responsibility

We believe that a fair, stable, and thriving society is built on education